EAST A HALF SOUTH

JOHN CURRY

COUNTYVISE LTD

East a half south was the magnetic compass course from Point Lynas to the Bar Light Vessel in my father's time, before the magnetic variation altered. It was also the answer often given by a pilot when asked a question, to which he did not know the real answer. Thus the vague; "East a half south," which was something the pilot did know, often followed by; "my father's a pilot," to round up the evasive reply!

First Published 2012 by Countyvise Ltd
14 Appin Road, Birkenhead, CH41 9HH

Copyright © 2012 John Curry

The right of John Curry to be identified as the author of this work has been asserted by him in accordance with the Copyright, Design and Patents Act 1988.

British Library Cataloguing in Publication Data.
A catalogue record for this book is available from the British Library.

ISBN 978 1 906823 72 6

Book and cover design by Charles McIntyre
Front cover photograph © Tony Kenwright
Rear cover photograph © Phil Parker

ACKNOWLEDGEMENTS

I would like to thank both of my good friends Marie Stacey and Robin Woodall for proof reading the manuscript, and for making the helpful comments which have been invaluable in improving the written text.

My thanks for the photographs not taken by me but, which are accredited to the photographer beneath. Similarly my thanks are also due to the poets, writers and playwrights whose work is quoted from in the text.

Any photographs or poems not credited are my own.

I would also like to thank Gill, for her support in the writing of this book and for putting up with the working life of the pilot, which relied upon time and tide.

PILOT OF THE FIRST CLASS

No. 110.

PORT OF LIVERPOOL

PILOT'S LICENCE

FOR THE

LIVERPOOL PILOTAGE DISTRICT.

𝕿𝖔 𝖆𝖑𝖑 𝖙𝖔 𝖜𝖍𝖔𝖒 𝖙𝖍𝖊𝖘𝖊 𝖕𝖗𝖊𝖘𝖊𝖓𝖙𝖘 𝖘𝖍𝖆𝖑𝖑 𝖈𝖔𝖒𝖊.

𝕿𝖍𝖊 𝕸𝖊𝖗𝖘𝖊𝖞 𝕯𝖔𝖈𝖐𝖘 𝖆𝖓𝖉 𝕳𝖆𝖗𝖇𝖔𝖚𝖗 𝕮𝖔𝖒𝖕𝖆𝖓𝖞. being the Pilotage Authority for the Liverpool Pilotage District, send greeting.

𝕶𝖓𝖔𝖜 𝖞𝖊 that........ JOHN L. CURRY.

aged 42 years, being 5 feet 6 inches in stature, having a FRESH complexion, and whose place of abode is 15 DEVONSHIRE ROAD, WEST KIRBY, MERSEYSIDE, L48 7HR. ......having in pursuance of the provisions of the Pilotage Act, 1913, the Liverpool Pilotage Order, 1920, and the Liverpool Pilotage Bye-Laws, and all other powers us enabling been duly examined on our behalf, and found to be qualified to act as a Pilot for shipping within the Liverpool Pilotage District, is, by this our Certificate, duly licensed to act as a **𝕻𝖎𝖑𝖔𝖙 𝖔𝖋 𝖙𝖍𝖊 𝕱𝖎𝖗𝖘𝖙 𝕮𝖑𝖆𝖘𝖘** for the Liverpool Pilotage District, as defined in the Liverpool Pilotage Order, 1920, from the date hereof until the first day of December, 1987 provided that he shall so long comply with the provisions of the said Act and Order, and of all other Acts and Orders binding upon him in relation to Pilotage, and with every Order, Bye-Law or Regulation made by us, the said Company, and shall conduct himself with propriety and prudence.

𝕲𝖎𝖛𝖊𝖓 𝖇𝖞 the said Mersey Docks and Harbour Company under the hand of their Secretary, this First day of December, in the year of our Lord One thousand Nine hundred and Eighty Six.

W.T. Bowie

Secretary.

FOREWORD

by Captain Robin Woodall, Master RD*, RNR, HCCM, FJMU

I was rather surprised, as a 'Blue Water Seaman,' to be asked to write a foreword to a book by a 'Brown Water Seaman,' and it was only on reading this excellent book that I realised that the one cannot do without the other.

Ocean going seamen, when arriving off a port can think; "thank goodness, the pilot can do all the work now" and in some instances this may be the case, but John's book well illustrates the many variations on this thought, from the one extreme to the other.

Until reading this splendid book I had not realised the arduous training that all Liverpool pilots had to go through to reach their First Class Licence, and it is interesting that John's 'Deep Sea Time' was much the same as mine, so I know what he has been through.

Even more interesting are the "ins" and "outs" of Liverpool pilotage, with the floods and ebbs of the tides, and the various swirls and eddies off the different docks of the River Mersey. Having sailed in the Mersey in a small boat, and been on many an ocean going vessel docking and undocking, I thought I knew the river well, but…

No!!! is the answer, and John illustrates so well the variations of the Mersey and Liverpool Bay, and why ship's masters and pilots should work as a team for the safe transit to and from the open water. Always remembering that you never know all about the sea, and what it can do. If you do not it will turn round and hit you very hard on the back of the head, and that can end in disastrous results.

John's book is a fascinating read, covering a significant time of the Liverpool Pilotage, enjoy.

Robin Woodall

Haven't you noticed that the people from out there
by the open sea are, in a way, a people apart?
It is almost as if they themselves lived the life of the sea.
There is the rush of waves, and ebb and flow too,
both in their thoughts and in their feelings,
and so they can never bear transplanting.

From: The Lady from the Sea, Henrik Ibsen

CONTENTS

East A Half South

Sun rising over flowerbeds
Which harbour springtime bulbs,
In berths where ships once lay.
Daffodils sound silent fanfares,
Whilst out on the river
Fog sirens and ship's bells
Herald early, dawn mists.

What cargoes will these stems bear?
Only language reminiscent
Of the straight stems,
Which once bore down on Liverpool.
Passengers for New York
Bade farewell to the Mersey Bar,
Looked westwards to Sandy Hook
And ground, which would nourish,
Transplanted, trans-Atlantic roots.

Canadian Pacific, Booker's Prize,
Cunard White Star,
Blooms, now faded into autumns
Of past summers.

May the new buds burst
And blossom, swelling
On the flood of a rising tide.
May Liverpool,
Long a haven in a storm,
Find peace within this bower,
And flourishing,
May both port and garden grow.

ONE FOOT ON A PILOT LADDER

The day was to be, for myself, as a young sixteen year old, not only one which I would always remember, but one which was to number amongst the most significant days of my life. I dashed into a red, public telephone box, complete with button A and button B, on the Pierhead. In my haste to reach the telephone, I had almost been knocked down by a Green Goddess tram rattling off on its railed journey up Everton Valley to Anfield.

The news, which I had for my mother and father waiting anxiously over the water in Wallasey, was momentous. I had, having presented myself with 'O' levels from Wallasey Grammar School before the full Liverpool Pilotage Committee, been accepted into the Service as a Liverpool Pilot Service Boathand. That was the Bye-Law title for a Liverpool Pilot Apprentice, one who had been chosen to learn the ways of the River Mersey in all her moods and safeguard the passage of the vessels navigating both the river and the channel approaches to and from the Port of Liverpool.

The time was early afternoon, on the flood of a spring tide. The Cunard White Star Liner *Britannic* was making a flood way approach to berth starboard side to on the Prince's Landing Stage. The autumn sun was shining that October day, and all was particularly well with both my sixthformer's world and myself. To begin with the news heralded the end to my schooldays and the opening up of the big, wide world beyond, when I would sail off to foreign parts, previously only read about in geography books.

The experience of being interviewed by the Pilotage Committee had been daunting. Some twelve youths were interviewed and six were accepted. The committee consisted of the Superintendent of Pilotage, two senior pilots, two ships' masters, the Marine Surveyor and Water Bailiff for the Port, the Marine Hydrographer, two independent gentlemen and the secretary of the Mersey Docks and Harbour Board. As formidable a line up for myself, as when playing in the school's first team scrum-half position, I had faced the back's line-up of Merchant Taylor's School on my own with nowhere to run.

Now, standing clear of the telephone box with the good news announced, I found myself on the brink of manhood, and stood proudly observing the full river flowing. On that tide, as in those of my apprenticeship, in the post World War II days, the river was always teeming with ships. Passenger liners, general cargo vessels, tankers, coasters, barges and tugs, both sailing and docking, jostled for space on the muddy waters of the Mersey. Timing was all, for time and tide wait for no man, and timing is the byword of the Liverpool Pilot.

The names of the ships' companies were known to me, as were their funnels and their house-flags. They were Cunard White Star, Blue Funnel, Elder-Dempster, Palm Line, Shell and Clan Line, amongst others. They would line up like magnificent blooms in a flower garden, as I was to write nostalgically in a poem, years later, when Liverpool held a Garden Festival to revive the faded life in the port's near empty docks. I make reference to the straight stems of the ships bearing down on Liverpool in fog, the air filled with the sound of sirens being replaced by the straight stems of daffodils with their silent, yellow horns waving in the gentle breeze of a misty, spring morning, many years and fortunes later after the ships had gone.

I will relate the fortunes referred to in a subsequent chapter, including reference to the contributory factors, which led to a fall, which was in turn to be followed by a subsequent rise, indeed a rebirth for Liverpool, a port so strategically placed and so vital to the commerce of the United Kingdom.

Clan Line was the name of the company, which was written on the formal letter of my acceptance into the Service, received at my home a few days after the interview. I was instructed to undergo a series of medicals, eye-sight tests, vaccinations and finally appear for an interview at the offices of Cayzer Irvine in the Liver Building, for it was with their then glorious Clan Line, that I had been placed as a cadet-officer to sail and gain deep-sea experience before entering the Service as a Boathand on one of the four motor pilot cutters of the time. The big shipping companies all offered berths to perspective Boathands in those days, realising the importance of the training of those who would safeguard their ships in future years.

The medicals and eye-sight tests along with numerous vaccinations were accomplished in company with my fellow successful interviewees, all of whom were to become close friends with the passage of time, the flowing of tides and the passing of storms and calms in the Irish Sea during the years, which were to follow.

Sixth form and school were suddenly in the past, and the hectic preparations of a young man about to set sail on his first trip to sea took priority. A visit to the Sailor's Home seaman's shop (Now sadly demolished along with the magnificent Victorian Building, which housed it, having been replaced with yet another multi-storey car-park!) and 'Ma Egerton's,' I believe it was called, seafaring outfitters, had me completely kitted out at great expense and not always to my satisfaction. I stand now, as I did then at five feet and four inches in height, but my mother, who accompanied me on the spending spree, insisted that I would grow and my regulation gabardine mackintosh was manufactured for a six-footer! Years later, as a Boathand, I was to give the mackintosh, in near mint condition, to a grateful tramp at Stan Water's Café on the Liverpool Landing Stage, one damp November morning.

In addition to this oversized mackintosh, there was the doe-skin No.1s full uniform complete with cap and badge, No.10s, the full 'all whites' for the tropics, and numerous other numbered outfits intended to be worn in various weathers in varied climates. Seaboots, black shoes, white shoes, shirts, shorts, vests, underpants, socks, ties and of course the books! *Nichol's Concise Guide* (to navigation), *Nichol's Seamanship*, *The Boatswain's Manual* and *Norie's* azimuth tables. No doubt someone would let me into the secret of what use these tables were in the fullness of time. Now in the days of Satellite Navigation they are virtually history!

At last I was fully equipped and I was given my first orders, which were to join the T.S.S. (Twin Screw Steamship, by then converted to motor) *Clan Brodie*, a vessel of some seven thousand tons gross. She was four hundred and eighty-eight feet long and sixty-three feet in the beam. She had been commandeered by the Royal Navy whilst still being built in 1940, and was launched to become an aircraft transport, fitted with a single catapult. The Cameron Class vessel was to serve as H.M.S. *Athene*, throughout the war years in the South Atlantic, and was returned, unscathed, to Clan Line in 1946. *Clan Brodie*, a relatively "big ship" of the day, was lying in middle-north Vittoria dock in Birkenhead, loading a full general cargo bound for India and what was then Pakistan, now Bangladesh. She lay on the north side of Vittoria Dock with another Clan Line vessel both to the east and to the west of her, whilst on the south side of the dock lay three Blue Funnel (Alfred Holt) vessels.

The morning of the big day arrived and with great trepidation, mixed with unbelievable excitement, I was driven by my brother, who, six years older than myself, was already a senior pilot apprentice serving on the Liverpool pilot cutters.

Above all, apart from the hustle and bustle in the warehouse sheds, where crates, pallets, more than one steam train, and other machinery were being loaded aboard, I remember the smells. Freshly cut wood, oil, tar, oakum, canvas and mustard seed-oil, with which the Pakistani crew oiled their hair, are the most prevalent, which in a dream world of remembrance, still can assail my nostrils if I close my eyes and concentrate.

Having been welcomed aboard by Captain Dalley, an old wizened salt, shorter in stature than myself, whose command the *Brodie* was, I was introduced to my fellow cadet, Peter Hardy and shown the cabin we would share for some four months, Hardy took me on a tour of the ship. She was five hatches long. Three hatches were situated forward of the bridge, one between the bridge housing and another block of 'island' accommodation and the fifth between this and the poop. There was no air conditioning and in the tropics we relied on electric fans and wind-ports, which were metal-scoops fitting into the open cabin portholes, designed to catch the passing breeze.

During my first tour of the vessel, I noted down below at the after end below the poop deck, some rather strange wooden constructions placed side by side over simple holes in the deck. By the stench, these were obviously toilets of some description and my heart sank. Turning a corner in the alleyway, I said light-heartedly that I needed the loo. To my great relief Hardy directed me forward to the mid-ships accommodation where the officer's toilets and bathrooms were situated. Going to sea appealed to me again once that problem was sorted out!

We sailed on a day tide of the 13th of November but it was dark by the time we were out in the river and heading out to sea. I was appointed my station aft with the second mate. The Liverpool Pilot, George Bender, piloted the vessel safely through the dock system, out into the river, which was crowded with ships, all lit with their approved navigation lights and the lights of buoys flashing magically in the darkness of the night. Pinpoints of light, green, red and white reflected in the dark waves. The pilot left us, disembarking, some fifteen miles out at the Bar Light Vessel Station and we were on our way. The ship's engines thumped away below, and the ship rolled in a low swell on her way with her cargo and crew to foreign parts, and I was part of it.

Peter Hardy and myself were put on day-work initially, for what I have not mentioned so far is that on the last day of loading, we received livestock. These were in total: a special type of eastern European sheep dog, which should have answered, but which did not answer to the name of Nutty, six polo ponies and a pregnant racehorse by the name of Star of Vintage. Until arriving at the port of Bombay, I was not to be a sailor at all, but rather a maritime stable boy! It turned out to be a full time job.

I will always remember the morning when Captain Dalley was making his rounds, and stood outside the open door of the racehorse's box on the port side of number four hatch.

Star of Vintage had turned round and was facing outboard with her relatively large pregnant bulk and very large equestrian backside presented to the open door. "Never forget boys," said the wizened old captain, "The head of a horse and the stern of a ship!" As he uttered these words of wisdom, he was backing into the box, holding a bunch of carrots in his gnarled hands. Before we could speak, he brought up[1] with his back to the large rear end of the horse. We all held our breath, but the animal was kind to the captain and moved not a muscle, let alone a hoof. Captain Dalley made it back to the door, unscathed, with both his honour and his wizened frame intact, although I suppose his honour was slightly tarnished, for after all, a really good navigator does always look behind, particularly when going astern!

We passed Land's End, crossed the Bay of Biscay and negotiated the Straits of Gibraltar to enter the Bay at Algiers to take on bunkers. Then on to a southbound passage through the Suez Canal. By now the temperatures were very hot indeed, in excess of one hundred and twenty degrees Fahrenheit as I recall. The ice-water tap in the starboard mid-ships alleyway was constantly visited! We turned north from Suez and steered up the Gulf of Aqaba, where we discharged cargo in the blistering heat, thinking of Lawrence of Arabia, surrounded by massive cliffs of stark red rock and the desert.

Having refuelled at Steamer Point, Aden and bought amazing battery operated mechanical toys for both my nephew and my niece, we sailed on, out into the Indian Ocean. The toys were made in Japan and had not as yet appeared in British Stores. I also purchased my first pair of flip-flops, a type of footwear, which I have worn ever since.

---

1 "Brought up" is a nautical expression for a ship to be all stopped in the water and therefore not moving.

My cadet logbook reads well for a sixteen year-old who wrote it, telling of islands passed in the Red Sea, of re-fuelling at Steamer Point Aden, of the arrival in Bombay and of the lowering of our ensign to the Indian Warship *Delhi*, formerly H.M.S. *Achilles*, which took part in the Battle of the River Plate.

From Bombay onwards I was to become a sailor as the horses were discharged there and my days spent as a stable boy were over! I have never forgotten, however, the morning that Captain Dalley told Peter and myself the importance of the simple lesson: "The head of a horse and the stern of a ship!"

The day's duties from then on included "tallying" stores and "tomming" off cargo, rope-work and other sailorising duties including the caulking of wooden decks with oakum and pitch. The sea was rough on many occasions during the voyage but my overall memory is of the oily, calm, blue-green waters of the Indian Ocean being cleft by the *Brodie's* bow to fall astern in a disturbed, white-frothing wake as the vessel ploughed her way ever onwards to the next port.

These ports were numerous: Colombo, Chittagong, Chalna, Madras, Galle, Calicut, Allepey, Cochin, and finally 'home' to Tilbury where I was to "sign off,"[2] no longer a "first-trip" cadet.

All the days of this voyage and the ports visited have stories as vivid in my mind's-eye as if it were only yesterday. For example, there was the excursion by bus from the mission at Colombo, inland to the Temple of the Tooth at Kandy, to see elephants bathing in the Katagastota River and to tour a tea plantation. There was the Christmas dinner alongside in Chittagong, where we were joined by crew-members from the *Clan Alpine* who were being flown home after their ship, which had, with both anchors down and steaming full-speed ahead, travelled twelve miles astern down the coast and four miles inland in the teeth of the strong winds resulting from an anti-cyclone. The storm was to take the lives of many. The story is well known in shipping circles of how as the

2 Legal requirement for registered crew when leaving a ship.

water receded, the vessel was found to be upright in a paddy field surrounded by palm trees!

There was also New Year spent at anchor in the Pussar River at Chalna. The two cadets were to keep the anchor watches. I remember that there were no fixed lights during the hours of darkness and the lights were camp fires in the bush, which died into embers and new fires had to be used for the anchor bearings! From the bridge we heard tigers roaring in the jungle in the darkness, which surrounded us, all enveloping in the stillness of the night.

Finally there was the channel battering so vivid in Masefield's *Cargoes* poem as we forged our way homeward to Tilbury, suffering that wonderful seaman's condition of growing excitement known as the "Channels" as we neared home.

I was to remain home for literally only a matter of days as an uncle who worked for I.C.I. informed me that M.V. *Clan MacLeod* was loading in Liverpool for a charter for that company and was bound for Australia. A phone call to the manning office in Liverpool with a request that I may sign on that vessel, resulted in my leaving Liverpool once more, this trip, bound for the other side of the world.

T.S.S. Clan Brodie

THE OTHER SIDE OF THE WORLD

Compared to the *Brodie*, M.V. *Clan Macleod* was "ultra-modern" and was even equipped with air-conditioning! She was classified at six thousand and sixty three gross tons. At four hundred and sixty six feet long, she was some twenty feet shorter than my previous ship.

In Liverpool, at the cadet-school, I was to meet my fellow cadet aboard, Andy Douglas, who was to become a life-long friend. Amongst many other achievements, Andy became editor of the shipping magazine *Sea Breezes*. We were to sail from Liverpool soon after this meeting in mid-March. George Cockram was the Liverpool Pilot outward bound from Liverpool. Unlike the stable-boy rôle aboard the *Brodie*, Andy and myself were to keep watches with the officers of the watch and I felt that I was on my way to stardom.

Once more we made the passage through the Suez Canal and out into the sultry heat of the Indian Ocean. One story, which I can never decide is either simply amusing or more a tale of a momentary failing in my responsible attitude to the preservation of life is the tale of the streaming of the ship's log south of Suez. Andy and myself were sent aft to stream the log[3] when the vessel was clear of Suez and heading southbound down the Red Sea.

A ship's log consists of a brass impeller made fast to the end of the logline, which in turn is made fast to the log clock to be slotted into a fixing, either on the after-end of the ship herself, or streamed from a boom off the quarter of the ship. The log in this case was to be streamed from a boom on the port quarter. Andy, being somewhat of a daredevil in his younger days, and the senior cadet, chose to stream the log, sitting out on the boom, holding the log-clock! My job was to push in the vaguely sexual, wooden, male plug into the vaguely female socket, when ordered to do so.

---

3 A means of recording distance covered in nautical miles.

"Now" came the shouted command from my senior-cadet, and I duly pushed home the large plug as ordered. For some reason, best known to himself, Andy was still holding the log-clock in his hands, apparently to "see if it worked," when the electrical current reached the instrument. I observed Andy, perched perilously above the shark-infested waters of the Red Sea, tossing the valued log-clock up into the air and screaming loudly each time he caught it, the current flowing through him briefly, before he tossed it back into the air. I am laughing now, proving my irresponsibility, but it was funny. With tears streaming down my cheeks, I shinned up to unplug the source of Andy's excitement and, yes, he did eventually forgive me, but never managed to see any humour in the situation whatsoever.

I note from my cadet logbook that many of the day-jobs, which we were given, were to check equipment. The Australian port authorities have always been renowned for their safety record, and as a result were renowned for the safety checks of equipment. Thus Andy and I checked just about everything on board which moved and everything which did not. I have never understood how the chief-officer could estimate the safe working load of an unmarked shackle! The mate would view the offending piece of unmarked kit, and with an experienced eye declare the number, which we were to stamp on it!

The vessel was to put into Colombo for bunkers before proceeding south to cross the Equator. I attempted to evade Neptune and his motley crew who vaguely resembled other members of our own crew but with the rest of the: "first time over-the-liners," I was eventually stripped, handcuffed to the ships rails and coated from head to foot in graphite grease! The atmosphere was light-hearted and fun. Once hosed down, the ceremony turned into a carnival with an enjoyable party atmosphere, with all those not on watch, joining in.

South of the Equator I was to notice that due to geostrophic force, bathwater drains out from a bath turning in an anti-clockwise direction as opposed to clockwise in the northern hemisphere! I was also to sight my first albatross following in the wake of the ship. For several days a storm was to force the ship off course to the south and west and we were to run downwind with a following sea, whose waves amazed me with their ferocity and violence. I have seen worse since, but these were frightening to a sixteen year-old. I would stand on the after deck, enthralled with the beauty of the crashing waters as the ship rose and fell on these waves, and albatross swooped gracefully in our wake, at home in the rolling troughs of the ocean swell.

At length, the storm abated and, having run a long way to the south, towards the Antarctic, we turned to the northeast and headed back towards Australia. The ship reached the south coast of Australia and coasted round Tasmania to head north and make the entrance to the magnificent, natural harbour of Sydney.

Whilst we were alongside in Sydney, we were able to go ashore and visit the beaches and the then new Sydney Opera House with its shell structure overlooking the harbour. I remember vividly walking across Sydney Harbour Bridge, riding in the funfair at Luna Park and visiting a distant relative, great aunt Patty. This wonderful lady was of a great age and she played the piano beautifully. I particularly remember her rendition of *The Laughing Song*, sung with a beautiful voice, which even now stirs tunefully in my memory.

With Andy, I visited the mission and made a train journey high up into the Blue Mountains, where we were to see and hear amongst others, whiplash birds. The distant mountains were, indeed incredibly blue in colour. We also visited Taronga Park Zoo and saw the native koala bears, kangaroos and wallabies. I recall an over friendly emu trying to swallow my tie! (Why I ask myself was I wearing a tie?).

The voyage continued north from Sydney to Brisbane, where I was to visit both relatives, (Great aunt Patty's son) and an old scout friend whose family had emigrated some five years earlier.

Back to Sydney and a brief loading of wool in bales for the homebound voyage before returning to Brisbane where we held an "official" party on board for, which I was to wear my No.10's, an all white full uniform, for the first and only time. I can remember a rather charming young lady who had been invited, Janet Waddel was her name, but I believe that I was far too young and immature for her to have even noticed me!

Andy and I also managed a trip north to Currumbin Beach on the Gold Coast. I have never been a strong swimmer, but when the beach guard's bell rang out from the watch-tower to warn that a shark had been sighted close offshore, I swam! Soon after I was reported to be flailing the sand some yards up the beach and well clear of the water's edge before I was lying safely all stopped on the beach.

The next port was to be Fremantle, and I recall the disappointment of not proceeding "north about" to call at Papua New Guinea as was first planned in the schedule but later cancelled. Two factors of this leg of the voyage remain clearly with me: one, I had a birthday and was seventeen years old. I was impressed that Andy had managed to save a bar of a particularly tasty Australian chocolate for me as a birthday present. I recall a black and white wrapper, square and with a male figure smoking a pipe on the top part of the paper.

The second is not such a pleasant memory. The chief officer, the mate, Danny Richards had "off-loaded" the gift of a large spider crab onto my unsuspecting self. Was I ill! They told me to report if I began passing blood. I did and I didn't, for I feared being left ashore in hospital in Freemantle. I simply wished to continue the voyage as planned.

Clan Macleod was to pass through the Suez Canal and call at Genoa, where a prostitute in a lime green blouse and a black pencil skirt chased Andy and me up a flight of stone steps near the harbour when we went ashore. It was not a case of playing hard to get, but rather that we were scared stiff! The lady hitched up her skirt and took off her very high-heeled black shoes. I believe that it was only because Andy and I had both been mile champions at school that we were able to escape I had no idea what!

We were to call at Dunkirk and Antwerp to unload our cargo of wool and skins before arriving at Manchester, which was the end of the voyage for me, as I was to sign off and return home to join the Liverpool Pilot Service within a few days as a "Boathand." The master of the *Macleod*, Captain Jean de Garis, had received a telegram to that effect somewhere on the homeward passage. The ship arrived in the approaches to the River Mersey and then it really was strange for me because we were "coming home" and then, we were leaving again, as the Pierhead fell behind us on our way to Eastham Locks and the Manchester Ship Canal. I signed off the following day, lost a bottle of gin to the policeman on the gate who said I was too young to carry it home for my parents, (bastard!) and said farewell to Clan Line.

When I look back on those days, I think of the film *On the Waterfront*, of 1953, starring a very young Marlon Brando, I remember the same methods of the handling of cargo on board the general cargo ships, which I sailed on. The dockers or stevedores, all used their own individual cargo hooks and employed a variety of cargo handling equipment such as: pallets, cargo nets, strops, snotters and slings amongst other specialised kit to cope with the varying cargoes. Their trade was altered overnight with the advent of containerisation. "Boxes to be loaded and unloaded with ease and carried on board even bigger boxes", which is one description of modern container ships and their cargo. The book, *The Boatswains' Manual* will enlighten anyone interested further. Suffice it to say that there are a great many "living dinosaurs" from the shipping industry like me, who experienced a series of revolutions in the shipping trade as dynamic as the change from sail to steam, and who still remember what could soon become, sadly, forgotten skills.

A note here is to record the loss of Peter Hardy, my fellow cadet on my first trip. Peter and Andy were to attend sea school, a mid-apprenticeship release at King Edward's College, London following the Australian trip. Returning to sea after the course, Peter was to sail as cadet on the ill-fated *Clan Keith*, which was to be lost, whilst she was outward bound off the North African Coast. This has always been a sobering thought for me, for if I had not been called into the Pilot Service, I would have been with the other two at King Edward's, and could possibly have been manned along with Peter as cadet on board the *Clan Keith*.

A further sad note is that Andy Douglas, who became a life-long friend, died in January of this year, whilst I have been writing this book. I read him the passage about the streaming of the log, and I am pleased to say that he did laugh at the memory. He will be sadly missed.

Cadet Officer, Clan Line

BOATHAND DAYS

Senior Lad on board No.3 1967

My orders were to join No. 3 Pilot Boat, the *Arnet Robinson* in Herculaneum Dock in the South Liverpool Dock System. The boat was refuelling ready to take up the western approaches or Lynas Station for the last week of her three-week cruise.

I was to relieve Ronnie Bradford, 'Yozza' in the sink. This statement of fact has often brought about mirth at the thought of me helping him to urinate in a washbowl! For the boathand it was far more obvious and simple. The latest junior boathand took over the position of the boathand who was his immediate senior on board the pilot boat, which he had joined. The junior boathand's duties included the unpleasant task of "washing up" the dishes for the rest of the crew.

My first memory was to be taken "down aft" to the boathands' quarters, where my lapel georgettes, which signified a cadet in the Merchant Navy, were ignominiously hacked from my uniform with a bread knife. Not even a sailor's knife, for there was a second selection amongst the boathands themselves. Suffice to say that this second selection was character building.

There were four pilot cutters in those days. One was on station at the Bar Light Vessel some fifteen miles out to sea. This station coped with vessels inbound from the north and with most of the outward-bound traffic. After one week manning this station the boat refuelled, restored and became the "running boat." That is to say she ran daily from the Pier Head at Liverpool with full complements of pilots on board to man the Bar Pilot Station Boat and on down to the Western Station Boat, which cruised off Point Lynas in Anglesey. She would sail at lunchtime and return towards midnight, depending on tide times. She brought back outward-bound pilots from both stations, who were then placed back on the working list of pilots.

At the end of the second week of the cruise, the boat would again restore and refuel, sail to Point Lynas, and this time relieve the Lynas Pilot Boat, whose station she would take for the third week of the cruise. After serving the vessels inbound to Liverpool from the west, and outward traffic consisting of large vessels or all vessels if the prevailing westerly gales were blowing, she in her turn would be relieved and return for what the boathands referred to as the "glorious week in dock!"

During my early days, we would work two days on board the boat in dock and keep watches if no watchman was assigned to the boat, but overall it was in the main a week off. We learned to be real seamen handling the boarding motorised boats called punts in extreme weather conditions and becoming good at it, for our lives and the lives of others depended upon nothing short of excellence. There were other stations kept by the station boats, such as Douglas Bay up in the Isle of Man, and these were dependent on existing weather conditions and the direction of the wind.

Having started as the lowest of the low, the boathand would work his way up the crew, until he reached the position of senior boathand on board, in effect, the chief officer.

As coxswain, about to board a pilot

The boathands were affectionately known as "Lads" even when they were "Senior Lad" and twenty-three years old!

From junior lad looking after the boathand's accommodation, serving up meals and washing up after the meal, the progression was to chart room lad who looked after the two masters' cabins in the six to eight evening watches. We worked four hours on and four hours off during the "cruise," breaking the pattern with the "dog-watches" of the "six to eight" each evening.

Then on to junior lad on deck whose specific task was to clear up after the day's work, cleaning paint brushes, coiling ropes and generally keeping the decks clear. This was the first position where you felt that you were becoming a recognised seaman, although all hands worked the punts when the boarding or disembarking of ships was taking place. These three junior positions tended to stick together and meet down forward to moan about their treatment and the rest of the crew towards the end of the six to eight!

I was fortunate after so long a long spell "Down Aft" as junior lad, to spend a winter in the next position up as log-man. This job entailed bringing the log-slate from the bridge in the six to eight, making a brew and copying the details of the ship's business into the official logbook to be presented to the Superintendent of Pilotage at the end of the cruise.

There followed the two positions of punts-men, whose job it was to service and refuel the punts. Then came the position of boatswain, who had the responsibility of making sure that the boat was always in an immaculate, and therefore safe, condition. Several times a year the boats were inspected for one reason or another, but particularly in the summer, when all boats were inspected by the pilotage committee out at sea.

The boatswain and the senior punts-man also kept the bridge watch in the six to eight to gain watch-keeping experience before they became the watch-keeping officers that the second lad and senior lad were. During the seven-year apprenticeship, this was the time it took on average to rise from the bottom of the crew to the top; each boathand would be sent "leadsmans" with serving pilots. This term was derived from the days when the apprentice pilot accompanying the pilot would indeed swing the lead.

The lead being a seven-pound weight attached to a rope, which is marked with different identifying marks at intervals marking the fathoms of line paid out to the bottom. A mixture of leather, white linen, blue serge, red bunting and cord, is inserted in the lay of the rope, and because of the different textures sensitive to the hand, which has swung the lead, the mark can be recognised even in the dark. The lead itself was "armed with tallow" so that the tallow in the cavity on the bottom of the lead might possibly pick up particles from the sea bed, so that the nature of the bottom could be identified and the knowledge thus help to fix the ship's position from information on a chart.

It is my opinion that a Mississippi paddle steamer would have had a draught of some ten feet in the water. This would account for the pseudonym 'Mark Twain' taken from when Samuel Langhorne Clemens was a "cub pilot," training with the "lightning" pilot, Mr. Bixby to be a pilot himself, as featured in the book: *Life on the Mississippi*. The importance of the sounding "by the mark twain" would, in my opinion be the safe depth for a riverboat to navigate safely. That would be, ten feet for the draft of the vessel in the water, and the safe margin of two feet underneath the keel, a margin Liverpool Pilots have always been happy to operate with in the channel approaches to the Mersey. This latter fact, of course being dependent on the slow speed of the vessel, progressing over shallows to avoid the phenomenon known as "squat" or "sinkage."

The name for the training trip of the young person in training to be a pilot, is still classified as a leadsman, even though electronic echo sounders and tide-gauges have taken over from the necessity of one hand standing in the chains: "swinging the lead!"

After each year's examinations and sadly, after either retirement or death, (many pilots died relatively young, or were invalided out from the service) the boathand would near the top of the tree and become a senior boathand, and be allowed to wear a single gold stripe on the cuffs of his uniform reefer-jacket. The candidate would, soon after, be sent back to sea at this point to gain the necessary sea time to sit for the examination of whatever maritime ticket was possible in the time left before his being called to present himself for the oral examination for a licence of the third class, which would allow him to pilot vessels up to six hundred tons net. (Sadly for Liverpool, there are still no female pilots in the service.)

These were very small coasters in comparison to the much larger starting vessels of the modern day standards. Qualifications of the present day for entrance into pilotage in Liverpool have altered through force of circumstances brought about by the changes in water-borne trade.

At present, the Liverpool Pilots require applicants to hold a 'Class One Certificate'[4], and to have been in command, before acceptance into the service to commence their rigorous training, to be an authorised pilot. This training includes the necessity to complete a number of "leadsmans," to and from all entrances on the river, where the trainee accompanies the authorised pilots on their duties and witnesses the operations of the pilot at first hand, just as the boathands had done before them.

I was delighted to find that I was to complete the "sea-time" necessary for the mate's home trade ticket required by being placed as un-certificated third officer with Booker Line. Bookers, (the same company, which awards an annual prize for literature in the United Kingdom) ran raw sugar from Georgetown, Guyana and from the West Indies to the United Kingdom.

Now that really was a different way of life from the previous hard years on the river as a boathand!

Liverpool Pilot Boat No.3. Arnet Robinson

---

4 A Class One Certificate is the qualification required for a candidate to be master in command of a foreign going vessel of the Merchant Navy.

WESTWARD HO!

John's gone to the Caribbean
He's gone and we know why,
John's gone to the Caribbean,
To the blue sun, sea and sky.

From: *Blue Sun Calypso*

My orders were to join M.V. *Booker Venture*, which was lying to mooring-buoys off Gravesend in the River Thames. The *Venture* was a bulk carrier of five thousand, six hundred and twenty five tons. She was four hundred and ninety feet long and was affectionately known as the 'Booker Line Submarine.' The nickname came from the fact that the *Venture* was of a very unusual ship design, which tended not to ride over the seas, but rather would, through preference, quite simply go through, or under them!

I was delighted with my new ship, my cabin with self-contained loo and shower, the crew and life in general. The mate was a dour Scot by the name of Bob Machechnie, whose accent I found difficult to understand at first. This fact is perhaps best illustrated by the keen young third officer, willing to please, who after believing that he had heard Bob say "My kingdom for a nail" offered him a box of nails, which I had noticed in my luxurious cabin. On producing the box, I was to discover that what he had actually said was: "My kingdom for an ale!" A box of which, I did not have in my luxurious cabin.

I had had the fortune to marry the girl of my dreams the year before this stage of my career, and I was delighted that in my new world Gill, my wife, was able to join me aboard for the weekend, whilst we were discharging sugar at Silvertown on the Thames. We were able to go up to London and I recall that we saw Alec Guinness in *Wise Child* at Wyndham's Theatre.

Afterwards, we walked around London, including around Piccadilly Square, and bought and ate hot chestnuts. I remember returning to buy a second bag of chestnuts particularly because, whilst Gill waited on the edge of the crowd for me, a young man came and asked her "How much?" Being somewhat naïve, Gill thought that he was inquiring about the chestnuts and replied truthfully: "A shilling." Whereupon the young man ran off!

We were to sail on the first of three trips early the next week and I can recall the mate sending me to use my diplomacy to extract the Liverpool crew from the pub across the road, minutes before the ship was due to sail. It is true to say that I have been through some tough times in the course of my career, and this proved to be one of the toughest; however, we were to sail on time, and with a full crew!

I made three trips with Bookers. Two to Georgetown, topping up with bunkers, homeward-bound in Barbados. The third and final voyage was as a tramp carrying phosphates from Bremen to Jacksonville and Tampa in Florida, before dropping south to Jamaica, St. Kitts and Antigua to pick up the sugar as the commodity came back in season again.

The first and second trips were made with Captain Ted Jones, and the third with Captain Armitage. I mention them both by name, for I learned a great deal from both men whom I respected. There were short leave periods between trips, as we signed off upon arrival in the Thames. On both occasions, anchored off, or lying to mooring-buoys, and awaiting a launch to ferry us ashore, I showed both my initiative and certain ingenuity by "thumbing lifts" on passing traffic in order to capitalise on the time to be spent at home.

On the first occasion, the official launch had departed before the crew had signed off, and I "thumbed a lift" for us all on a passing bunkering barge. A whip round of ten shillings (old money) a man was little enough to pay the delighted barge crew. The second landing was to be a lone landing, as the rest of the crew did not believe that I could pull such a landing off again. But, having my faith in fellows of the river from my earlier Liverpool days, I did, and a passing river police launch obliged, and dropped me in the middle of nowhere. I was ashore, however, and made it to Euston Station and a homeward-bound train, hours before the rest of my shipmates even managed to get ashore.

From many mainly happy memories with Bookers, I remember numerous events, which now, as memories, flit lightly, like bats through the cloisters of my mind. I remember watching the angle of repose on the sugar as it poured with that warm sweet smell into the holds. The vessel always being loaded to: "bad draft" for maximising cargo. That is to say that she was loaded down by the head, so that with squat[5], she would level out to cross the shallows of the Georgetown Bar on an even keel at maximum draft.

I see vividly the huge wave, which stopped us dead in the water and flung the *Venture* onto her beam-ends. We were heading north, bound for Tampa and it was in the forenoon watch. I gripped the chart table as my legs flew out horizontally to starboard. I watched the young deck boy, who had been on the wheel; hurtle past me at eye-level to end in a heap in the forward, starboard corner of the wheelhouse. As the ship, thankfully righted herself, I leaped to the wheel and spun the helm hard-to-port to meet the next wave. Captain Armitage ordered that we were to "heave-to," and we rode out the rest of the storm ticking over dead slow ahead, the ship's head end-on to the teeth of the howling winds and the blown spume of the tortuous seas.

I recall being concerned about the course laid on the chart over shallow water in the Yucatan Channel between Mexico and Jamaica, and shining the Aldis Lamp into the waters during the evening watch and sighting the sea-bed! Captain Armitage heeded my concerns and ruled off a shallow "no-go" area for future voyages!

---

5 The sinkage experienced by a vessel travelling at speed, which increases her draft. With small craft, such as a speedboat for example, by the stern, for large vessels, by the head.

I had learned from a fellow boathand who had sailed on board the *Venture* before me what we called the "noon sight" trick. Sextants were not in our daily navigation on board pilot cutters, so both the instrument and their science were alien to us.

The trick was to stand between the captain and the second-mate at the noonday sight and listen carefully. The degrees were not a problem, but the minutes and seconds were the exacting part of "shooting the sun." during the sight, with the sun at its zenith. With ears pricked, the third mate could hear the captain mutter his reading and soon after the second mate would mutter his. Go for the minutes and seconds of arc between the two, and it never failed! "He's got it right again Second!" would be the declaration, which never failed to upset the second-mate!

On one crossing to the west we did not sight the sun for days and as it eventually took three weeks, it is important to note that the weather was appalling. Gales from the west the whole voyage had us proceeding astern at times. We did not know where we were and then I remembered my close reading of the Boatswain's Manual, and a reference to the 'Dutchman's Log'.

This makeshift method of dead reckoning is quite ingenious and entails throwing over the bow, ahead of the ship, a floating object. The mate who throws it, flags up the moment the object passes abeam of him and the mate on the bridge clicks the stopwatch. The object is timed down the known length of the vessel to be clocked again abeam of the bridge. "Hatch wedges Mr. Mate," ordered Captain Armitage, and "Bring me a stopwatch." We were all pleased to find that the resulting position from the speed calculated was, indeed not far from the ship's actual position when we were eventually to see the sun again. I remember that the second-mate was not too pleased with me over that one either!

A pilot's strike was threatened, after we had anchored off Savannah-la-Mar. This natural harbour was made film-famous in the James Bond thriller *The Man with the Golden Gun*, for it was the setting for the man with the golden gun to shoot the poor bird out of the tree in front of 007. I spent a pleasant day in command of the ship's motor lifeboat with two A.B's and a sounding lead, charting the depths between the anchorage and the open sea. The pilot had warned against us leaving without a pilot if the strike had gone ahead because of "the shoal." The soundings proved that there was no hidden shoal, and I smiled as the pilot, who had not gone on strike, put in a "dog's leg" to port to illustrate some point on the straight forward southerly course to the waiting pilot launch.

Whilst we were loading sugar from barges at anchor in the bay, I remember that the second mate on this trip, who shall remain nameless, owed me so much watch-time by the arrival in Jamaica, that I was able to leave the vessel in Savannah-la-Mar and travel by local bus across the island to Doctor's Cove Beach in the north.

I waited in the darkness of early dawn for the arrival of the dugout canoe, fitted with an outboard engine, which was to ferry me to the hard and the early morning bus. As I stood on the deck, there was the sweet smell of the sugar; the air was loud with the incessant howling of "pye" dogs and a hundred cockerels crowing, heralds of first light.

The bus journey was incredible. The route lay round to the southwest of the island with names such as Tortugas Cay, Brimstone Hill, Mosquito Cove and Negril Point. The bus bounced on the dusty, pot-holed track. Passengers laughed and chattered as their goods, which included hens and piglets and other livestock, as well as masses of fresh vegetables, bounced, squawked and grunted on the dented roof above.

I spent the afternoon on Doctor's Cove Beach in Montego Bay before returning on another local bus, which travelled due south over the mountains. I noted the large cruise liners anchored off, one I believe was the German Cruise Liner *Bremen*. Ships' lifeboats ferried the passengers ashore to pay to stretch out on the magnificent sands, whilst I observed the scene from the free local's beach, fenced off from the tourist's world, but no less magnificent with the same gleaming white sand.

On the return journey, there were delays, and when I arrived back on board the crew were relieved, for troubles had broken out in Ian Smith's Rhodesia, which had had political repercussions in the West Indies. Captain Armitage had been concerned for my safety. I can only say that my fellow bus passengers had made me so welcome, and had even shared their food and drink with me during the course of the lengthy journey in the tropical darkness back to the south. The second mate said that he intended to make such a journey one day, but I doubted if that day would ever come.

My sea time completed, I returned home for a short leave and a holiday with Gill in Ibiza before attending the nautical school at Liverpool, Byrom Street Polytechnic, as the present John Moores University was then called. After a summer of study and successful examinations, I was nearly there. I was soon back on board Number Three Pilot Boat the *Arnet Robinson* as Senior Boathand, with only weeks before I was to be called before the Pilotage Committee to be examined for a licence of pilot of the third-class in the Port of Liverpool.

I had grown a beard on the first trip. As soon as we cleared the Thames estuary, I threw my razor over the side. After a few days out into the Atlantic, the master, Ted Jones, expressed the opinion that with my reddish-blond stubble, I looked like "a rat peering out of a bale of oakum!"[6] I wanted to know, like most young men, if I could indeed grow one, and then there was another reason. Although I was twenty-four years old, I looked like a teenager. At best I could be taken for an eighteen year old and I was concerned about the question of authority when I came up against some of the "old shell-back sailors," whom I knew to be in command of the world's merchant fleets of the time.

A splendid Scotsman of the old school, Lieutenant-Commander Hill held the position with that grand title: Marine Surveyor and Water Bailiff for the Port of Liverpool at that time. I was concerned

---

6 From the 'Boatswain's Manual:' Old rope yarns teased out and tarred.

that appearing before the examination-board with a beard might jeopardise my chances of being licensed.

The day before the examination in August of that year, I travelled over to the Port Office Buildings on the Pier Head to both sight the latest charts and to seek possible permission to retain the beard. Lieutenant-Commander Hill looked at me with a withering glance for some moments before declaring: "I dinna like beards Curry, but I tak' your point, ye can keep the beard." I believe that that made me the first boathand ever to present himself as a bearded candidate before the committee. The following day I passed out as pilot of the third class. Ambition achieved! I was to collect my licence the following morning. Now for the ships!

The Booker Line submarine

Liverpool Pilot

Out in the Bay,
Where the wind and spray
From the north-west are driving,
And the bitter sleet
With its winding sheet
To hide the track is striving.

Through the fearful night
Gleams the flashing light
Of the buoys in the channel rolling.
And the warning knell
Of the floating bell
In the pilot's ear is tolling.

On the oceans wide,
The ship may ride
Whilst the crashing waters thunder,
But the clutching hands
Of the Crosby Sands
Would tear her bones asunder.

Through the cruel ranks
Of the shoals and banks,
The pilot steers undaunted,
Midst the swirl and fume,
And the white blown spume
By its secret fury haunted.

From the lofty bridge
He can see the ridge
Where the tidal race is swirling
And he dare not tack
From the twisted track
Where the broken seas are curling.

On past the cruel hands
Of the Crosby Sands
The laden ship is creeping,
Whilst the tempest tries
To tear the prize
From the pilot's trusty keeping.

Until at last,
She's swinging fast
Where the lights of the town are gleaming,
There, the pilot's wife
Of the water's strife
And the deadly shoal is dreaming.

What an emptied name
Is the moneyed fame
Of the market's vulgar brawling,
To the stern renown,
An age long crown,
Of the pilot's lonely calling.

An anonymous poem, written by a female passenger, a nurse on board the SS. *Nirvana* for my father, Walter Curry, when he was returning home from Suez, having been recalled to become a Pilot in the Port Of Liverpool in 1928.

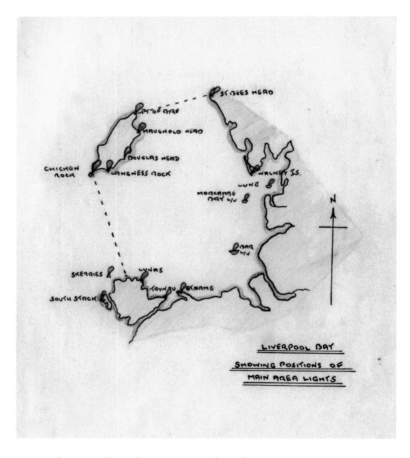

A rough map taken from my Boathand's mark book, showing the
Liverpool Pilotage District as defined by the 1913 Pilotage Act.
This area was to be considerably reduced under the Pilotage Act
of 1988.

THE WORLD IN MY BRIEFCASE

"Your true pilot cares nothing about anything on earth but the river. The pride in his occupation surpasses the pride of kings..."[7]

I was to sign so many documents on the insistence of the shore-master the following morning dressed in my piloting suit. The suit, which conformed to the Pilotage Bye-laws, was tailor-made from navy-blue hopsack and was very expensive. It was also only to last three months! My parents had insisted on paying for this, my first professional pilot's clothing. The suit looked superb initially but could not cope with the rigours of a pilot's life.

The cloth was constantly splashed with salt-water from breaking waves, it was slept in when a few hours could be snatched, possibly at anchor, and occasionally it was brushed with wet paint or oil, possibly grease, on the deck of a ship. The Liverpool Pilot's "uniform" was, Bye-Law, a nautical blue suit, a nautical peaked cap and a watch, set to committee time! Added to this, a pilot carried a bag in which were charts, a wash-bag, a novel, and in later years, a V.H.F. radio. A pea-whistle, an 'Acme Thunderer', was the method to communicate with tugboats before technology progressed. A blue gabardine mackintosh was the favoured outer garment, but being short of funds and it being the swinging sixties, I cut down a shiny-black, Dock Board issue, oilskin-coat into a serviceable and "Carnaby Street, trendy," waterproof jacket of the '60s.

The death of a pilot from the Port of Preston by drowning heralded the swift advent of the Sea-Safe "floata-coat," which incorporated a lifejacket, a whistle and a strobe light. But that was to come in a few years down the line.

My outfit was completed on the day with a touch of youthful independence mixed with 1960s rebellion, by the wearing of a pink shirt and a flower-power tie!

---

7 'Life on the Mississippi,' Mark Twain. Chapter 7.

After the signings, in total trust, for, amongst other things, membership of the Liverpool Pilots Association and the 'Henderson' fund as I recall, I was then given that most essential piece of piloting kit, a book of tide tables by the shore-master and manned on my first ship: the Motor Tanker *Falmouth* bound from Eastham Locks to sea on the ebb of the tide that afternoon. I have often stated that a true pilot could go out to sea stark-naked, the only essential piece of up-dated knowledge in addition to that gained through experience he would need to do the job, would be the time and height of the tide, which he was working on!

The August day was fine with clear blue skies and sunshine. Gill, and I had recently bought a very nearly "clapped-out" Sunbeam Alpine, two-seater sports car in readiness for the new life. Gill had recently qualified as a teacher and, as it was the summer holidays, she was able to accompany me, driving me down to the Eastham Locks. (Gill was also to accompany me forty one years later, actually on board my last ship, M.V. *Atlantic Compass*, when I sailed off, literally into the west and the setting sun!)

I left Gill outside the pilot rooms and with a mixture of eager enthusiasm and a certain healthy trepidation, I walked over to Eastham Locks, to where the vessel had been brought by a Manchester Ship Canal Pilot. The "Good Afternoon Captain" and the questions of where bound, what draft and who the agents were, are somewhat lost in the mists of that exciting afternoon, but what I do remember vividly is what happened after the ship had been guided safely out of the lock and into the Eastham Channel. The pilots' rooms lie on the Cheshire bank as was, just to the west of the middle of the Q.E.II Oil-Dock lock, and there outside the rooms, sitting on the bonnet of a white sports car, was a: "little blonde!"

The captain grabbed the bridge binoculars and focused in on the apparition. "Look at this pilot…" brought about the swift realisation that the captain was about to inadvertently come out with an expression he might, and I certainly would, regret and invoked the stern warning: "Before you say anything further Captain, be aware that the blonde on the bonnet of my car is my wife!" He blushed and I took the incident as a compliment.

The two hour or so passage outward-bound on that particularly bright and clear summer's day, passed uneventfully, and all too soon I was taken overboard by one of the boarding-punts of No. 3 Pilot Boat, my own boat! On board the pilot boat there was much in the way of congratulations bestowed on this, the latest Liverpool Pilot. On the bridge "genial" (as he was once described in a local newspaper) Captain Harry Littler, 'The Boy Captain,' and the man who made sure that his crew was ultra-efficient, asked me how I now looked back on my training under his supervision. My truthful reply startled him and to some extent myself: "Captain Littler Sir, you taught me above all else, one important lesson in life-skills, and that is the fact that you may command respect, but you cannot demand respect." He took it well, but he did stop smiling!

The following afternoon, I was to conduct a similar tanker on the same passage without incident. She was the M.T *Teesport*, a vessel Captain Littler had sent me a leadsman on board down the Menai Straits to Caernarfon, a month or so earlier.

My third assignment was a move from Eastham Locks to Birkenhead, West Float on board a very small tanker called the *Onward Enterprise*. The move was memorable only in the fact that when I had manoeuvred the vessel, inbound, close to the berth on Ilchester Wharf, which is situated on the south side of the West Float dock, with a strong southerly breeze blowing, for the inexperienced life of me, I could not get her alongside!

It was by now late evening and dark and I could not even drive her close enough for the crew to successfully throw a heaving-line to the waiting linesmen. I shall never forget that my problem and embarrassment were to be resolved by the young mate forward, who, having tied a heaving-line around his waist, dived over the side and swam with it through the murky waters of the West Float safely to the quay! With a line ashore, we were soon able to heave the vessel alongside.

I had been placed in Group One, Black Section and the group had been on leave and now were "turning to." This meant that I was to move from "Long-Shore Turns" (manning outward-bound vessels) to "Sea Turns" (bringing them in) with my own group. I had the honour to serve for three months in the same group as my father, the late Walter 'Curly' Curry. I did not always see eye to eye with my father, particularly in later life over issues such as fostering and adoption matters. Such issues were dear to both my, and Gill's heart, but difficult for my father and my mother with their concern for my well being. Such matters were alien to their way of life.

With regards to piloting, however, my father was for me, and not because he was my father, the best. He had an attitude, which could possibly be described as that of a laid back professional. It would seem to me that he had a judgement of speed and distances in a tideway, on no matter what size of ship he was aboard; that marked him out as something very special, a natural ship-handler indeed, and he was spoken highly of in marine circles. Off the bridge though, he could be very "silly" in the specific meaning of the word, with a total disregard of what anyone else might think of him or his behaviour. I shall refer to him from time to time later, but suffice to say that I believe that, happily, something of his piloting skills rubbed off on me and I certainly believed, as he did, that I kept on learning up to the moment, upon which I retired.

I remember being very proud and knowing that both my father and my brother Brian shared in that pride, when just once in the early hours of a winter's morning, shortly before my father retired in the November, I came overboard from an outward-bound coaster, to find the pair of them waiting for me in the starboard embayment of the Bar Pilot Boat. It was the only time in the three months that we were to be together on a pilot boat as pilots.

On my first tour of inward duty, I was to pilot two small tankers, one bound to Waterloo Dock and the other bound for Eastham Locks before I was to be sent to Point Lynas to bring in my first vessel from the Western Station. She was the Dutch coaster *Trim*, bound for Huskisson Dock via Sandon Locks. Not the easiest of locks to dock into but the over-riding memory of this passage is of the captain's toothache! The vessel called up an hour or so before arrival, not so much to confirm his E.T.A., but to urgently request that the pilot bring with him a supply of aspirin tablets to ease the captain's acute toothache. The said captain insisted on staying on the bridge, moaning and groaning every second of the five-hour passage up to Liverpool.

In the September I was to pilot the Dutch coaster *Tridale* up from Lynas bound for Langton Lock with the choice on the ebb, of backing in against the ebb tide or of my first opportunity of utilising the manoeuvre known as 'The Aeroplane Spin.' This manoeuvre makes use of a flood set, which manifests itself at about one hour's ebb on a tide, when the submerged, remaining ruins of the old Canada Half-Tide entrance, act as a block to the main flow of the tide, and an eddy is formed, which forms a flood-set back down the wall in front of the lock entrance.

After the lock was opened by Her Majesty Queen Elizabeth II in 1962, (I was the junior boathand on board No.3 Pilot Boat when the Queen boarded the *Arnet Robinson* in the lock to sail into the system for the official opening) a pilot approached the lock on a small coaster to lock-in on a big ebb tide intending to back in stern-first. He was amazed to find that the tide quite simply spun the vessel round, head to the lock because of this flood-set, and he docked by default, head first! It is indeed a simple and impressive manoeuvre, but daunting for the first time on your own.

I approached in the dark, apprehensive and unsure as to whether or not to attempt the spin. Another coaster, a Polish vessel, transporting from Eastham Locks was to lock in ahead of me. I will watch and observe his approach and act accordingly I decided.

The *Wrotzka* approached from the south and swung to make an ebb-way approach. It was a near disaster as the vessel spun off the wall with the ebb-tide on her port bow, and came sideways to the north, narrowly missing, first: the west pier-head of the lock, and then the Canada Wreck Buoy, before hurtling clear of me to the north in the grip of the tide.

Right, my turn now, and I edged the *Tridale* gently in towards the wall. I cleared the west bull-nose of the lock, judged the distance and began the controlled spin. Whap! Round she came and almost before I knew it, there I was, all fast in the northwest corner of the lock. The *Wrotzka* was now making his second approach.

I observed carefully. This time the pilot of the *Wrotzka* had decided on an approach, which I never chose to use, and this was the dash; close down the wall from the south, initially with the tide behind, heading north for the lock. He made it, bringing up in a flurry of spume and spray! Somewhat messy and not very neat, but the ship was safely in. I took the ship's binoculars and peered round the corner of the wheelhouse, trying to keep out of sight, for whoever the pilot was, as I was the most recently made up, he had to be senior and therefore more experienced than me.

In the darkness I could make out a figure on the bridge of the other ship, with a pair of binoculars, peering as I was round the corner of the wheelhouse, trying not to be seen. It was my good friend and colleague, the now late David Temple. David was my immediate senior, having been granted his licence, only two weeks before me!

I now reach a point in this account where I believe that, rather than recount stories relating to various incidents from my career in chronological order, taken from the names of ships recorded in my copies of the tide tables, I will range, as I have done so often during my lifetime, in telling tales of the sea. I intend these tales to follow as they present themselves to my literal mind. They will not necessarily be the one more important than the other, but they will follow a mind pattern that has so often pleased and intrigued others during the telling of them, throughout my career.

Where better to continue than with a tale of dense fog and a ship with no radar! I set the scene with the description of the Island of Anglesey on a particularly warm and sunny, late autumn-day in October. The tones of the golden-brown, yellow and red leaves were at their most intense and, the fields on the island were ploughed and the soil ready for the sowing of the next year's crop.

I was now into the second year of my first licence. I had travelled to Point Lynas by train to Bangor and then across the island by taxi to the port of Amlwch. From the Port, along with a dozen or so colleagues, I was ferried by motor-punt to the pilot boat cruising offshore. It was late in the afternoon and the sea was flat calm. We would have said "mackerel conditions" if it had been earlier on in the summer. On the bridge, each man took his turn to peruse the list of ships written on the schedule of ships expected inbound, speculating on what the future had in store for him personally.

"Two ships rounding the Skerries," came the cry, and binoculars and telescopes were focused to the west. The two ships sighted were both to turn out to be Dutch coasters and both were to require pilots. A third ship hove into view, somewhat larger and one, which turned out to be a second-class Booth Line vessel. The three pilots, who were to be manned, had all noticed "something else" inbound from the west on the light westerly breeze as they scanned the horizon to identify the inbound ships. This "something else" was a light white cloud covering the entire horizon to the west, astern of the ships. It was a summer fog. It appeared like wispy, cotton wool, and had been conjured up by nature through the day having been very warm indeed, and now, as the sun was losing the heat; the cold of the sea froze the air's moisture into a heavy mist.

In those days, not all ships had radars. That is not to say that they did have radar, which was non-operative, but is to say that they simply were not equipped with radar. We, who were newly licensed pilots in the immediate post-war period, are now certainly to be classified as living dinosaurs in effect, for the changes afloat from the end of the Second World War to the present day are unbelievable, and certainly vie with the one major change, which is so often quoted, which was the change from sail to steam.

No radar scanner being visible was the obvious telltale sign in daylight through binoculars, which indicated that the coaster's owners had not paid out for the then relatively new, and now essential equipment.

The third ship sighted arrived first, and took my good friend and colleague Bob Swift, then a second-class pilot and who had been best man at my wedding in 1966. Bob was to reach the river in dense fog and then get himself into all kinds of trouble before he eventually docked the vessel safely into Brunswick Lock the following day.

The first of the two coasters was to be boarded by Chris Jones, also my senior, but still third class. Chris's ship was bound for the Manchester Ship Canal on the night's tide, but as he chose to drop anchor off the Orme's Head later in the passage, he was not to dock for several days. The vessel anchored in the dense, blinding whiteness of this long-lasting autumn fog.

I was to be home by midnight, sipping a hot chocolate before curling up in a warm bed and how this was achieved I trust, makes an interesting and an almost unbelievable tale.

Years later, when I was operating at the Marine Research and Training Centre at Port Revel near Grenoble in Isère, France, I was to learn the difference between a fairy story and a sailor's yarn. The first begins with the words: "Once upon a time..." and the second begins: "And this is no shit..." I always feel that this tale really fits into the second category!

I leapt aboard the Dutch coaster *Martinistad* minutes before we were to be overhauled by the fog. A swift exchange of greeting and pleasantries over, I quickly took a bearing and distance from Point Lynas Lighthouse, and laid the resulting position out on the Admiralty chart. I looked up from the chart, glanced ahead and was dismayed to discover that the visibility was such (or perhaps more accurately non-such) that I was unable to see the fore deck of this relatively small ship.

Whoops! "Right Captain, now we know exactly where we are on the chart, where are we bound?" The answer floored me. "Penmaenmawr Stone Jetty Pilot," came the reply.

Suffice it to say that few Liverpool Pilots had ever been to Penmaenmawr by sea. Yes, we had all passed through Penmaenmawr station on board the train from Chester to Bangor, but not on a coaster inbound from sea. It was admittedly in the district, which I had been examined for, and I knew where it was, but knowing and actually going, is an entirely different matter. I set a course to the east of Puffin Island, down towards the Conway River, and set off on half-speed, about five to six knots, and noted the depths of water on the course line from the chart.

Looks good, I thought to myself excited by the challenge. It was the last of the morning tide's ebb, and the only good memory, which I had before the fog closed in, was that there were no other vessels to the southeast of Point Lynas on the chosen course line. The *Martinistad* plodded slowly towards the land. To the north, we could hear fog-sirens, ships' bells and the dull thudding of ship's engines and propellers thrashing the still waters.

I felt confident but slightly uneasy with the fact that I was to some extent going into the unknown, even in my own district. I constantly checked the readings from the echo sounder against the soundings on the chart. This method of navigation is known as "following a line of soundings." We were nearing Puffin Island, or should have been, and the noises from other ships had died away to the north, leaving only the throbbing of our own ship's engines. It was then that I noticed the other line of almost identical soundings.

Not far from, but to the west of our desired course line and unlike our clear passage, these ran directly into Dinmore Quarry! What if the ebb had been stronger than I had anticipated on our slow moving ship? Perplexed, I looked up and noted only clear blue sky. The captain had picked up my obvious anxiety and was astounded when the pilot ordered: "Keep her going, as she goes Captain" before disappearing into the fog by climbing up the ladder on the mainmast to the truck of the mainmast, high above the ship's bridge!

The next words that the captain was to hear from aloft, were words obviously mixed with both relief and delight: "I can see everything from up here Captain. We are on course and will be anchoring off the jetty in about twenty minutes." It was unbelievable. The dense fog was extremely low-lying, perhaps no more than fifteen to twenty metres above sea level. Ships' funnels and masts could be seen clearly away to the north. Best of all for me was the fact that the ruin on Puffin Island was exactly where it should have been, abeam to starboard and the clock high up above in the quarry, to which we were bound, was both clearly visible and illuminated, and a signpost for me to be able to find the jetty.

I anchored the ship some two miles off the stone jetty in deep water to await the flooding tide. When we were to lift anchor, the fog had cleared close inshore and we made it without further incident to moor starboard side to on the jetty. My job satisfactorily over, I dashed up the jetty and onto the mainline railway track just in time to catch the last train of the evening from Penmaenmawr Station to Chester. From Chester, having missed both the last train and the last bus, I was to thumb a number of misty lifts home along a foggy A540 to West Kirby. Once safely home, I was soon tucked up in my own bed with a contented smile on my face, knowing that in the dense fog it would still be "hell out there," and dreaming of my good fortune and of the day's events.

'CRISPIN'S DAY'

Saint Crispin's day is traditionally set for the twenty fifth of October. Saint Crispin and his brother, Saint Crispinian, according to my Dictionary of Saints, are the patron saints of cobblers, shoemakers and leather workers. My Crispin's day came in my first year as a pilot and was much nearer to Christmas.

No. 1 Pilot Boat, *Sir Thomas Brocklebank* was sheltering from a northerly gale in Douglas Bay, to the south of the Isle of Man. With the wind from south round to the northwest, Moelfre Bay in Anglesey, southeast of Point Lynas, offers shelter for operating a pilot station in complete safety, both for inward and outward vessels. With the prevailing wind in the Liverpool Bay being westerly, and often strong to gale force, the Lynas Pilot Station is of vital importance to the Port of Liverpool.

Unfortunately for operational purposes, unlike the Isle of Wight, which lies close to the major Port of Southampton, the Isle of Man lies some fifty two miles to the north of the Liverpool Pilots' Bar Station. When the wind veers to the north of northwest, problems are presented for operating in the Liverpool Bay. In the days of the four pilot cutters, the Lynas Station Boat would proceed to the north to the shelter of Douglas Bay, sometimes in the most appalling conditions. In the present day, pilots are flown to the island to be boarded by a fishing boat, chartered as a pilot launch.

The week of Christmas in 1968, I found myself the only "tonner," or "short-hand" pilot, on board the Lynas Pilot Boat, which, having made the passage to the north, was cruising in Douglas Bay.[8] Captain Leighton Eddleston was master and he had a problem. I was the only tonner on board, indeed I was the only pilot on board that particular morning and there were no vessels small enough to take me expected in the near future. He solved the problem

---

8 A pilot whose operations are governed by the tonnage restrictions (now length restrictions) on the licence, (now authorisation) which he has been examined for, and holds currently.

sensibly by boarding me on a vessel, which had orders to dock on that afternoon tide. My orders were to proceed to the Bar Pilot Station, where it was to be arranged that I pick up a pilot of the appropriate class, who would relieve me of my charge and take her to dock.

The Booth line vessel M.V. *Crispin* looked beautiful as she made her way up to the pilot boat from the southwest. Her paintwork gleamed in the winter sunshine; the air was clear as was the blue of the sky, and crisp, white snow lay heavy on the backdrop of the island.

I was warmly welcomed on the bridge by the captain. The vessel was homeward-bound from a voyage to South America and the crew would be home for Christmas. I have mentioned the "Channels," the condition, which affects a homeward-bound crew and the whole ship was buzzing with an air of excitement.

We proceeded south on the flood of the afternoon tide with both wind and tide behind us. I explained the position regarding my boarding and the captain was only too happy to have me on board. On my part, I was also only too happy to be on my way home until the situation began to go, as so often happens at sea, not according to plan, and my adventure began.

As we approached the Bar Light Vessel, we discovered that the pilot assigned to the vessel was on board the pilot boat, which had been forced to proceed to the Northwest Light Vessel, a large buoy moored some seven miles to the west-northwest of the Bar Light Ship. She was engaged in boarding an inward bound tanker, which was considered too large a ship to bring in amongst the large number of vessels then anchored at the Bar Anchorage.

If we were to divert to the west, having to dock into the South, or Brunswick System on the level at high water of the tide, we would miss the tide. "I have a pilot on board," announced the captain who was determined to be home that evening. I explained again to him that his ship at around two thousand gross tons was far too big for the licence, which I held. "Nonsense!" came the reply, "I trust you, and so DO something about it."

Now the tide moves in mysterious ways, and as the old pilots constantly reminded us, there is always another tide! To catch the tide, which is currently in motion, however, is always a challenge if there is even the faintest of possibilities of doing so. I thought carefully and offered a possibility.

If the captain and the pilot on board the Bar Pilot Boat agreed, I could navigate the vessel up into the river and pick up a pilot from the pilot launch off Woodside Landing Stage, which would indeed, allow the time necessary for us to catch the afternoon tide. It was agreed, and caught up in the excitement and now faced with the challenge of the situation we found ourselves in, I pulled out all the stops focusing my powers on the knowledge of the passage and both the swiftest and safest way that I could make it.

I entered the Queens Channel between the Q4 and the Q6 Buoys, where we had water, as it was little more than an hour to the high water of a spring tide and we were running out of time. At moments like this it is all too obvious to be aware of the stark fact that, as I have mentioned earlier: "time and tide wait for no man". Avoiding all other traffic, of which there was a lot, all proceeding both ways at a slower pace than me, I hurtled out of the channel on the other side at Q17 Buoy to cross the Askew Spit, ostensibly for a re-entering into the Crosby Channel at C17 Buoy amidst a great excitement, which was growing with every second of the passage. In effect I had cut the corner of the Crosby Bend, and in cutting this distance, I had saved a considerable amount of time.

Then came an unexpected blow. For some reason, best known to himself, the lockmaster at Brunswick Lock, a fully fledged master mariner, decided that unless the vessel was crossing the lock-sill at high water Liverpool, he was intending to close the lock gates "to conserve water" in the dock system. For a brief moment the captain was crestfallen, but his young pilot was to have yet another ace up his sleeve. I was aware that for just one month before final closure, Herculaneum Dock Entrance, an entrance also into the South Dock System, was re-opened after being out of use for many years. So long had the entrance been closed, that I had not been in it since pilot boat bunkering days and never on a leadsman. I called the lockmaster on the appropriate V.H.F. Channel, and spoke to a Captain Crowe. "I will give you until twenty minutes ebb young man. See what you can do with that."

Now with a ship of the *Crispin*'s size, which was heading north in the system, the correct docking procedure was, with two tugboats, a swing in the river and a docking stern-first into the entrance, which was just eighty feet wide. I knew that there was not only no time for a swing, but also that there was no time to slow down to make the tugs fast and certainly no time to pick up the first class pilot, Michael Wright, who was waiting in the river on the pilot launch *Puffin*.

"Will you trust me Captain?" I asked in hope. "To the ends of the earth Pilot if needs be, but certainly to Herculaneum on this tide." came the reply. Right, so be it! I cleared the manoeuvre with the trusting Michael Wright, ordered the tugs to follow me into the system and began slowing the vessel to a docking speed as I headed to the east towards Herculaneum.

At this stage, a pilot on a large tanker bound for Tranmere, who had not picked up on the situation regarding the opening of Herculaneum Gateway for the last time, sighted *Crispin* rushing past him as he made his approach for the jetty. "Look at this Captain," (he was reported to shout) "this vessel is about to be wrecked. There is nowhere for him to go, the gate there has long been closed. He is heading for a stone wall and certain destruction." The two on the tanker watched with bated breath as the *Crispin* sped on to disappear into the hole in the wall made available by the opening of the gate. On board *Crispin*, I judged the speed, trying to bring her down to a safe manoeuvring speed, but found that I even needed a kick back on full speed ahead in order to whistle safely between the pier-heads of the gateway.

Clear of the pier-heads, (somewhere close to the position of the present Otterspool Road roundabout, where one exit leads to a Chinese restaurant on the river wall,) I grabbed the bridge telegraph handle myself, and rang a "double ring full astern" to the engine room. They obliged, and feet short of the "empty of water" dry-docks and their closed gates on the south side of the dock, the swirling wash of the vessel's pounding propeller caught up with us, and we were all stopped in a flurry of white foam. The white of the foam echoed the white of the deep snow covering the entire dockland-world in a winter glow, gleaming in the sunlight of the day.

I looked astern to see a pilot launch close behind, followed by the two tugs booked for the vessel. These tugs were in turn followed by another vessel; a Bulgarian of a similar size to us, with two tugs fast, as she also had been turned down at Brunswick Locks. They all made a truly magnificent sight for me on this successful occasion. Michael Wright arrived on the bridge and offered that I should continue to the berth with him, but with the adrenalin still flowing, and my personal contribution of the job well and truly done, I chose to leave the vessel by means of the pilot launch, which was waiting for me alongside. I landed on the Herculaneum Dock Wall, and danced northwards, all the way to the Pierhead in the snow.

'SHORTHAND TO FULL HAND'

Following the excitement of the *Crispin*, I was to pilot many more third class vessels. In the August of 1970, I was to be examined for, and pass the licence for pilot of the second class. This licence enabled me to pilot vessels up to two thousand tons gross, which were considerably larger than those I had been piloting for two years. This size of vessel is comparable to the vessels, which the present Liverpool Pilot rules allow fourth, or lowest class of pilot, to pilot when they first qualify. Following the Pilotage Act of 1988, the authorisation of United Kingdom pilots, by law, is now based on the length of the vessel, and not on the tonnage.

I note from my tide-tables that after piloting four hundred and fourteen ships in the first two years of my career, on Wednesday the twenty sixth of August 1970, I was to be licensed as a pilot of the second class. On the following day I was to pilot the *Tibana*, a second-class ship, from Alfred Locks, Birkenhead, to sea. More than the name, however, I cannot remember, so it must have been a straightforward passage, but the first of many second class and further third class ships, which I was to pilot in the next three years. Three years it was, it should have been two, but the second class pilots in the port at this time were sacrificed for some deal as a bargaining ploy to improve an overall pay increase.

The increase in the size of vessel was noticeable, for the ships were so much larger and also many were to involve an increase in dock-pilotage monies, which was extra financial reward for the individual pilot. One factor, which had a bearing on this financial aspect, was the manning of the second pilot on the large tanks for Tranmere. The second man, or "heart attack" pilot as he was referred to, was there to cover the pilot himself in case of illness through stress and strain. He was also there to ease that strain, for in effect the second man was the communications assistant who, as a radio operator, handled the calls both to and from the vessel to allow the pilot himself to concentrate on the actual piloting of the vessel.

Now the older pilots of the time viewed this as a duty, which excluded them from earning dock-pilotage, and chose to have the position covered, if possible, with second-class pilots. This was the first time that I became involved with the politics of the service. As young pilots, we saw this manning as unjust on two counts, for it prevented us from the hands-on experience of learning our trade on the bridge of our own ship, and in addition it reduced our income accordingly.

The second-class pilots turned out in strength at one of the monthly meetings in the old purpose built pilot office on Canning Pier Head. It was on this occasion that my colleague and friend David Devey, and myself, were to work together for the first time politically. I was to propose the motion that second pilots aboard tankers should be manned from the first class pilots of the port for the reasons of safety. David was to second the motion without waiting for the discussion, for then, we had reasoned, the motion had to be voted on.

There followed a heated discussion with the older experienced politicians of the service working towards an understanding that it would be done, "if possible". At this point, I reminded the Chairman of the resolution and the rule, that as it had been seconded, the motion had to be voted on. It was, and we won. Justice had been achieved.

The second-class ships were so much bigger to the young pilot and, many of them entered the dock systems and required tugs to assist them. The work involved took on a whole new rôle with respect to both responsibility and excitement. There were, for example, four vessels registered in what was then Yugoslavia. They were on a regular run from the Mediterranean. Initially they ran to the Manchester Ship Canal and later to the Brunswick South Dock System. In strong winds they certainly required tugs, but in calm conditions they handled beautifully, and, a small amount was offered by the agent to supplement the dock-pilotage rate if tugs were not employed.

The names of the four were: *Krushevo, Titov Veles, Cavat,* and *Korchula.* They were splendid ships and rated third in my estimation of ranking for cuisine when it came to eating on board ship. The first ranking being the French, whilst in second place lay the Spanish. All three of these countries ships served wine with the meals, which might have had some bearing on the matter! The Dutch, with luke-warm coffee, cocoa-paste and cheese sandwiches for breakfast, were fairly low down the list!

Meals on board ships were accepted to be free to the pilot who was to find himself on board at mealtimes. Occasionally a Japanese ship's master would ask for a signature to confirm that the pilot had indeed been fed. Once on board a German ship, running for Gracechurch, bound for Garston, I had a delicious breakfast one Sunday morning. During the afternoon, the agent was to ring me to confirm with me if I had indeed had the meal. I confirmed that I had, and understood that the agent was not pleased that he had been given a bill, which included the pilot's breakfast from a mercenary German captain.

Later I was to find out that Dave Davies, my good friend, the agent had recovered this cost. It was in the early days of photocopying and the German captain had left the ship to ask at the Gracechurch offices if he might photocopy some documents. "Certainly Captain, go ahead," was Dave Davies's friendly response. The captain completed his work and was leaving the building to return to the ship. Dave stopped him from leaving. "Excuse me Captain but that will cost you two pounds and fifty pence." It was of course the cost of the pilot's breakfast!

There are many stories concerned with eating on board ship. They range from the sublime to the ridiculous. The latter, best illustrated by the British coaster's excuse for an evening meal consisting of sweet tea with condensed milk served in a cracked cup, this beverage accompanying a dubious looking sandwich, which arrives complete with the greasy thumbprint of the sailor who brought it up to the bridge on the outside ladder. He would have been holding the offering on the plate with his unwashed thumb, so that it was not lost overboard in the teeth of a howling gale.

One summer's evening, I arrived on the bridge of an Everard boat around about eighteen thirty hours. After the captain had shaken hands with me, his first statement was that the ship was non-federated. I thanked him for the information and was surprised when he repeated the fact again. I thanked him again adding that I did not actually see what that had to do with me. He replied that it had everything to do with me, for being a non-federated ship, only one meal per day was supplied, and I apparently had just missed it. We had an eight-hour passage up to Garston Docks, and I survived on tea and a thin slice of stale cake, which was discovered for me from I dread to think where.

One of the finest meals, which I can remember, was aboard a magnificent French first-class container-vessel by the name of *Caraïbe*. The vessel arrived at the Bar Light Vessel late morning to dock on the late afternoon tide. I boarded and the charming French captain invited me to lunch. He suggested that we anchored, so that we could enjoy the meal at table, in the saloon. We had the time as we were waiting for the tide, so I anchored the ship to the northwest of the Bar Light vessel. The captain showed me to the pilot's suite, where I could shower before lunch. I duly did, and joined the captain in the bar for aperitifs.

Then to the table and a meal, which I swear comprised at least a dozen courses of the most excellent French cuisine. With each course there was a different wine and when we came to the brandy, I realised that if I drank the digestive, then, the ship would certainly not be docking. I requested that I leave my brandy until the ship was safely alongside. This was agreed to, and I left the ship in exceptionally good spirits, with a large bundle of fresh French baguettes under my arm. The captain had heard the news that Britain was suffering a bread strike, and insisted that the French would help out at least the pilot who had docked him safely in the port.

There must now follow the story of the worst meal I ever encountered, and one, which I could not eat. I was once boarded on a Faroese coaster, which had missed the night's tide. The vessel was bound from Belfast to the Manchester Ship Canal in ballast. She had discharged a cargo of fishmeal in Belfast and had missed the tide because the crew were cleaning hatches prior to docking, north of the Bar.

Both on deck and in the wheelhouse there was an extremely pungent smell of fish. We proceeded up-river to anchor over lunchtime to await the afternoon's tide. The captain was ecstatic, for it was some special Faroese feast day and with that went a lunch of a Faroese delicacy. Safely anchored in the Middle-Deep anchorage off Bromborough, we left the bridge and went down to the tiny saloon for this special lunch.

All hands were there except for the mate left on anchor watch. All five or six crew were wearing ganseys, oiled-woollen, knitted, seamen's jerseys, encrusted with stinking fishmeal. The galley door opened and in came the piping hot delicacy on a large silver platter. Now, I had become used to enjoying the delights of the food of many countries, and nothing had defeated me until this day. Something was wrong for me, as the silver tray was whisked under my nose. The meat on the tray looked magnificent, for it appeared to me to be roast lamb. I gingerly took a small portion, but the captain grabbing a dagger from his place setting, speared what appeared to be a complete shoulder of lamb and dropped it on my plate.

At this point, noticing that an extremely unpleasant smell of fishmeal, coupled with something else about, which, I was not at all certain, had assailed my nostrils, I asked what was so special about the dish. The answer gave me cause for concern. The meat was indeed lamb, which had been slaughtered some three months earlier, and had then been buried as raw meat in the ground until this voyage, when it was exhumed in time for the special-feast day.

Right, so I was confronted with a plateful of cooked, but rotting meat. I took a leaf out of my children's books when confronted with unwanted food and, who ask for a drink to swill the offending matter down with. "Please may I have a beer Captain?" I asked politely. The captain barked a reply: "We do not have beer on board." This was followed by a command to the cook: "The pilot is thirsty, bring him a glass of milk." This was too much for my stomach to contemplate, rotten lamb to be washed down with milk! I began to retch. "Captain, forgive me, I have just remembered a V.H.F. call, which I have forgotten to make." I fled to the bridge, where I hung over the dodger breathing heavily. I was not sick, but I did not return to the mess. When the captain came back on the bridge, he never mentioned my departure from the table, and the ship was to dock safely at the Eastham Locks. I have often wondered what I missed.

Many ships were to be piloted, with me being provided with many splendid meals as a second-class pilot. During my three years as a second-class pilot, I was also to be boarded on a first-class tanker bound for Eastham Locks by mistake. On this occasion, although the vessel looked big, it was not "that big," and it was not until the captain signed my card when the M.T. *Olau Nord* was safely in the lock in the February of 1971, that I sighted the gross tonnage. There was not the excitement of the *Crispin*, however, as I had navigated the channels in the darkness of night, to dock in the early dawn of the day.

I was to become a first-class pilot, capable of handling any size of ship on the twenty ninth of August 1973, having piloted nine hundred and seventy six ships. Following an accident on the river in 1968, which involved a young first class pilot on board a large tanker, the pilotage committee was to place a further time limit on the handling of the very large vessels. On the occasion, a large tanker arrived far too early on the tide to berth at South Tranmere Oil Stage, and demolished the North Stage, thankfully without any human casualties. I was to witness this near total disaster from across the river, standing in the pilot office.

The result was that the young pilot now had time to gain more experience on larger vessels, although there was no further examination, and in effect the licence held was, under the Bye-Laws, a licence for all vessels.

It was not, however, until the tenth of October, on the day tide, that I was to sail my first "Full Hand" ship, my thousandth ship, the M.T. *Iliad*, from the Q.E.II Lock to sea. With my love of Greek literature, I was delighted that the name of the ship echoed the beautiful face of Helen, the face that launched a thousand ships, all bound for the siege of Troy.

I had taken the day after my exam as a leave day, and Gill and I set off for Stratford to camp one night on the banks of the River Avon. We were to spend the evening at the Royal Shakespeare Theatre, where we watched a production of *Coriolanus* with Ian Richardson in the title rôle. I had made it, ambition achieved at the age of twenty-nine.

THE CHANGING FACE OF WATERBORNE TRADE

Cobbleweed

A bollard-dwarfed yellow
Midst the green
Slime-grown,
Iron wood growths
On the sea wall.

Chain-rusted links
With a port's past
Are interwoven with grasses
Beneath gull-clouded skies.

Rain-lashed reflections,
Shimmer in industrial rock pools,
The yellow cobbleweed glows
Above the oil-soaked shallows.

Looking back at my tide-tables of those early years, I see so many names of ships repeated, each with their own stories. *Hannes Knuppel, Siegerland, Frieda Graebe,* Stroom Boats ('Stroomies'), Robbie Boats, Everard Boats, Saint Boats, Craig Boats and so many other regular coasters. These were the vessels on board which the young pilot was to cut his teeth and learn his trade.

The first three mentioned were of the new class of post-war German container vessels. Germany had lost the Second World War, but with grants and other monies poured into the broken country, Germany came back with a vengeance and took the coasting trade by storm. The ships built in their shipyards were fast container vessels.

On one occasion, whilst docking a small German coaster, fourth ship into the Eastham Big Lock, at four hours to high water on the flood of a spring tide, the German captain, who had been extremely pleasant up to this moment, suddenly drew himself up to his full height.[9] He was then to utter the statement: "Zer you see! Vot Hitler could not achieve, vee have now achieved." Finding this statement somewhat uncalled for, and somewhat unpleasant, I asked him for clarification. "You see Pilot, vee are zee fourth ship in zee lock, zee ozzer sree, zey are all German!" I had no answer to this now obvious truth.

The Great Western Railway had offered a container service in the mid-nineteen twenties, a door-to-door furniture removal service with a wooden container delivered by road to your door as one of the facilities offered in the carriage of freight. The "box," once loaded, was transported to the nearest station and then transhipped to the nearest railhead to the final destination in the same manner as the collection.

The idea was not to catch on until the early sixties, however, when a minor battle was fought between the concept of container trade and that of palletisation. Pallets may be loaded into containers, however, and although Stroom line, for example, built at least one ship designed to carry pallets, containers were to win, as we are all only too aware as we look at the heavy container traffic on the motorways today.

The Germans were the first to capitalise on the idea and built many fast feeder-ships capable of twelve to fourteen knots and were quite simply, the first of many: "fast boxes for carrying boxes." Shipyards such as Sietas were to build pre-fabricated vessels, which could be ordered at any length. Ninety-six metres, a hundred and ten metres, one hundred and seventeen metres and so on were the most popular initially. The bridge layout on a Sietas-built ship was

---

9 Docking fourth ship into Eastham at four hours to high water was one of the most difficult manoeuvres a Liverpool Pilot was ever called upon to execute. The other in my book is the large deep-drafted bulker inbound for Gladstone Lock, which, because of the draft, is necessarily running late on the tide.

remarkable. Designed to be practical for single-handed bridge-control, they resembled the spacecraft flight decks of rocket ships, which were then involved in the race for the moon.

The captains in command on board these vessels were also of a new breed of sailor. Proud of their commands they, with the new technology of the bow-thruster installations, were in the main, superb ship-handlers, and we young pilots were to learn a lot from them. Heavy landings became a thing of the past and the finesse of gentle landings could be perfected with a pride, particularly in adverse weather conditions, which added to job satisfaction.

Captain 'Manny' Coral on the Craig boats was one such ship-handler, sailing from Belfast to Garston on vessels built to the maximum for locking into and out of Garston. Manny was to marry a Liverpool girl and live on the Wirral. Mrs Coral was to sail with him and on one occasion I can remember her scathing comments in the early dawn of the day, referring to the fact that she had advised him to leave earlier, for he had missed the day tide. My account is missing the choice language, which she herself employed as she raged onto the bridge!

Then there was Willy *Friede Graebe*, who was a difficult man, and did not particularly like young pilots, whom he objected strongly to having on board. At the other end of the scale, there was 'Uly' Schultz, master of the *Hannes Knuppel*, who wore a bush shirt, and in the breast, cartridge-pockets, carried the twisted brown-paper wrapped Underbeg liquor bottles for when the going got tough! Uly was unfortunate to have a chief officer who got into serious difficulties on two occasions, one, which involved a death. Fortunately for the sociable Uly, German maritime law, unlike the British equivalent, has the officer on watch responsible for incidents, which occur on the watch, and not the master below, as Uly was on both occasions.

Manny too, was to have a serious incident, which highlighted the problems of minimum manning on these fast, make money and sail with minimum crewing level vessels. The German crews, having successfully seen off the competition of the Dutch, the British and the French in the coasting trade, were themselves to fall foul of the accountants who now rule the waves. Their wages were "too high" for maximum profit, and first the crews were replaced with Philippine or other "third world" nationalities, and then the masters and chief engineers with Polish mariners. Various combinations of "cheaper" crewing options are now to be found on all sizes of ship, sadly for the United Kingdom, ever fewer British.

An interesting observation about nationalities and the times we live through, Polish officers have always been mariners with a high standard of competency and during the Soviet years, so too were the officers of the Soviet fleet but, when the Berlin wall "fell down," so too did the standards on board what were previously Soviet ships. It was inexplicable, almost as if along with each ship's party member, the commissar, the top-rate officer-class, was removed from the ships. The hammer and sickle was no more on the funnels of either the White Sea or the Black Sea Fleets and the Russians I was to meet on flags of convenience ships, were often more interested in improving their English language than they were in the navigation of the vessel.

When I graduated to second-class pilot, licensed to pilot vessels up to two thousand tons gross, in the August of nineteen seventy, I was to find myself inviting a Russian captain "home for tea."

I had been boarded on a Russian second-class vessel, the *Kolymales*, a regular of the Black Sea Fleet carrying timber to Garston. The weather turned nasty, preventing our docking on the tide, and as the wind veered northerly and strengthened to gale force, we were obliged to run for shelter in the lee of the Isle of Man.

I was anchored in Douglas Bay for forty-eight hours, almost obliged to watch the Soviet-Hero propaganda films kept on board to both amuse and instil the crews with a patriotic spirit. The master of the vessel was one Boris Revunenkov, whose home was in the then major port of Leningrad, now St. Petersburg. Boris's English was very good and we chatted in his cabin with a glass of vodka or two, Russians never drink just one! There is always "The other Leg!"[10] before dinner. He was old enough to be my father, and I both liked and respected this elderly, grey haired man who had been a child during the Russian Revolution.

We docked eventually, without incident, in Stalbridge dock, where the vessel was to discharge a full cargo of timber. Several days later, I was to berth second off to the *Kolymales* on a coaster. I landed by climbing a ladder back on board the *Kolymales*. I took the opportunity to visit Boris, "en passant," as it were. After a glass of vodka with him, I invited Boris over for a meal with Gill. The offer was immediately refused, with an excuse that guests were expected. After the second glass of vodka, Boris asked if I would listen to a forty-five record, which he had bought and wished me to write down the words for him. The record was the recording of *Those were the Days my Friend* by the Welsh singer Mary Hopkin and it was, (and is if you listen carefully) sung to the refrain of an old, Russian tune of the nineteen-twenties. Boris excused himself and left the cabin whilst I wrote down the words for him.

Boris returned from his absence from the cabin and was excited, almost behaving like a schoolboy. It transpired that he had been to visit the vessel's commissar, and had been given permission to come to dinner. There were restrictions: I was to collect him in my own car from the ship, he was to meet no one but my wife, and then be returned to the ship after dinner and after visiting nowhere else but my home.

Boris came to dinner and we honoured the restrictions and it was a most pleasant and enjoyable evening. We live in a very large, semi-detached, Victorian house and at the time we had no children. Despite our protestations, which were later to become

---

10 The second, and therefore "balancing drink," the concept being of one going down each leg!

true, that we intended to fill the house with children, Boris found the fact that only two young people were living in such a large house unusual.

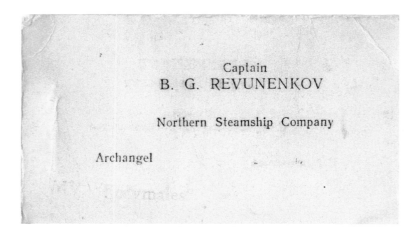

Captain

B. G. REVUNENKOV

Northern Steamship Company

Archangel

Boris was to figure years later in a conversation, which stemmed from his only apparent concern in life, which I was to have with the commander of a British nuclear-powered submarine, in the conning tower of H.M.S. *Superb* outward bound from Seaforth Dock, Liverpool. Handling a nuclear powered submarine in the dock-system is not easy, even with two tugboats. I have likened them to being similar in behaviour to a large, semi-submerged log on a pond, which a child might push from the bank. It, like the submarine will go easily in a straight line. Turning the craft, even with the rudder propeller, which helps, is difficult. I am told that submerged, they move like a porpoise with positive elegance and grace.

We were safely clear of the lock, head north, tugs away and building up to full manoeuvring speed. As so often on board naval vessels, the commander will express his thanks for the handling of the vessel in the dock system before announcing that: "My No.1 will take her now, but do keep an eye on her Pilot."

Keeping 'an eye on her' is second nature to a pilot and in doing so an impish impulse made me think of my friend Boris. Knowing perfectly well the answer, I asked:

"What exactly is the vessel's purpose Commander?"

"She is a hunter-killer Pilot."

"That sounds drastic! Who exactly are you likely to hunt and kill Commander?"

"The Soviets of course."

"Oh, have you ever met any Commander?"

"No actually I haven't." He had inadvertently fallen into the trap!

"Well, I have met a great many as we have a large number of Soviet vessels running in and out of Liverpool."

I elaborated with the specific story of Boris Revunenkov finishing with the statement of the fact that Boris's only concern was that his daughter, who was a lecturer in mathematics at the University of Leningrad, and being single, might not produce the grandchildren both he and his wife desired.

The commander went quiet. When asked if I had said something wrong, he replied that his only daughter was going up to Oxford in September to read mathematics! I did not have to make the obvious comment that we were not so different then. I am sure he would not have hesitated in the firing of torpedoes if it had been necessary to do so, but I know I had given him food for thought.

Another story of events on board a Soviet-Russian vessel was in the early years of my time on the river. The vessel was a small container feeder-ship running from Riga to Coburg Dock, Liverpool. I had been invited down and booked early to have lunch with various dignitaries before sailing outbound, via Brunswick Lock on the afternoon tide. This I thought was a splendid gesture.

After lunch, we repaired to the bridge for sailing. The vessel had a revolutionary rudder-system, which consisted of three rudder blades, which, in turn each joined as one when the helm was put hard over. This meant in effect that the small coaster would swing on a sixpence! The Russian captain was a very tall man and had been both polite and welcoming over the meal table. On the bridge, however, he stated that categorically he was to handle the manoeuvring of the vessel in the dock. I was then to watch in frustration as the captain failed to turn the small ship one hundred and eighty degrees to proceed outwards from the narrow dock.

After his umpteenth attempt, I was not only losing my temper but I was embarrassed, because a large contingent of press photographers who were standing on the quayside, along with the dignitaries, was recording this debacle. "Right Captain that is enough! Put the vessel back alongside and I will go ashore, walk round to Brunswick Lock, and, if you make it there in time for the tide, I will pilot you safely out." In those days, the dock-pilotage was not compulsory and commanded an extra charge.

Fortunately, the captain swallowed his damaged pride and agreed to accept orders for the necessary manoeuvres. From bows west in the middle of the dock, with the helm, and therefore the three rudders joined together, and a kick of half-speed ahead, the coaster spun on a sixpence, and we were on our way.

Whilst approaching the lock. I became aware of a "clicking" sound. Looking round, I observed no less than three crewmembers taking photographs of me from different angles and I burst into verbal protest. "Captain, get these men off the bridge at once. You are fortunate to be visiting the democracy, in which I both live and work. If I was in your country, doing what you are doing here with your cameras (without even asking permission) I would certainly find myself in some Gulag concentration camp before nightfall. Please, do not abuse the privilege, which you are enjoying."

The cameras vanished and we proceeded safely to sea. Weeks later, a colleague who had subsequently piloted the ship, presented me with a photograph of myself on the bridge of the ship, standing behind the binnacle, wearing my piloting suit, along with my pink shirt and flower-power, sixties tie, looking fixedly ahead. "I was told to give this photograph to: "that angry 'OLD' pilot who had us out first trip!" I was only in my mid-twenties!

"That angry old pilot!"

By the time I became a first class pilot in the port, having been sacrificed along with my contemporaries for some pay deal, and having had to complete a third year as a second-class pilot, there were still vessels of the post-war cargo fleet plying the oceans. I was honoured to pilot most of the "big" companies' ships including two Clan Ships. The first was a boarding, inward bound for the same berth, from which I had sailed from in Vittoria Dock as a cadet-officer, the *Clan MacGillivray*, late one evening for the night's tide on the fifth of March 1975. As I climbed over the rail, there was the cadet waiting with the officer to take me to the bridge. I followed him with an unbelievable elation, sensing with pleasure, all the old familiar Clan Line smells, which assailed my nostrils.

The second occasion was not such a happy one for, it was Christmas Day, and the vessel was the next to last Clan Boat, sailing from the Mersey, to leave the river forever. The last was outward bound from Eastham Locks behind me on the same tide. Mine was the *Clan Macintosh* on the Christmas Day tide of 1976. The end of yet another, well established shipping company, marking the end of yet another era.

The reason for the big company's demise was quite simply the container. The simple box! A different type of vessel was required to carry this new form of cargo transportation. A best simple description of such a vessel is the one used earlier: a large box for carrying boxes. These container ships were to grow ever bigger. A.C.L were to perfect the system for Liverpool with the G3 container ships, the largest vessels to fit into the Liverpool dock system, which I was privileged to pilot in the last decade of my career.

As I write, A.C.L. are designing an even larger vessel, even if only by centimetres, which will still fit into the system and replace the G3's! We bear in mind that the *Penelope Maersk* class is the largest class of container vessel afloat, at nearly a hundred metres longer than the A.C.L. fleet and twenty metres wider. There are few ports at present capable of handling these ships. It is my belief that the optimum size of container vessel will eventually be somewhat less in size, both ways, than this class.

Liverpool certainly cannot handle these vessels without a river berth, and even then, the main channel would have to be kept dredged at a considerably greater depth than it is maintained, at present, to cope with these deep-drafted vessels on a one-off, let alone on a regular basis. Add to this a breakwater, which would be necessary to protect and shelter the proposed site of the terminal in the north river, and the costs could well be prohibitive. What, if any alternative is there, costly though it may be, is the all-important question so vital to the future of this great port?

Liverpool was ill-prepared for the container trade, in fact it would be true to say that the Mersey Docks and Harbour Board was totally unprepared, and as we had no facilities whatsoever, we were to see the "non-profit making" Board withdraw their trade from the port. The board was made up of ship-owners. We were to be abandoned through the lack of vision and foresight, and the Board itself was to go into receivership. These became dark times indeed. This was the first time that we realised that we had too many self-employed pilots with too few ships to pilot.

I once stood on the Woodside Landing Stage, waiting for a launch to take me out to the Bar Pilot Boat. In the dawn light I saw the Arthur Dooley, then red *Tatlin Tower*, metal sculpture, then positioned to the left of the Mersey Docks and Harbour Board building on the waterfront of the Pierhead. To me it looked like: "a wound in the Board's capitalistic heart, bleeding into the river." I was to write that line in a poem about the port's misfortunes. The Board was to declare itself bankrupt, and the port was to be taken into receivership.

The container revolution was to revolutionise cargo goods trade as radically as the Suez Canal Crisis in 1956 revolutionised the carriage of oil in tankers. With the enforced closure of the canal, the size of the oil tanker now required to navigate round the Cape of Good Hope was almost limitless, and they grew overnight and every night from then on. When I sailed on my first trip with Clan Line, the tankers were big, but not that big, because most of them would still fit into dry-docks in Birkenhead.

As a first class pilot, I was to witness, but not pilot, the largest tankers in the world, the five hundred thousand tons French B-Class, moored at the ill-fated Single Buoy Mooring off Point Lynas in Anglesey, close to our Western Boarding Station. The S.B.M. was ill fated because the Shell Oil Company did not take Liverpool Pilots' advice that the currents were too strong for the large tankers to hold position on their own. This proved to be true, and after a relatively short period, 1972-1990, the S.B.M. was removed, for the towage bill for the necessary tug required for safety in the tideway, was prohibitive, even for the oil companies.

During the period of the S.B.M's existence, we were to witness the shrinking of the tanker size to a standardisation of the "big-ones" being of two to three hundred, thousand tons, all of which are capable of entering the Mersey, albeit in a lightened state, for the channel approaches are too shallow to allow them to enter fully laden.

The port was eventually to construct both oil stages in the river at Tranmere for the large tankers, and build a container terminal at the Royal Seaforth Dock. After years of hardship, the port was back in business.

A NEAR DEATH EXPERIENCE

Spring buds of May were in full flower, but nobody had made the situation clear to the winds. They were still of a mind to be operating on their winter schedule.

During the afternoon of the *Rhine Ore* near-disaster, I had been interviewed for a German language 'A' level oral examination. I had taken up learning languages since I had become a fully-fledged pilot of the first class in the Port of Liverpool. This simple academic fact is relevant, as will become clear as the tale unfolds.

On the evening tide of the same day, I was manned to sail M.V. *Rhine Ore*, a twenty-six thousand tons, iron-ore carrier in light condition, from Bidston Dock in Birkenhead, to sea, via Alfred Locks on the night tide.

I was a young first class pilot, at the tender age of just twenty-nine years old. I was initially horrified to board the vessel at the appointed hour, to discover that she was listing some fifteen degrees to port! You may take it from me that that is a serious list on a big ship. Climbing ladders to the bridge was difficult, but when I reached the bridge, the German captain assured me that all would soon be well as the engine room staff were sorting out some failure in the ballasting situation of the now discharged and completely empty, iron-ore carrier. What he did not tell me on that near fateful night, however, was that the reason for this failure was due to the inexperience of the majority of the crew. Only the captain and the German deck officers, along with the German chief engineer had been on the ship for any length of time. The rest of the crew, who were Spanish, had only signed on during that afternoon, only hours before me in fact.

As the darkness closed in and the list was corrected, the wind strengthened from the southwest, reaching a good force six on the Beaufort scale. Rain fell from scudding dark clouds, and as the undocking manoeuvres commenced, the Liverpool Tidal Theatre of Life opened the curtain on what, by midnight, almost became a tragic drama.

At approximately one-and-a-half hours before the high-water of that spring tide, the ship was manoeuvred stern first out from the lock into the fast-flowing, dark-swirling waters of the River Mersey, swung with her head to the north to stem the flood, and with the tugs all gone and clear, the engines were engaged ahead and the passage was commenced, outwards towards the safety of the open sea.

As the *Rhine Ore* built up to full manoeuvring speed, which was about nine knots over the ground against the last of the flood tide, and as she was approaching the then operational Rock Lighthouse off New Brighton, I was aware that there were many other vessels moving on the tide. In particular, and of note was the ninety thousand tons tanker, *World Faith*, which had been negotiating the Crosby Bend as my own charge had been clearing Alfred Locks.

Now, as we first sighted her through heavy rainsqualls, she was three miles to the north and was reducing her speed on the approach to North Tranmere Oil Stage. Our combined approach speed was later estimated to be around sixteen knots, which if translated into a collision impact speed, with twenty six thousand tons versus ninety thousand would have meant, almost certainly that the *Rhine Ore* would have simply been rolled over with the certain death of both myself and her thirty man crew. At that moment of sighting, however, there was no danger and I was happily speaking German with the captain, whilst keeping a weather eye on our outward progress.

"Hard to starboard the wheel Sir and we are still swinging to port" was the alarm in the cry of the Spanish helmsman. Blood does run cold, and mine did just that as the vessel began what was an immediately obvious, irreversible hard-to-port swing, to sheer across the bow of the incoming tanker. What I am about to describe next will take a lot longer to relate in words than it took in the actual reality of the horror.

In judging correctly that a steering failure somewhere in the link between the ship's wheel and the ship's rudder had occurred and that there was no doubt that even if rectified, the present swing was irreversible, what I can only believe was a mixture of dedicated training and self-preservation linked to my professional responsibility for my charge, resulted in the actions, which I am about to describe.

Leave the engines on full speed ahead to have any chance of crossing the incoming vessel's bow and possibly avoid the collision was the first thought, which hurtled into a brain, which seconds previously had been taxed with what had appeared to be a straight forward safe, outward-bound passage involving giving only the necessary compass courses to the helmsman whilst continuing to practice my 'A' Level German on the captain.

My hand had grasped the V.H.F. handset transmitter automatically and the clear, stern but amazingly calm young voice, which was recorded in the Vessel Traffic Control Centre, was contacting the pilot of the inward bound tanker.

"Mister Mackay Sir, my vessel is ahead of you and as you will have observed, she is swinging rapidly to port. We will not I repeat not, recover from the swing. DO NOT alter course to Starboard (as the collision regulations would have required him to do) but please order "Hard to Port." The Shell Appropriated Pilot James 'Jock' Mackay did indeed heed my request, and claimed that he did not manage to steady the ship from the resulting double swing for the next two miles of his inward passage!

The next V.H.F. call, which I made, was to the three Alexander Towing Company tugs, which I had noted were hanging off Gladstone Lock awaiting the arrival of an inward bound G.1 Atlantic Container Line vessel, now in the Crosby Strait. "The three tugs waiting off Gladstone Lock, we have an emergency just to the north of you. If all is well, you will be needed to assist my vessel *Rhine Ore*. Please get yourselves down here with all speed."

The final call, having established that the three tugs were indeed on their way, was made immediately to Mersey Radio, the V.T.S Control, directly beneath whose tower the drama was rapidly unfolding!

"Mersey Radio, You will have gathered on this channel (twelve) that *Rhine Ore* has a problem river north. I will keep you informed."

Seconds later, the *Rhine Ore* swung only a few metres clear of *World Faith's* bow, or perhaps more accurately, *World Faith's* bow swung clear of the *Rhine Ore*. The bow itself loomed ominously, high above us, a curving wall of rain-soaked steel, close, and threatening in the swirling darkness.

With the amazing revelation that a collision, which would have resulted in both dire and deathly consequences, had been avoided, and that we were both still alive and still afloat, I ordered the main engines to be regulated to "Stop." This, the now panic-stricken second engineer on watch below did with such efficiency and aplomb to the command given on the engine room telegraph, by my own hand, that he literally stalled the main engine and it did indeed stop!

My next rung command for "Full Astern" was superfluous. My charge, now literally a floating hulk, continued her port swing, and though slowing in speed over the ground, sped towards the clutching hands of the Burbo Sands and possible destruction on the stones of the Training Wall off New Brighton[11].

"Let go the port anchor!" rang out my voice, the voice of a young, but rapidly gaining in experience pilot. "Let go the port anchor!" The order given for the second time, the only sound in the otherwise dark silence of the wheelhouse. Then the third and final command for the anchor to be let go was given, my brain registering that if she goes now, we will sit on it, but at least it would look good in the report. No anchor left the hawse pipe, and later it was established that the language problem being experienced between the new

11 The main channels for the Port of Liverpool are lined with stonewalls to hold back shifting sand and assist the self-swept channels to maintain depth of water.

Spanish sailors and the German chief officer at stations on the foc'sle, was to account for the failure of the foredeck crew to obey the commands.

The vessel rushed inelegantly onto the sands, which was simply at the point that fortune chose, and was incredibly, the only position where the sands of the bank had edged eastwards and covered the hard unforgiving stones of the training wall to the west of the safe buoy line marking the channel. The impact of the grounding threw the bridge team, and probably everyone else on board who was standing, ignominiously to the deck.

If I had looked at my watch at this point I would have noted that a mere ninety seconds had elapsed since the helmsman's first desperate cry. I too find this fact hard to believe, but V.H.F control had the recorded tapes of the transmissions, and ninety seconds it was.

There was to be more crying, for as I leaped to my feet, the sobbing from the shadows on the deck below me came from the captain. "Get up man! Pull yourself together there is work to be done and quickly. We are running out of time for the ebb will be away before long and so must we be if it is at all possible. Send one hand to sound the hatches. Send the rest to stations fore and aft, all of them. Make the tugs fast as soon as they arrive. Make the *Albert* (Ah! The magnificent, brand-new, single-screw tugboat *Albert*) fast forward, and the other two fast aft. The tide is turning and I have no intention of ending my career tonight." "I have only just begun it" was registering vividly in my young mind!

After agonising minutes, which seemed like hours, where nothing seemed to be happening, the tugs reported that they were all fast as requested and with the stern boats towing with full power to the east, and the *Albert*, both holding the bow and pulling to the east, just as the tide was turning, some twenty minutes after the grounding, *Rhine Ore* slid thankfully astern and into the safety of the deep water of the Crosby Channel. I brought her to mid-channel, head north, with a Shell tank passing outward bound on my starboard side and the A.C.L. container vessel passing inwards on my port side. "What the hell!" I thought with an uncontrolled elation, "I am afloat!" The three tugboats had done a wonderful job but I have always maintained that it was the work of the *Albert* in particular, which saved us.

My thanks at this point, go particularly to the three tugs and to their captains and crews for their speedy response to my summons and for their excellent seamanship. Also my thanks are due to all my colleagues involved, particularly to James Mackay on the *World Faith* and also to the late Peter Dawson on the A.C.L. and to the late Malcolm Lacey on the Shell tank, whose ships all passed me safely by.

"At least there will be a second dock-pilotage charge to be paid to me after I have re-docked the vessel dead-ship, and before I am reprimanded and possibly relieved of my Licence" I thought ruefully. No incidents at sea, I believed at the time, resulted in any party involved being free of some percentage of blame. But no!

"We are not taking any water pilot. The main engine is running again and the steering has been restored and tested. (The breaker had been pushed back in to its rightful electrical, contact spot by the gravely concerned about his own future, German chief engineer.) We shall proceed to sea."

It was, as with a child, who had observed that his glass of lemonade had been knocked to the kitchen floor by his own careless hand and wants to both believe and deny that the accident had ever happened. In the captain's case there was no broken glass and apparently everything was back in order.

I pointed out what I believed to be the error of his thinking, emphasising the fact that we had not all lost our balance on a whim and that our charted position both on our own chart and on that of the V.T.S. radar plot, "all stopped", showed that we had been both out of the channel and on the top of a sand bank! There had been a terrific impact at which point the ship had stopped moving and that there must be serious damage to the hull.

The captain did eventually accept the fact that the ship had been aground and later together, outward bound to the Liverpool Pilots' Western Station at Point Lynas, we agreed on the grounding report and the timing and events, which led up to it.

I reflected on the 'First Laws of the Sea' made in Henry II's reign at the time of a Crusade[12]. Pilots were embarked off the Isle d'Oleron at the mouth of the Gironde River, France, to pilot the crusaders' ships safely into the Mediterranean. One of the Laws of Oleron runs roughly so:

"If a pilot shall run his ship aground, then shall he be taken to the forecastle and there, without trial, shall he be beheaded!"

My father, the late Walter 'Curly' Curry, as a Liverpool Pilot, had told me this, and to my knowledge the law had never been repealed! I gently felt the delicate skin at my throat before insisting that if we were to proceed outward-bound it would be to an anchorage to examine the ship's hull in daylight with divers. We would let the tugs go but not dismiss them until we were clear and away from the dangers of the channel. Once might be considered an accident and even an "Act of God," (as it was eventually to be described legally) but twice...

Once clear of the channel the captain insisted that he continue his voyage and after warning him of the possible implications of such a decision if there were to be undetected serious under-water damage of the hull, I accompanied him to the Western Pilot Station to leave him on passage for Puerto Ordaz in South America. The ship was to load iron-ore back for Birkenhead. I left him some four hours later without further incident, and after disembarking on the Lynas Pilot Station Boat, returned to my home.

The ship reached her destination safely but never did load that cargo of iron ore, for divers examined the hull and discovered it

---

12 The Laws of Oleron are attributed to Eleanor of Aquitaine. Eleanor was to marry Henry II in 1152.

to be "rippled" from abaft of the ship's stem aft to forward of the bridge, which was situated amidships.

The nightmare on that darkly flowing spring tide in the River Mersey had indeed been a reality, which I had lived through and survived and not the stuff of an exaggerated fiction.

I was left an older, wiser and exceedingly lucky young man, having had an experience, which I could well have done without!

I was congratulated for my actions by the Pilotage Committee, particularly for giving the orders and advice, which led to the avoidance of a possible collision of dire consequence and was given permission to claim salvage! It was then that I learned that if a vessel under pilotage goes out of the pilot's control through no fault of his own, he ceases to be the pilot and further, if he saves the ship, he becomes a salvor in the eyes of the law. In retrospect, although this was to bring some solace, and although this was to give me experience for when something similar was to happen to me again, on a subsequent occasion, I would rather, quite simply, have remained the pilot.

RISE AND FALL TO RISE AGAIN

Rise and Fall

Liverpool,
I see you Liverpool,
In the mud-fingered ebb,
Sand seeping seawards.

I see you,
In the dawn
When the young flood
Races over the bar
To caress upriver reaches.

I see you,
Through the masts of tall-ships,
And from the watery ways
Of charted channels
Where bell'd beacons rock,
Ringing out mournful chimes.

I see you,
Held in the grip of the powering tide.

The rise, and maintenance of Liverpool as both a great city and a number one port, has not been a simple progression. There have been many complications, which have presented obstacles to a smooth and natural development. The fact that we had a container terminal finally built at Seaforth, and two river oil terminals constructed at Tranmere, on the then Cheshire bank of the river, along with a "fitting out and repair" river terminal at Rock Ferry, did go a long way towards resolving, but did not completely resolve, all of the complex problems, which Liverpool was beset by.

The incredibly swift increase in the physical size of ships themselves, brought about many of these problems. The South Dock System, entered from the river in the latter stages by Brunswick Lock following the final closure of Herculaneum Gateway (not long after the *Crispin* was safely in) was obsolete, almost overnight. The ships were simply too big. I personally piloted the last three what were then "Eastern Block" ships out on consecutive day tides, a Russian, a Bulgarian and a Yugoslav, all around the two thousand gross tons mark. Certainly there were yet small coasters still afloat, and although initially the gates were left open at Brunswick, making the system tidal, the grain silo at Brunswick dock remained operational for some time. The inbound pilot would present the master of the coaster with an indemnity form for him to sign, acknowledging that he was to accept total responsibility for entering the dock, going alongside the silo, and for his time inside the system.

The operation was to dock before high water on the tide. It was a bit like shooting rapids in a canoe. The starboard anchor had to be dropped over towards the west of the middle of the dock, and the vessel swung and brought alongside port side to, ready both for cargo operations and for departure. On one occasion after I had successfully "shot the rapids," the mate forward, paid out too much anchor chain. This extra chain allowed the vessel to slide into the Brunswick-Coburg gateway on the swing and consequently jammed the ship's after rails on the port quarter in the bridge-way on the still rising tide.

This unwanted situation required an acetylene burner to cut the rails clear, and a small passing barge-tug, *Cherrygarth*, was called in to make fast and pull the vessel clear of the gateway. I went back over to the vessel at low water to see the master and assess the situation with regard to the siltation. The starboard anchor was in the mud over to the west, but it lay in a position above the coaster's bridge height, the anchor chain leading skywards from the hawse-pipe! Shortly after this incident the coasters ceased to be booked in and the silo was demolished some years later.

Although the Port of Liverpool has many docks, only one is actually in Liverpool! Stanley Dock is the one, which was dug out of the land, the rest are all built on the foreshore of the Mersey. The Mersey Docks and Harbour Board had jealously guarded both their land and their possessions. The Company initially followed this policy, but thankfully with the formation of the Merseyside Development Company, the obsolete South Dock System was eventually to be handed over to them for both preservation and development. The Brunswick lock gates were closed and the system was saved.

The Albert Dock is built out into the river on greenheart piles, and if allowed to dry out, these piles would quite simply have rotted, with the result that the superb Jesse Hartley construction, with all its magnificent and historic buildings, would have collapsed and tumbled into the river. Today, we see the realisation of the development with a yacht marina, hotels, offices and flats, shopping complexes, museums and art galleries. This complex, now borders on to Liverpool One, the development accomplished during the lead up to and following Liverpool being declared the European City of Culture in 2008. The city with all its history, bathes in a new light for the future.

Sadly to the north, the development is not nearly so advanced. There are new hotels and office blocks following the conversion of the East Waterloo Dock grain silo into apartments, on the same lines, and at the same time, as the conversion of the Wapping Dock apartments, and the Albert Dock developments to the south. I have to confess that I sighted the largest rats that I have seen anywhere in the world regularly, when I joined or left a vessel moored at the grain silo in East Waterloo Dock. A.C.L. main offices are to the west here on the river wall, with a wonderful view to the north, but further north from here, there is still much dereliction and much yet to be improved.

It was fun to take vessels into the North System via Waterloo Lock, and Sandon River Entrances. One interesting passage, which did take place on occasions, was from East Waterloo Dock to sea via Gladstone lock, a distance of about two miles with a chicane in the middle in the form of Nelson Dock. Here the gateway from the south and Salisbury Dock was to the east, with the exit gateway to the north and Bramley-Moore Dock lying to the west! In the days of "Dock Pilotage" this would incur the maximum fee. That is the full price for the size of the ship, plus ten per cent per gateway up to fifty per cent. With the starting price for a coaster being the princely sum of two pounds fourteen shillings and sixpence, the total was not a lot by today's standards, but it was a great deal to a young pilot with a young family in the 'seventies.

The charges for shipping at this time were taken on the gross tonnage of the vessel for both inward and outward pilotage. The Port Authority under the Pilotage Act of 1913 charged this fee, but once in the dock system, dock pilotage came into force, and this, unlike the compulsory pilotage in and out of the Mersey, via the channel approaches, was voluntary. The money went straight to the individual pilot. Some pilots were more fortunate than others, for in the luck of the draw, which was the manning system, some acts of pilotage were worth more than others. Later, before the Pilotage Act of 1988, this was to change, and compulsory pilotage was to be levied both to and from the vessel's berth.

The Pilotage Act, which came into force during the years of the Conservative Government of Margaret Thatcher, was inevitable. As I have already explained, the ships had all got bigger, and although eventually more cargo was being shipped, there were fewer ships and quite simply too many pilots worldwide. Liverpool was no exception. The major problem faced by the government was that all pilots were self-employed and, therefore excess numbers could not easily be disposed of. There was a certain irony in these bitter years, for most pilots were staunch conservatives by virtue of their professional calling.

A book could be written on the events, which took place in the mid to late eighties and into the late nineties, for in this period,

Liverpool pilots were to be drastically reduced in numbers, those remaining were taken forcibly into employment, and after a nine year political battle, were to fight their way back to self-employment in the June of 1997.

On the 30th of September 1988, the Mersey Docks and Harbour Company, which was about to become the Competent Harbour Authority, or C.H.A., under the Pilotage Act of that year, allowed us to "close the port!"

The pilots, both serving and retired, with the addition of all our loved ones held what was to be called 'The Last Muster.' We took over the southwest corner of the Albert Dock buildings and we held a party. The following morning, when the port opened again we were employees.

We were spending monies, which were in the Liverpool Pilot's coffers, which we believed should be shared. In hindsight, what we should have done after the ball was over, as it were, was to order more champagne, and gone and sat on the river wall, to watch the tide flow in and wait for the C.H.A. to come and find us. Then our bargaining power would have been immediately effective. We did not, and the first pilots, who included myself, were on board ships within hours, and the long battle for a pilot's rights in Liverpool began.

The "battle" was to last nine years, but the Liverpool Pilots were finally successful in winning the day.

Suffice it to say that being employed was not a pleasant experience. On the bridge of the ship life was the same, but on landing, there was something extremely unpleasant about daily life in general. This was brought about by the Company's treatment of the pilot, who is so often now considered to be a "necessary evil" by those who would do well to appreciate the profession's true value, which has always been to provide safety at sea from time immemorial.

A good friend who is both a master mariner and an academic with a PhD., retired V.T.S. officer Roy Williams, found a literary piece during the course of his studies of Greek writings of the fifth century B.C., which related to pilotage. The writing is in the form of a guide to merchants on the importance of engaging the services of a good pilot: "They, (good pilots) could be recognised down in the harbour and identified by their badge of office, which was the steering oar, which each pilot carried. They were not paid very well in those days apparently, as one Ariston, stated in a letter to a friend asking why this was so, and why these good fellows were paid less than those who sold bad fish in the marketplace?"

Another of Roy's translations tells of the retiring pilot's plans for his retirement, which included walking inland carrying his steering oar, claiming that eventually when he met one who would stop him and ask him what the strange looking shovel on his shoulder was, that then he would halt, and settle in that place, helping the other with his or her labours!

Pilot with steering oar, Corinth

During the "Battle Years" as we came to call the years of September 1988 to June of 1997, I became Chairman of the Liverpool Pilot

Service, for I apparently had the ability to keep order at meetings and help clarify argument so that both sensible and useful decisions could be made by the body of men. My friend and colleague, David Devey led a team of representatives who fought our case to the eventual freedom of a return to self-employment. Sadly for friendship, the facts that my insistence that the political movement must be based on a majority, and therefore democratic decision, in every case, did not always please David. Our friendship was to be become strained over these dark years. With a strong Chairman, however, and a strong representation coupled with a dedicated following of members, the Liverpool Pilots became a political fighting force to be reckoned with. Eventually we were to win our way back to the desired freedom of self-employment in the June of 1997.

I remained as Chairman for some years before standing down to hand over to the younger element of the service, for, as I have always insisted, it was their future and that they must capitalise on the good fortunes, which we had won for them. In telling my younger colleagues this fact, I always emphasised that although their future was important, even more important was the future of those not yet born, who would eventually follow them. I trust that this future is in safe hands.

When the arrangements for the 'Last Muster' were being made, I was asked by colleagues to write a poem to commemorate the event. The poem was printed on the back of the menu for the evening's dinner. 'The Feather's' provided the meal.

The poem has been my most successful poem to date, being widely published, broadcast, and even used by the late Lord Derby as his text for his address at a Bluecoat School speech day! The poem's second outing, much to my surprise, was when taken by the Reverend Canon Bob Evans as his text for his address on the Sunday morning following the 'Last Muster.' On this occasion the Liverpool Pilots filled the Liverpool Church of the Sea, St. Nicholas's, at the Pier Head for a service of thanksgiving for the past years. The poem is universal, for it offers hope.

Guardians of the dawn

Centuries long,
The river has flowed
Through an hour glass.
Carrying in suspension
The sands of time.

Tides have turned,
Carrying our changes of fortune,
All our histories.
Gull shades of our ancestors
Swoop on dark, estuarine waves.

We men of the dawn
Came from seawards.
Learning the river's ways,
We mastered
Our business in her waters.

From the bridge,
We have seen
Calm seas, prosperous voyages,
Tempests, and have heard,
Bell'd-buoys tolling in the storm-torn night.

Now, on the eve,
On the flood of another tide,
How fares the wind for Liverpool?
We must set yet another course,
There's a new dawn breaking.

September 1988

M.V. *KHUDOZHNIK ROMAS* AND A FEW MORE GREY HAIRS

I was to experience another near grounding disaster years after that of the *Rhine Ore*, and managed to resolve that one before touching the bottom. Five Russian vessels of the Baltic fleet were at one time, shortly before the fall of the Berlin Wall in 1989, running containers from the continent, via Liverpool, to Montreal for Anglo-Soviet Shipping.

The vessels were sound, thirteen thousand, nine hundred tons gross, well built, but they were in a poor state of repair because no money was being spent on them. No paint, little oil and grease and the excellent crews were poorly paid. As soon as the Berlin Wall came down, the fleet were among the many vessels, which were immediately impounded with writs on the mast for debts unpaid. Two were to be laid up in Canada, one on the continent and two were in Liverpool. They were to sail, months later, three of them ostensibly on the same trade, under the flag of Moore Line.

The incident, which I am about to relate, took place on board the *Khudozhnik Romas* on the evening tide of the first of March 1992, some months after another incident with the vessel, where I was called upon as an outward bound pilot, to be boarded back inward-bound, having had to relieve a colleague who was taken ill on board the vessel as he was approaching the channel entrance.

On the second occasion we were outward bound, and by coincidence, the same colleague, whom I had relieved, was on the launch, this time, also outward bound and waiting for me, before we were to return together. He was to have a long wait!

We had left Gladstone Lock on the flood of the tide. The vessel was deep, drawing nine point five metres. I had piloted the ship safely outward bound in the Crosby Channel and we had just cleared the bend into the Formby Strait, when the helmsman started to shout. "Oh dear", I thought. "I have been here before, years ago!"

I was very swiftly to be proven right. The vessel was commencing an unwanted and uncalled for, hard to starboard swing on this occasion, and the helmsman was indicating that he had the helm hard to port. The speed over the ground was about twelve knots, and to swing to the north at this point would take us over the Queens North Training Wall, and this time with our draft and no sand to save us, we were on our way on to the unforgiving stones of the training wall.

The engines were on manoeuvring full speed ahead and I ordered "Stop Engines" and immediately ordered the mate forward, to let go the port anchor. Events happened swiftly now as in the case of the *Rhine Ore*, I ordered the stopped engine to full speed astern and ordered the mate to let go the starboard anchor, even though the port anchor chain was still running very swiftly out. This he did at once, but the engineer was less successful as his engines were tired and in need of a long overdue service and failed, grinding to a still, silence, more noticeable by the lack of vibration than by any lack of noise to indicate lost power.

The wind was southerly, about force six and strengthening. I waited moments to await developments and to assess what if any success had been achieved by letting go both anchors. The first sound to break the silence was the captain's screamed assertion that I personally had lost both of the ship's anchors! I smiled bitterly and contradicted him. "No Captain that is not the case. I believe that we have indeed lost the port anchor and some eleven shackles of cable, but ask the mate to look again closely over the starboard bow and I believe that he will see the starboard anchor cable leading close under the forefoot of the vessel. We are stopped Captain and something is holding us. We are still in the channel and nowhere near aground thankfully, so that must be the case. Now call up the engine room and have them sort out some propulsion."

My report to the V.T.S. on this occasion and queries about the possibilities of tug assistance was bleak. Only one tug, still in the dock system, could be mobilised and she was hours away. When the tide turned, the vessel would swing head to both wind and tide and, ground on the stones so close to the north of our position. I thought of the *Pegu* lost during 1943 on the Crosby Bend in similar circumstances outward bound in a convoy. Her remains now lie in two; each part occupying a section of stonewalls, which lie to the east of the channel. "Captain, our best chance, maybe our only chance, is for the engineer to come up with some power, even if it is only for a short period of time and not even full power."

The chief engineer did a grand job, and shortly before the ship was to swing to the ebb tide, we had engines turning ahead, albeit only just! The mate was able to heave up the starboard anchor and we limped to the west, the channel entrance and the open sea.

Almost there, the engines failed again and I was forced to drop the starboard anchor again. This time, with less speed on the vessel, the one anchor held, so that the bow was perilously close, but clear of the Q6. Buoy. This time we had engines more swiftly and were able to lift up the anchor again, and limp to the position for a safe Bar anchorage, where she was to remain for about a week for repairs.

Just before I left the bridge for the waiting launch, the pressure on the captain was too great and he snapped. "Mr. Pilot you are responsible for losing my port anchor and eleven shackles of anchor chain." I replied brusquely for I too had been under intense pressure: "Yes Captain that is unfortunately true, but in losing it I have saved your ship!" We shook hands, and he thanked me for my swift actions, apologising for the unnecessary comment.

There is a lovely rider to this story, for during the whole incident I had not put any position on the ship's chart but of course I was well aware of distances off the frightening red-flashing of the port-hand buoys in the darkness, and of our exact position in relation to them. A day or so later I was at home, the wind had died and the Mersey Docks and Harbour Company salvage vessel *Vigilant* was out in the Formby Channel searching unsuccessfully for the lost anchor and chain.

It was, I believe in the early days of mobile phones. My good friend, Brian McShane was then a surveyor in the port, and in command of the search operation instigated for the lost anchor. He called me and stated that they had been searching for some time but with no success, had I any advice to offer to help in the search.

"Take the vessel to Q10.Buoy," I replied, "half a cable off in the channel, and steam outward bound parallel to the buoy-line. You will pick up the cable about one third of the way towards Q8. Buoy." Less than ten minutes later Brian called me back to say I had been spot on, and they had both found, and were now recovering the anchor and its chain. This news was gratifying, particularly when I learned that the anchor had been returned to the *Khudozhnik Romas*, still anchored where I had left her, and still undergoing repairs.

Again I would have preferred not to have had the experience, but as I was again awarded salvage for saving the ship, Gill and I were able to make a trip out to Indonesia during a period the following year whilst Gill was studying batik art for her Master's degree. I would look at the sun, sea and the sand, but not far from my memory was the darkness of the near gale-torn night, the waves breaking and the stones threatening the stricken ship.

MATURE STUDENT MUSINGS

Following my success at becoming a first class pilot, I began to think of other pursuits to tax my mind in addition to piloting ships. In the early seventies, the traffic was changing as I have already explained. We were still, however, following the ruling of boarding all vessels on arrival, whether at Point Lynas or at the Bar Light Vessel. If the vessel had orders to dock within forty-eight hours, the pilot was to stay aboard. That was a long period to be on board a ship, when you were not actually part of the crew.

All ships are, required by law, to provide a pilot's cabin. On board small coasters, however, a narrow settee in the captain's cabin or even a bench in a cramped messroom might be all the sleeping space available. The pilot, after a long passage, would often be tired, when having the necessity to anchor. The ship might be waiting for the tide, or be in dense fog, or possibly even with engine problems. Sometimes the captain of the ship had, even though English is the international language of the sea, only a very limited knowledge of it.

The captain may be Greek, Turkish, Russian, Italian, or indeed be of any nationality, and he may be friendly, and then again he may be indifferent, or even hostile. I have always believed that a pilot was a guest on board the vessel, a guest with a very important job to do, using other people's expensive property and equipment. My policy was always, that when a pilot arrived on the bridge of a ship, it was his responsibility to find the level, where he could work and therefore do his job with the utmost efficiency. I have frequently said that a pilot's life is often a lonely existence.

In the first week of my days as a first-class pilot, I was to pilot five German vessels in succession. I noted terms such as "Lautstärke," (volume control on a V.H.F. set.) "Voll Voraus," (full ahead on the ship's engine-room telegraph.) "Steuerbord und Backbord," (Port and Starboard.) and many others, and I realised that here was an opportunity, par excellence, to learn a language.

I bought myself a German pocket-dictionary and set to, translating the seven initial basic questions, which a pilot asks on reaching the bridge after exchanging greetings with the captain: "Where bound, where from, what is the draft, what is the cargo, what is the name of the agents, has the vessel any defects, and what is the full speed of the vessel?"

I boarded a German coaster soon after at Point Lynas, she was bound for Liverpool. I greeted the Captain with "Guten Tag Herr Kapitän!" (Good day Captain) and proceeded to ask my translated questions. The captain, a certain Captain Horry Knoll, fell about laughing. My literal translations were way out, but by the time we had reached the Bar Light Vessel, the captain, as my teacher, had helped me to write out correct translations, and I had managed to learn them.

On board the next German ship, I made the point of asking the questions successfully before I had to admit that I did not speak German. I learned some more on that passage, and so over the years, both my vocabulary and my ability with the language improved rapidly. So much so, I revised my "O" level French and embarked upon the pursuit of "A" levels in both languages, which I was finally to achieve. A lifelong, love and fascination with languages was established.

Following the "A" level successes, I looked around for further ways of exercising my mind, and I became an "F" registered student with the Open University, which had been Harold Wilson's brainchild under his Labour Government. I was to embark on both the Arts and the Mathematics foundation courses, and was to specialise in the Arts, reading a second level course on Renaissance and Reformation, followed by three third level courses to complete my basic degree. I chose Drama, the 19th Century Novel and 20th Century Poetry. I followed the basic degree with two half credits in both classical and modern art. Then, I realised that the problems of the port with over-manning and fewer ships could give me an opportunity, which I had been considering for some time.

Some of my colleagues had gone abroad, to pilot in such far off lands as Saudi-Arabia and Guinea, West Africa, but I saw another possibility. I applied to the University of Liverpool to read a Joint Honours Degree in French and German, and I was accepted to begin in the autumn term of 1982. I became a full-time student and a full-time pilot!

With most of a pilot's work, 76% at the last count, being at night, I did not get much sleep during the weekdays of my university career. The completion of my first year at Liverpool was to be counted as a credit by the Open University, and I was awarded an Honours Degree by the senate of the O.U.

Gill and I had four children at this time, three adopted and one of our own, but Gill supported me in the venture, even to the time I was able to spend abroad in my third year, the "Year Abroad." It was a wonderful period in my life. The tutors and lecturers were superb, many were my own age, and have become friends over the years. The main body of students were female and exactly twenty years younger than myself, but they made me so welcome and part of their 'University Years.'

When, on the occasions that I had been out all night at sea, I would sit at the back of the lecture theatre between friends who would make sure that I was wide awake if there was something of particular importance to appreciate, or if I was being asked a question! If I was to miss any lectures or tutorials, these same friends provided me with their notes to copy so that I could keep up with all my courses. During the three years of actual time spent at the University, I was to miss, on average, only one hour per week of contact time. This I believe was less in total than many of the hours missed by younger fellow students.

There was one amusing incident, which took place on one of the days "missed," which is worthy of note. There was, during one term-time, a whole week's exercise throughout the United Kingdom, which took place, on the theme of 'The Defence of the Realm.' All the regular services, the Royal Navy, the Army and the

Royal Air Force, were pitted against their Territorial counterparts. A 'Dad's Army' affair. All aspects of the ports and their personnel of the United Kingdom were informed about the nature of the exercise, *Operation Brave Defender*, except marine pilots!

Tanks, artillery sentry-boxes and sandbags were to appear in the ports during the course of the week, but at first, when I boarded a small tanker, inward bound from Point Lynas, running late for the tide at Langton Lock, we knew nothing about the operation.

I first noticed, as it was daylight, a minesweeper to the south, and some miles astern of my ship, on the same course. The grey funnel was I noticed, unusually painted white and red. Later we were to discover that this was the Royal Navy playing at being part of the "Soviet Fleet attacking the British Isles." I carried on my way until I was entering the main channel when I observed that the minesweeper had come up to the north, and was directly astern of me, and closing fast.

I had only a rough idea of her draught, and as I was passing to the north of the Formby Light Float to cut a corner and save time to ensure that my ship would not miss the tide, I was concerned that she might have some equipment lowered beneath the hull and be too deep to follow me safely. I knew that there was no pilot on board, so I called her up on the V.H.F. radio:

"Minesweeper following the red-hulled tanker *Maria Therese* into the Formby Channel at Liverpool please reply." I called several times with no response, so I called her again using the 'M' number painted on her bows.

The reply was both immediate and icy! The commander was a unit of the opposition, and was attempting to enter the channel in broad daylight using my vessel as part of his radar-target, so that he would remain undetected! In broadcasting the minesweeper's official number on air, it appeared that in the rules of the contest, I had sunk him! He followed me up channel to be taken into custody by the Liverpool University naval-unit's launch.

The local evening newspaper, the *Liverpool Echo*, and the following day's *Liverpool Daily Post* newspaper, ran an article, with the headline: "John torpedoes 'Russian' attack." I discovered the following day just how many university lecturers actually read the *Daily Post*!

Liverpool Echo, Thursday, September 12, 1985

Britannia rules the waves

John torpedoes 'Russian' attack

GENERAL Sir James Glover missed the unsung hero of his imaginary war when he met Merseyside's Brave Defenders, in the armed forces defence exercise.

But today the Echo can reveal the story of the man who scuppered a daring "Russian" invasion of the Mersey — simply by doing his job.

River pilot John Curry was on board an inward-bound Danish coaster when he suddenly noticed a warship following.

Collision risk

Although the strange red and white funnel markings were foreign to him, the mine sweeper had the look of a Royal Naval vessel.

Completely unaware of her intentions and worried about the risk of a collision in the channel, John called up the mysterious stranger on the radio.

When two attempts to make con-

tact were met by silence he tried again using the warship number 2003 he saw painted o n the side.

This time a slightly exasperated voice answered identifying the ship as the Baltisky Waveny — now sunk and out of the game!

The ship he had spotted was in fact part of the "Russian" fleet carrying crack invasion troops on a mission to take over the Liverpool docks.

Said John, from Devonshire Road, West Kirby: "Although we have nothing to do with Brave Defender, I realised what was going on and called my own control to be told, 'You've blown her up'.

"It seems a little unrealistic for anyone to believe that a Russian warship could get up the Mersey in broad daylight without being seen but I suppose that he was attempting to avoid radar recognition by using us as a shield."

My "Year Abroad" was made possible by the generosity and encouragement of my colleagues of the Liverpool Pilot Service. I was allowed to take my leave periods over two years, when I required them. With a young family and a mortgage it would not have been financially viable if I had simply taken time out. This arrangement meant that, including two summer holidays, I was able to spend a great deal of time of the year abroad both in France and in Germany. First of all I was to spend time both in France and Germany during the summer of '84, which period allowed me to visit Port Revel near Grenoble, the Marine Research and Training Centre. I was interviewed, and as I was offering my services free of charge, I was accepted as a translator, interpreter and instructor at the centre for two months the following summer.

I also won a scholarship from the German department to spend a month at the University of Freiburg, picked up another scholarship during the February of the following year as the winner was unable to accept it, and spent the time at the Goethe Institute in Staufen also in Breisgau. I completed my "Year Abroad" with a month spent at a summer school at the Sorbonne in Paris during the summer of 1985. Boris Becker won Wimbledon for the first time whilst I was there. The family joined me for my final week and stayed in the Cité Universitaire, before we set off to the south for a holiday in Provence. Including holidays with the family, I believe that I managed to spend seven months abroad, which the university was to accept, as it amounted to more than a full-time university study year.

Yes, the whole experience was as wonderful as it sounds! I made many friends, both old and young in my travels, circumnavigated Paris "en velo" (on a bicycle) whilst staying in the Cité Universitaire, was fortunate to have student accommodation in both Freiburg and Staufen, and found "Ma Chambre" within the home of the family Darbon, now my French family, close to Port Revel, at a small village called Marcollin in Isère.

I studied hard and was eventually to be awarded my degree with Joint Honours in the summer of 1986. I had found that my best subject was medieval French, under the guidance of Professor Glyn Burgess. He was to become my mentor and set me off on, at first, a Master's Degree, and then because of the nature of my research, my studies were upgraded, and I embarked upon a PhD., following, in literature, Saint Brendan across the Atlantic in the twelfth century work *Le Voyage de Saint Brendan* by Benedeit.

This proved to be increasingly difficult for me to be able to devote time to, as pilots were being reduced in numbers leading up to the Pilotage Act of 1988, under Margaret Thatcher's government. Something drastic had to be done politically, as, for the reasons described earlier, there were too many marine pilots in every port in the world. With the reduction in numbers, my studies have had to be put on ice. I would dearly love to continue them, and even hope to do so when this book is published in the fullness of time.

Back at full time operations, I devoted myself to piloting, but also continued to write articles and poetry. I had had, through the misfortunes of the port, managed to experience another career, as I taught at the University in the Department of French for almost twenty years, teaching Medieval French Literature. As a result of my interest in the study of the "Old French" language, I was to come up with a possible theory for the origin of the name of the port, in which I was a pilot.

Coming home from teaching tutorials on one occasion, I stopped at red traffic lights close to the Royal Liver Building on the Pier Head. Looking up at the eastern-most bird on the tower, I had what I believe is described as a "Eureka" moment: "Li" is an old French version of "the," "ver," I took as "springtime," as in the Italian "primavera." Now then, what about "pool?" When I reached home, knowing that the original spelling of the name was "pul," as in the document handing over the port to King John by a knight by the name of Fitzwarren in 1206, I searched my dictionaries. The document is kept in the vaults of the Liverpool Library. I was not allowed to sight it, even with a university request, but I was sent a photocopy!

Now, when a word cannot be found in Medieval, or Old French, in either a modern English or a modern French dictionary, the secret is to turn to the Latin. I was delighted to discover, that the seventh meaning of words beginning with "pul," was: "pulvinarium," meaning anchorage! The Anglo-Normans, who used Latin in official documents, were engaged in omitting some Latin endings as we see most obviously in "Londinium" becoming London. Thus we have: the 'Port of the Springtime Anchorage.' This makes sense for me, because even now, with the prevailing westerly gales, the port is more accessible in the spring and summer months. John would have been engaged in developing the trade, which we still have, between Ireland and his possessions in England.

I have published this idea and believe that this is indeed the origin of the name. The Romans avoided Liverpool and the strong tides of the Mersey, in favour of the wider, more easily flowing, River Dee. They described the River Mersey in their sailing directions, apparently as: "A rocky creek in the vicinity of Deva (Chester)." With the more substantial long-ships of the Normans, the navigation of the Mersey would have become more desirable, with the wish to trade from the north through the waters of the Mersey.

Another set of terms used in the laws of the sea; I also believe come from Anglo Norman French. These are the four legal terms regarding loss at sea:

"Flotsam," from floter to float off the deck of a ship.

"Jetsam," from jeter to throw overboard from a ship.

"Lagan," from lagan, "the gain", débris or goods thrown overboard and buoyed in the hope that the owner would recover it, at a later date.

"Wreck," from 'wrec,' quite simply wreck, and irretrievable.

Whilst I was involved in my full-time degree, I had many memorable occasions, which are vivid in my recollections. I remember that, when I arrived at Port Revel, for example, the other instructors were wary of me. I believe that they might have suspected, wrongly, that I was after their job. For several days after my arrival and after Gill and two of my children, Becky and Nathan had been waved goodbye to at the station in Grenoble, I was to feel very much alone. The train had weaved its way slowly northwards, leaving me with our bright orange Volkswagen camper van, complete with orange canoe lashed to the roof (rather like a Fisher Price toy) to fend for myself.

I was given an office opposite the secretary's office. Monique Chapel was, and is, a delightful young woman full of fun.

Monique is now married to the present Director of Sogreah, the firm of port builders, who run the Marine Research Training Centre. My first task was to commence an overhaul of the teaching manual, removing all Americanisms and replacing them with good English.

After several days of working on this project, late in the afternoon, there came a call for me to join the senior instructor at the southernmost jetty. The "estagier," or trainee, was a young American chief officer with Exxon, who was returning from the course to be master in command of his own ship. I was to board the "maquette" (model) tanker, taking the engineer's position, forward of the captain/operator's position. We were ordered to leave the stage, proceed and go alongside another stage and then return. The American was having all kinds of trouble leaving the jetty, so I muttered instructions in a low voice, and we set off. Upon our return, the chief instructor, Philippe de la Salle, who was to become a friend, ordered a change of places and instructed me to take the tanker back to the garage, where she was to lay for the night.

The trainees were given a preliminary lecture about the models, and allowed: "to play" during the first morning to become conversant with the handling of them, but for me it was in at the deep end. Philippe turned on his heel and disappeared into the trees, but I knew that he would be watching this latest arrival at Port Revel closely. I gave the "engineer" my instructions. In fact, I believe that it was more truthful to say that I read him the riot act! My reputation, and thus the reputation of Liverpool Pilots, was at stake.

I had gathered through observation that the models moved approximately five times faster in the swing than the real thing. And that the Doppler-log speed of two knots was accurate in scale and thus, close to land or jetties, the model could be handled similar, to the tanker, which she was modelled on. This was a model of a one hundred and twenty thousand ton ship, and therefore in reality she would have been a "big boat"! I took her off the jetty and out into the bay to get the feel of her before attempting the approach to the garage. The American was with me and was giving me confidence with his support.

I made a lazy swing for the garage on the port helm, and began the approach, watching the Doppler all the time. We entered the gloom of the garage making approximately a knot and a half. There, standing on the jetty was Philippe and the full team of four highly skilled technicians, who themselves could handle the models superbly well. I could never understand why Sogreah did not put them on the real thing, under supervision, to prove the point of the model training.

Philippe was pointing to his feet, which stood at the end of the narrow, barely model width, which was our berthing position, between two other models. I edged her gently in, constantly demanding the Doppler-log speed over the ground until we came to a halt, a centimetre off the quay and with about five centimetres on either side, without touching. The reception committee spun on its collective heel, without comment, and left the garage. I had passed the test!

I just happened to have a bottle of whisky in the camping-wagon, and after dinner at the Hotel Bonnoit down in the valley, I offered "my engineer" a drink to celebrate my acceptance at Port Revel. The hotel where the "estagiers" stayed was also the hotel, which provided the "haute cuisine" lunches up at the lake and the cuisine was, indeed excellent. The hotel was a favourite of President Mitterand when he was watching the Tour de France down in the south. It was then that I learned that Americans have a penchant for drinking in their hotel room. After several, or more, large whiskies, I took my leave of my newfound friend and attempted to leave the hotel. It was by now the early hours of the morning, and to my blurred dismay, the hotel was well and truly locked up for the night.

For sometime in the dark, I endeavoured to find an unlocked door, which I could open, or even a window, which I could slip through, but to no avail. Eventually I ended up in the wine cellar and also could find no way out of there. On coming back up the cellar steps, to regain the main hallway, I was aware of a shadowy figure standing in the darkness above me. The figure turned out to be Madame Bonnoit herself, brandishing a key. Madame said nothing as she opened the door and let me out. Next day, being Saturday, I returned to the hotel with a large bunch of flowers to make as a peace offering. To my relief, Madame laughed and forgave me, finding my midnight prowling mildly amusing in fact, and we were to become firm friends.

My most enjoyable week at Port Revel was the week when we had eight French pilots attending a week's course. One pilot was from Bordeaux, (so, like Liverpool pilots, he was a sea, river and dock pilot) two of the pilots were from Le Havre, and so were breakwater, harbour pilots, and the other five were all Seine River pilots.

The adaptability to the models showed, for the Bordeaux pilot was outstanding from the start, the Le Havre pilots were next in line for coming to terms with the models, and the Seine River Pilots, who never, as I understood it, actually berthed ships alongside a quay or dock-side, found the exercises the most difficult.

Mealtimes at the centre during that week were memorable. The food and wine were magnificent, both provided by the Hotel Bonnoit from the valley below the lake. Jean Graf, the director of Port Revel, led the story telling as always. I had been there some weeks by the time the French pilots arrived, and Jean had integrated me into a kind of double act, which helped the conversation to flow.

This time it was different because the whole conversation and the storytelling were conducted in French. The gathering insisted that during the course of each meal, I was to tell two of my stories in French. This was wonderful for my need to improve the language, which after all was the reason for my being there at all.

As it was 1985, Margaret Thatcher, 'La Dame de Fer' (The Iron Lady) and her approach to the French was a constant source of the gathering ribbing me, and my country. I coped, and waited for the last mealtime, and my last story. For this occasion I chose my father's true tale of the visit of a French destroyer to Liverpool. Upon arriving off the lock, the commander of the warship was not pleased. The booking clerk for the tugs had impishly provided the vessel with the tug *Nelson* to tow ahead, and the tug *Trafalgar* to tow astern.

The gathering went silent as I continued. I explained that the commander was naturally angry at this arrangement and insisted that the same tugs were not to be present for the sailing. The tug company complied and instead provided the destroyer with another two of their tugs. The *Wellington* was to be the head tug and the *Waterloo*, the stern tug.

I sat deliberating upon whether I should make a run for it, as perhaps I had misjudged my friendship with my French colleagues. Then, realising that they had made me suffer over "butter mountains, wine lakes and New Zealand lamb," (all parts of Margaret Thatcher's Anglo-French policies apparently) the mumble of "Ça va John, ça va!" grew and the laughter broke out. I was forgiven, and I had, to some extent, got my own back for the week's barracking.

Back on board real ships, I remember one amusing incident, which took place after my degree. I usually spoke German on board German ships in order to continue to improve my spoken language, and simply because I enjoyed doing so. There was one of the Craig Line container vessel's captains, who was Polish born, but was a naturalised German.

This captain and myself played a language game. He spoke English to me and I corrected him, and I spoke German to him, and he corrected me. This game led to the story of 'Harry Bannerchek and the Optrex.'

"A Liverpool Pilot, out of his district!"

The time of year was near Christmas and it was to become my colleague's favourite tale over the festive season. Gill had the use of the one car, which we owned at the time, and as it was daylight hours, I was to catch the train from West Kirby to Hamilton Square Station to join a morning launch in time to be boarded on the *Craigivad*, bound for North Dock, Garston, on the day tide.

Walking through the park, I was aware that the wind was quite fresh, from the northwest, and a cloud of blown dust blew a speck of grit into my eye. Ouch! Not to worry, the chemist opposite the station was open, and I was able to buy a bottle of Optrex and an eye bath. I cleared the offending particle from the eye on the train and placed the Optrex in my piloting bag. I always carried a black leather brief case, that is, until I became an A.C.L. pilot when I was to buy a tan briefcase from 'The Bridge.'

Out to the Bar on a pilot launch, and then on board the Craig boat and into the language game, which was undoubtedly beneficial for both of us. I had been told at the university that the best way to learn a language was to find a 'Long-Haired Dictionary!' I knew, however that Gill would not have been happy with that arrangement, and Harry did not exactly fit the description, but he was better than nothing.

We navigated the vessel safely up to Garston chatting in our language game until we were to swing, head north, before entering the Old Dock, and berthing in North Dock, where the container base was situated. On the southwest corner of the Old Dock, lay a coaster discharging something, very brown and very dusty by grab into a waiting lorry.

The stiff breeze was still from the northwest, and just as we were directly downwind of the discharging operation, the grab opened, depositing several tons of brown powder into the lorry. The wind took the lighter part, and it hurtled towards us in a dense, dark, swirling cloud. "Vorsicht!" (Lookout!) I shouted and ducked below the dodger along with the German chief officer. (Yes, there was a witness to the tale.)

Now Harry, being Harry, although master of a German container vessel, was not always the brightest of individuals, and he obeyed my warning as an order. Harry's head vanished into the brown cloud; eyes wide open, staring fixedly ahead. When he emerged from the cloud he was totally blind, or "blind," as it is the same in both languages. "Fear not Harry, give me the controls and sort your sight out!" I ordered. This he dutifully did, and by the time we had entered the next dock he had, what might be called: "blinking vision." "I have it, I have it." He growled gruffly, taking the controls back. "Harry," I exclaimed, remembering the Optrex in my bag, "I have just the thing for you." I dashed off into the wheelhouse to fetch the bottle of Optrex and the eyebath from my briefcase. I poured the liquid into the eyebath on my way back. "Here Harry, Optrex." I said, handing him the eyebath. "Was ist, was ist?" (What is it, what is it?) He asked, but before I could answer: "Augenspüle," (eyewash.) he raised the eyebath to his lips and drank the Optrex down in one gulp!

The mate and I fell about laughing. The sequel to the story is that as Harry, upon realising his silly mistake, laughed too, so much so that he cried. In doing so he proved with his tears, that Optrex is capable of being effective if taken internally as well as being administered externally!

In 1993 during the celebrations of the 50th anniversary of the Battle of the Atlantic, we were to use leave pilots to cover the increase in the numbers of ship movements because of the visiting warships. Most of the volunteers piloted three warships. I was delighted to find that one of my extra vessels was to be the German U boat: *U 25*. (S174.) The whole crew had obviously watched the television series 'Das Boot.' as they were all dressed like the crew from the film, and the commandant was the very likeness of 'Der Elter!'

It was a pleasure for me both to pilot the vessel and to speak German to the commandant.

□ Leaving of Liverpool – a German submarine glides away, as the Royal Yacht awaits her turn to head out to sea   Picture: FRAZER BIRD

U 25 clear and away from Alfred Locks, Birkenhead

'IN FOG, MIST, FALLING SNOW, HEAVY RAINSTORMS AND ANY OTHER CONDITIONS SIMILARLY...'

So read the start of the old collision regulation rule sixteen, relating to the speed of ships to be moderate in these conditions. As Boathands, we had to learn all thirty-two of the rules off by heart for oral examination purposes.

The rules of the road at sea lay down every aspect of lights, signals and behaviour required of both vessels and seaplanes in all conditions. Rule sixteen dealt briefly and efficiently with fog and reduced visibility. When asked the question, most navigators would prefer a full-blown gale to dense fog if given the choice. Basically, even if it is blowing hard, navigators can still see where they are going on most occasions. Falling snow is perhaps the worst condition of all, for radars cannot see through snow, and if out on the wing of the bridge, the snowflakes blind the eyes.

I have related the tale of the *Martinistad*, which was to close with such a happy ending. Indeed, all of my reduced visibility experiences were to end happily, but that is not to say that on many occasions the going was to get both tough and demanding.

In the first year or so, I always had in my mind the old pilot's view, that if you could not navigate the channels without the use of a radar set in dense fog, you were not worthy to call yourself a real pilot. As noted in the *Martinistad* incident, many small ships were not equipped with radar when I first became a pilot. With no Clean Air Act, fog was very definitely more of a possibility than it is subsequent to the Act. The opportunity came to test for the "real" pilot within me, quite early on in the third class pilot period.

I was boarded in dense fog out at the Bar Light Vessel on a coaster bound for Birkenhead. It was daytime, and the grey swirling mists of the fog enveloped the vessel from stem to stern. Two outward-bound first class pilots had requested a passage back with me, so that they might land earlier than they would have done if they had waited for a pilot launch. On the way across from the pilot boat, as the pilot boarding punt felt her way through the all-enveloping mists, I had requested that both my colleagues sit down in the mess-room, and leave me to my own deliberations, but promised if I were to need another pair of eyes, that I would call them to the bridge.

I had noted the boarding position from the pilot boat's radar, and laid it off on the coaster's chart. Allowing for an estimated set and drift from both the flood of the tide and the light breeze I timed the estimated ship's speed on my watch and much to my delight (but not total surprise) I came upon the Q1 Buoy at the entrance of the main Queen's Channel. From here, over the next two hours, I successfully navigated the channel approaches and the river from buoy to buoy until, after swinging to the flood of the tide off Alfred Locks, the vessel gently touched the south side of the North Lock and we were there with myself, the exhausted young pilot vowing, that, unless I was caught out, I would never do such a passage again!

My father always emphasised the importance of "getting as far as you can when you can" for no one knows, even with weather forecasts, what the future will actually hold. This being applicable to wind conditions as well as to reduced visibility.

Dad backed this advice up with a story about a pilot, long ago, who was boarded on a ship without radar, down at the Lynas Pilot Station on a beautiful summer's evening with clear visibility. The ship's orders were to dock at Brunswick Lock in Liverpool on the following day's tide. The captain and pilot opted to anchor the ship in Moelfre Bay, have a few beers, turn in,[13] and to lift anchor to proceed up to dock after a leisurely breakfast.

In the event, they awoke to find themselves engulfed in dense fog, and were not to dock until several days later. If they had

---

13 Nautical expression for getting into a bunk bed and going to sleep.

proceeded up to anchor off the lock they may well have been able to dock on schedule.

In my early years, the Rock Channel was still buoyed, although the buoys themselves were chequered, black and yellow on the starboard hand and red and yellow on the port hand. Conical buoys on the starboard hand, can buoys on the port hand, numbered from seawards. They were coloured so as a secondary channel, and to indicate that the channel had not been positively swept free of wartime mines! The channel ran from the Rock Lighthouse at New Brighton, first to the west and then seawards to the northwest, off Harrison Drive.

I note from my mark book[14], that these buoys were removed from station on the twenty fourth of May, nineteen seventy-one, but for almost three years, I was able to make regular use of the channel. Inward bound, or outward bound in those days of dense traffic on the tide, the channel, when sufficient water for the ship to float was present, provided an escape for a small coaster from the main flow of traffic in the Queen's and Crosby Channels, particularly desirable in dense fog. I was to use the unmarked Rock Channel once, after it was closed, much later in my career when I tided it round from the Port of Mostyn to Bromborough Dock on a Dutch coaster called the *Hoop*.

Fortunately, not that long after I became a pilot, it became maritime law that all vessels were to carry at least one radar set. It was however, still possible to be caught out, and on one occasion, after 1986, I was boarded at the Bar on a Norwegian vessel of about fifteen thousand tons, gross. A retired pilot, John Woodfine was on duty in the Radar Tower. The ship was eventually found in conditions, which I had not experienced before, and was not to experience after. The wind was a good force six and the fog was both dense and swirling, rather like the frightening sequence at the start of the film *The Wreck of the Mary Deare*.

---

14 A mark book was the term for the Boathand's study/notebook.

One of my first questions to the captain was: "How are the radars Captain?" The reply came back that they were in perfect order, so we commenced the passage and passed the point of no or difficult return, for a big ship, which is the Q1. Buoy. Once passed the buoy, the radar I was looking into became suspect, with a great deal of what we call "clutter" on the screen. The captain advised the use of the second radar "which was a much better picture." On viewing that screen, I was to discover that there was no picture at all! Returning to the first one, I discovered, to my dismay, that it had followed suit. Calmly I ordered a reduction in speed, and settled down for an unwanted channel passage "on my watch."

I requested that John confirm my starting position from the shore-based radars, and swung the vessel into the Formby Strait, where relief came as both radars burst into new life and we were to continue safely into the dense, swirling, "cinématique" mists.

Another relief situation was found on board a large Korean grain-carrier, outward bound from Gladstone Lock, in ballast. The ship had been under arrest and my orders came at short notice to hurry over to the berth, and attempt to sail on the tide, on which the legal writ had been lifted from her mast. It was early on a fine summer's evening and it was a neap (small) tide. The vessel was manoeuvred both swiftly and safely into the lock. The warm sunny day was becoming noticeably cooler, but no fog had been forecast.

I left the Gladstone lock, swung to starboard with the tug to head north, but half way on the swing, New Brighton disappeared, and the mist, which had not been forecast, came swirling in from the west. The tug skipper was not happy and declared that he would have to let go as he "could not see the ship." I replied that that was strange, and that he was not to worry, for I could see him! I promised that if the fog was to shut visibility down totally, I would give him a course, and watch him on my excellent radars until he was safely back in Gladstone Lock. We completed the swing, I kept my word, and the tug was soon safely back in the lock. Now it was going to be "head in the radar time."

I settled down on the outward course, and was soon aware of what at first, could be described as a light giggling. Now most Asian registered vessels, as well as ships of Her Majesty, the latter for obvious military reasons, tend to have large numbers of personnel on the bridge when the vessel is under pilotage and in coastal waters, so the giggling was noticeable. The giggling grew steadily into gales of Asian laughter, and I became both uncomfortable and not a little angry, for I believed that the laughter was for some reason directed at me, and caused by me, for some reason I had undoubtedly become a figure of fun. I looked up and swung round to turn on those who had chosen to take me as the subject of their uncontrollable mirth, to discover that the visibility was as clear as the proverbial bell, and that we could have seen America on this beautiful summer's evening if it had not been well below the horizon.

On another occasion, I inadvertently became a successful "radar technician" on a Silver Line tanker, outward-bound from Eastham Locks at the entrance of the Manchester Ship Canal. Visibility was about three miles and it was daytime, the captain had two defects for me to report. One was the low volume of his V.H.F. radio, and the other was that his radar would not work.

We sailed from the lock and I insisted that an officer stood close by the V.H.F receiver in case someone was to call us. As I settled in, I was to learn that the whole crew had only just joined the ship at the loading berth in the Canal. With experience already recounted about what can happen in such cases, I ventured to turn up the volume control on the V.H.F. to hear Mersey Radio blasting out the two hour to high water broadcast! The captain was delighted and apologised for the simple error saying that he wished that I could do the same for the radar. I jokingly gave the radar a firm thump with my fist, and it too sprang into operational vision! I was indeed the captain's favourite pilot that day.

Twice I can remember racing a fog bank for the safety of the harbour wall. In my "shorthand" days (second or third class licence days) I had made a passage on an old Kelly boat, bridge amidships, from Point Lynas to Garston Docks, and ended up racing the predicted fog bank up the Garston Channel. On this occasion we were overtaken, short of the lock. On reduced speed and with no radar, I asked the mate, forward to shout as soon as he saw anything. He did, although unfortunately it was the wooden jetty, which runs from the east side of the lock seawards from the lock, and it was on the starboard (wrong) side of the bow of the ship. A hasty astern movement arrested our slow progress and, with the jetty on the port (right, that is right as in correct) side the vessel entered the lock safely.

Later in my career, on board an A.C.L. container ship, I was leaving the lock, inward bound for the berth and, looking sideways from my control position, I noticed a white finger of cloud. This was the start of a dense bank of fog, forecast for later, arriving from the south, and which would lie over the port for several days. Now, you cannot hurry an A.C.L. The vessels are approximately thirty metres longer than the *Titanic* was, and a third wider, and the pilot using the bridge controls "drives them" like a motorcar. I pushed as hard as I dared, and did manage to find the berth by the lights of the container cranes only.

Later that evening the authorities closed the port for the first time in its history, save for the tide of 'The Last Muster.' All vessels were locked in the system. On the Sunday, when the fog finally cleared, I entered the bridge of a very modern Scandinavian tanker with all the latest equipment in the Q.E.II Lock to be greeted by a scathing welcome of: "Decided to do a bit have we Pilot?" Years of experience helped me to control my temper and I replied: "I am going to pretend that I did not hear that Captain. I am going to leave the bridge and return immediately, so that we may start again." The vessel sailed, shortly afterwards with the apologetic captain and pilot the best of friends.

A story, which shows how a pilot may be caught out and yet still must cope, is the story of a light scrap ship bound for Liverpool with an Indian master. As I neared the river on the road from my home, I realised that the visibility on the river must be near zero. It was a winter fog, cold and depressing. Upon boarding the pilot launch, I realised that the newly made up to coxswain in command was not happy with the situation. He actually lit up two cigars, one immediately after the other, without realising it!

"I would like you to sit up in the wheelhouse next to me if you do not mind Mr. Curry."

"I can assure you Coxswain," was the reply, "I have no intention in these conditions of sitting anywhere else."

We sailed, relying on courses and the radar, finding the ship, anchored in a position northwest of the Bar. "Right Coxswain, stay alongside, for in these conditions, I am not intending to dock." Caught in fog, as in a storm the pilot has to do something about it but it would be a fool who sailed into either without the necessity to do so, unless there were mitigating circumstances. "I will be right here by the ladder, Mr Curry." came the relieved reply. Up the ladder I went, and onto the bridge. Standing with my back to the forward bridge windows, I commenced my delivery upon the reasons as to why we would not be docking on the coming tide. The captain was looking at me strangely in the darkness of the wheel house, so much so, that I turned to look behind me to the east, and to my surprise, I could see three miles. I ordered the anchor to be heaved aweigh immediately, and dismissed the pilot launch.

Visibility reports throughout the channel and the river were all three miles, so we made all speed and hit the dense banks of fog, which had come rolling back in from the land on the Formby Strait. An excellent three-centimetre radar helped me to reach the Rock Lighthouse for the swing, and I knew that an equally excellent ten-centimetres radar would assist me to find the lock, when we were at close range.

Two, now amusing exchanges, took place between myself and the captain, whose English was superb, but pronounced with a Peter Sellers' Indian accent, which as he was Indian, was not surprising! The first came as I was slowing the speed for the port swing. The tugs had failed to find me on this occasion so the swing had to be made without them. "Mr. Pilot, how wide is the lock?" I replied casually, without looking up from the radar, that it was thirty-nine metres wide. "No, no, no, Mr. Pilot, I mean how wide is the lock?" I replied in a slightly louder and more authorative voice that it was indeed thirty-nine metres wide. "No, no, no Mr. Pilot you misunderstand me, I mean how wide is the lock?" Now my head was out of the radar and the swing, not quite forgotten, could wait, for I was anxious that I might have indeed "lost it" and given the man false information. I whipped out my tide-tables and my pocket torch (essential piloting equipment), turned to the correct page and pronounced, that as I had said, the lock was indeed thirty-nine metres wide. "Oh, deary, deary me." came the mournful response, "My ship is thirty-four metres wide!" "That's no problem Captain, she'll fit" I replied somewhat relieved, and put my head back in the radar.

Half way round on the swing and it was on the flood of a spring tide, the captain came out with another unusual statement: "Mr. Pilot, I am so pleased that I have a pilot." I dutifully asked him why that was the case, and he replied: "Because I don't know where I am." If the truth were told at that moment, neither did I, exactly! I knew where the ship's position was when I had commenced the swing, and where I was when we were head north, stemming the tide, but the sweep in between when he made the statement was anybody's guess within a relatively large expanse of river!

With the tugs finally fast and the vessel safely in the lock with thanks to the use of the ten-centimetre radar we were, or more accurately I was, to have a stroke of luck as the fog lifted. I was able to make the short passage to northwest Gladstone scrap-berth before the fog descended like the proverbial blanket once more.

There is a sequel to this tale, for earlier, I had spoken to an older colleague who was inward bound from Point Lynas on a splendid, "flash" container ship, also for Gladstone Lock. I had spoken to my colleague and friend, and in describing my unwanted situation, I was warning against him following me into reduced visibility.

The colleague, however, continued inbound, and whilst I was being entertained in my captain's dayroom, metres away, the other ship was to demolish a gatehouse on the west wall of the Seaforth Cut, after he had suffered a compass failure. I was to wend my weary way home, blissfully unaware of the drama.

Once on a day tide, when dense fog had started to clear after several days of the old "pea-soupers"[15] before the Clean Air Act, I entered the main channel on board a Polish vessel. There was an air of clearance in the morning light, and indeed it was the case that the fog was clearing from the west. I ran up the Crosby Channel in clear blue skies with three miles visibility ahead, whilst to the east of the channel, to port or on my left, a solid white wall of fog hid a fleet of anchored ships awaiting the clearance, each cocooned in a ghostly silence of mist, as the tide swirled silently past their hulls.

My final foggy story, chosen from many, is one, which took place in the February of 2007. The vessel was a ship of one hundred and fifty seven metres in length, with a draft of eight point four metres, by the name of M.V. *City of Glasgow*. She was a container vessel running for Yeoward Lines, for whom I was an appropriated pilot.

I had with me a "leadsman," Adrian Sedge, a young pilot gaining experience for his next class of authorisation. The fog had been hanging around the Bay for some hours, but with the "early on the tide" docking time, thanks to the relatively shallow draft of the vessel, with no other movements, and excellent radars, I believed that I was in with a chance of docking the vessel, which I had piloted numerous times before.

---

15 Colloquial term for dense fog.

Once aboard, I crept up the empty channel, much as I had done those years before on the Indian vessel. I was to swing with a bow-thruster and main engines, without tugs, and make them fast when the vessel was head north. The swing was accomplished without incident, except that the vessel was a little further to the south of where I would have wished to be in an ideal swing. The visibility was as zero as it could be for most of the time and one of the tugs had a problem to find me. As the ship was equipped with a powerful bow thruster, I gave that tug captain a course to steer for the lock bull-nose for him to wait for me there and wait to sight my bow for me coming, hopefully in line out of the fog, and made the other one fast aft.

I edged the ship up against, and across the flood tide with the cheerful encouragement of my good friend Larry Larkin, with whom I was to share many manoeuvres in both difficult weather conditions and in unforeseen circumstances, we were soon to be safely moored in the Gladstone Lock. Larry was the skipper on the tug, which had made fast, and yet again he was to see me safely through another difficult job.

Subsequently, I had good fortune, and the fog cleared somewhat in the dock system, in time to allow the ship to berth successfully. When I asked my young colleague what he had thought of the experience, he replied that he was most favourably impressed, but added that he would not be doing any such manoeuvre in his foreseeable future.

I took the comment as a compliment, and assured him that in the fullness of time, I believed that with experience and confidence through practice, I was sure that he would, and even enjoy the challenge as I had done.

MUSINGS ON BOTH BROMBOROUGH AND GARSTON DOCKS

From Garston North Dock Wall

Sun setting golden,
Turning the mangled, rusted iron-scrap,
"Englische Stückgut"
(English General Cargo!)
To fiery sculpture.

Flood tide, bubbling
Over mud flats
Patterned with pitter-patter gull-feet.
Air fragrant with mud-oil, salted scent,
As sinking rays
Transform débris
Into object beauty
On Garston North-Dock wall.

Both of the dock systems in the title were relatively small. Bromborough, or Brombro' as the latter port was often referred to, is now closed, and indeed filled in. It was constructed at the mouth of the small River Dibbin as part of the Lever operation, which set out to handle African produce, in particular palm oil and rubber, from the plantation to the final manufactured products derived from the raw materials. The Lever Estate "built" the whole operation from seed-sowing to consumer, including housing for the workers, both in Africa and in the United Kingdom, the necessary factories, the transport, which included a fleet of ships, and the docks required to handle them.

Port Sunlight, the Lever village on the Wirral side of the River Mersey exists today as a prime example of the "town" built to house the workforce. It includes shops, recreational spaces, and even the famous Lever Art Gallery, built for Lady Leverhulme. In the Congo, Lord Leverhulme built Leverville for the African workforce.

Garston Docks, on the other bank of the river, is still in existence as a port although only small ships may be handled there, and like Brombro' was, it is a tidal basin, with big ships, too large to lock in, having to dock on the high water of the tide, and await the following tide, twelve hours or so later, for the earliest time at which they may sail. I ran as pilot for Gracechurch Container Line (now Borchard Line) as an appropriated pilot to Garston for many years. As the ships were part of a container service, both to and from the Mediterranean, being "locked in" for the tide lost valuable time, and the operation was eventually to be moved north to the Seaforth Container Terminal in the Port of Liverpool.

Of many exciting moments, which I experienced at Garston, I think initially of a New Year's Eve docking, and a New Year's Day sailing, which for complete contrast could not have both been more dissimilar, and therefore more notable. The years were 1986, turning inevitably at the midnight hour to 1987.

I had been sent down to Point Lynas to board a "chartered vessel"[16] for Gracechurch, by the name of *Express*. "She is just the same as our other ships, apart from the fact that she has two cranes on the port side," were the agent's parting words as he handed me the ship's mail in Gracechurch's "town office," the Baltic Fleet public house.

Later, the following morning as the vessel hove into view, sadly too late for the day tide, something did not look quite right, and it took me a minute or two to fathom out what appeared to be wrong. The two cranes were on the port side, but if they were, then, unusually the bridge was for'd. It turned out, however, that that was indeed the case. Now entering Stalbridge Lock up at

16 A vessel not owned, but rather hired by a company.

Garston was always considered difficult enough on the last of the flood tide, but entering, literally standing on the bow, with the majority of the vessel behind, was something else!

The forecast was not good, strong winds from every direction, and so I decided to make the passage up into the river in the daylight, in order to anchor off Birkenhead in the Sloyne Anchorage, to await the night's tide. The captain was German, and as his full crew were from the Philippines, he was delighted to meet a British pilot who spoke German. We proceeded on passage up to a safe anchorage. As we anchored off Monk's Ferry Slip, the storm clouds were gathering, scudding low and grey over a darkish-green, streaked with the mud-brown of the river, and the gulls were winging inland in an unearthly light.

We heaved up the anchor in good time for the tide. The wind was from the southwest, blowing an estimated force six to seven. The traffic was busy, both inwards and outwards, and a number of ships were going to be in trouble before midnight. I proceeded up Garston Channel in the darkness. The speed was fine, the vessel was handling well, we were on time and only about two ships' lengths off the Stalbridge Pierhead, when, WHOOSH, the wind veered in a split second to the north-northwest, and strengthened to storm force ten. "We must turn round" screamed the captain in English. "No chance" I replied simply, "We are too close to the lock's pier head, wind and tide would sweep us across the entrance to the lock, and, once there, we would be wrecked on the stones of the bull-nose.[17] No, the only chance is to increase speed for steerage-way, and steer for the middle of the lock."

We increased speed and shot between the pier-heads. I had a momentary thought as the bow entered, that we, standing forward, were safe, but I did not like to look behind to see if the rest of the ship was following in a straight line! Fortunately it was, and as we cleared the lock with engines full astern, and the bow thrust full to starboard, the vessel whipped round on the starboard helm,

---

17 The rounded end of a lock, in this case on the seaward side.

until she was end on to the storm force winds. We were safely in, and from here on, with the wind on the bow, there were no further problems in manoeuvring the vessel northwards, through Old Dock and up to the berth, starboard side to on the east side of the North Dock.

That night, others were not so lucky, and several slow, underpowered ships were caught by the storm. A number of such vessels were in difficulties both in the river, and in the channel approaches.

Sailing was a completely different story, for on the following evening, New Year's Eve, the storm had passed over and it was flat calm with clear skies. We sailed without incident, and were in the Crosby Channel as the midnight hour, the dawn of a new year loomed. The crew were all assembled on the bridge to partake of a glass of pink champagne, provided by the captain. I took the wheel to allow the whole crew to join in the toast. As the clock struck midnight over the still, calm waters of the channel, I was to witness a sight, which I had never seen before and have never seen since.

From the far west, down towards the Ormes Head, round behind and astern of the ship, over the Cheshire and Lancashire Banks, up to the north and Saint Bees Head in Cumberland, the dark, clear skies were to be illuminated with the vivid reds of ships' distress parachute flares drifting gently downwards. At this time it was a custom to fire off out-of-date rockets, to dispose of them. As we may imagine, it is now illegal to do so. That night was magical, with the whole sky illuminated with a smoky pink, and the bright red of the glowing flares reflected in the calm waters below, creating a burning curtain of drifting air and waterborne light.

When I landed back ashore, some hours later, I made it to, and revitalised the local neighbourhood party, regaling the revellers with my description of the sight, which I had witnessed only hours earlier, far out in the Bay.

On another occasion, I set off for an outward bound tanker from South Bromborough Dock, on a winter's evening with the northerly wind blowing a good force eight, bordering on force nine. I took my car to the berth, and remarked to Gill as I left the house that I would be back within the hour. A ground rule for sailors is that if you are caught out at sea in forces nine to ten and stronger, then you have to cope, but only a fool would leave a place of safety to sail out into a storm. We only have to think of the ships out in the open sea that are seeking shelter from the same storm to recognise the common sense in the ground rule.

To my dismay the master was desperate to sail, for it was late January, and the crew, having missed Christmas, wished to be back in Germany for their relief as soon as was possible. I strongly advised against sailing. Then the captain challenged me, asking me if it was an emergency, did I think that I could extricate the ship from the dock? I thought carefully and replied that I could try, but could not guarantee success because of the strength of the wind, adding that the main problems would begin out at sea even if we managed to clear the dock.

"My ship is seaworthy and I know my command and her capabilities, so please Pilot try and sail the vessel, so that once clear of the dock, I may make the passage home." With the use of a great many ropes as springs,[18] I managed to manoeuvre the vessel in the darkness, from the south side of the dock to a position, bows north, and starboard side to on the east side of the dock.

From this position, with no less than four ropes deployed as springs from the starboard shoulder, and almost maximum power ahead on the main engine, the helm hard to starboard, I fought the stern of the vessel up into the wind, and we slid into the lock, which was open to the river. As we held position in the lock for some minutes to give us time to heave in the many ropes, I pointed out the fact that the wind was strengthening, and emphasised the wisdom of returning to the safety of the berth. The German captain, bound

---

18 Ropes used as levers against the forward or after thrust of the engines.

for Hamburg, home and the aftermath of Christmas, opted to continue on passage. The vessel was non-hazardous, and a launch was able to take me off in the shelter of the river, and I lost sight of the vessel in the darkness of the night, pitching in the swell, lashed by rain and spray.

The following morning, the pilot's shore-master, who manned up the vessels requiring pilots with the available pilots, rang me. His news was thankfully not of a disaster, but that the German tanker had only made it to the Rock Lighthouse at the entrance to the river, and had been forced back to the safety of a river anchorage, and was now requesting a pilot to take him to sea as the storm was abating!

Going in the opposite direction, inward bound on a parcel tanker by the name of the *Lucor Manor*, in daylight, in flat calm conditions on a spring tide from Point Lynas, I was to experience another thrilling experience. The excitement on this occasion was to be caused by a human source, namely the dock-master at Bromborough Dock.

I had been boarded on the vessel, after breakfast down at Lynas. She was late on her E.T.A., and we were running for the tide at Brombro'. As soon as I boarded and had requested maximum speed, I contacted the dock-master at Brombro', explaining that we were running late, but as she was a fast ship, about fifteen knots as I recall, with a distance to cover of around fifty miles, and it being the flood of a ten metre tide, we should make it for high water. "High·water it will be pilot, I am closing off on the dot." "I have been here before," I thought, thinking of the *Crispin*. The captain explained the amount of money that it would cost if we were to miss the tide. "Please ask the chief engineer to open her out to maximum speed, and I will do my best, but Captain do bear in mind that safety is all, and that there is always another tide."

Off the Ormes Head, I called the dock-master again and reported that we were running for high water, but reminded him that we would have to slow down for docking. Now it must be stated that the length of time the gates would remain open after the high water, often depended on the mood of the dock-master on duty. The previous and following tides were similar heights, so he was not going to lose water in the dock if he were to leave the gate until even half an hour's ebb, which had been done many times. "High water or nothing" came the stern and adamant reply.

Off the Bar Light vessel and the Rock Lighthouse, the E.T.A. was the same, and so was the reply: "High water or nothing." At this point in the passage I was thinking of slowing down, for with the spring tide we were making around nineteen knots, and flying past all other traffic. High water it was going to be, but what about this excess speed? The captain was convinced that I could make it, for he wanted the ship to be in, and we were so close, less than a mile away, but you cannot dock a ship at that speed.

One more try at this close distance and only minutes before the deadline! "High water or nothing" came the unrelenting reply. "Right Captain, tell the chief I require immediate action on the engine room telegraph requests, and tell all hands at stations that requests for ropes, anchors, or whatever is ordered, must be complied with at once. The ship sped on. "Hold fast John," I said to myself, "we have passed the point of no return and this ship is going in." I reconciled myself to the fact, that, as in the *Crispin* adventure, that there would be no time for the two tug boats waiting for me to make fast. On the V.H.F. radio, I requested the head boat to stand-by to the south, and for the stern boat to stand by on the wooden jetty end to the north, in hope that he might manage a push in on the starboard quarter of the ship, to "nudge'" the stern into the line of the lock, for it was necessary to make a turn in the region of ninety degrees to enter safely.

I ordered the engines to half speed ahead, and was horrified that she immediately sheered to port. "Full Speed Ahead," and the helm hard to starboard corrected the sheer and put a starboard sheer, towards the lock entrance on. In retrospect this, the two initial sheers, that is, must have acted as a rudder cycling movement[19], and commenced the reduction in speed. The next few minutes flew by in a whirl. The sky was blue and the sun was shining on this February day. I spotted Joe Webber, the then pilots' senior representative on the north side of the lock. Joe's ship had cancelled outward bound, and he had opted to wait in hope that we would travel back together.

At this point the captain, who believed in me, had dashed below to reappear with a bottle of whisky. He placed it on the edge of the forward bridge windowsill. "If the bottle is still there when we are in, it will be yours pilot," was his promise, and the last words he was to utter for some minutes. His confidence in me, and his humour, gave me that extra belief that we would be safe.

The fact that the committee would have an eye witness in Joe Webber if this went wrong occurred to me, but only fleetingly, for we were on the swing and the wall was approaching rapidly.

The weak bow-thruster was full to starboard, but the effect was little more than that of an egg whisk. The stern tug is the answer to the final few feet of the swing I believed, and gripping my V.H.F., ordered: "Now! Starboard quarter, push now with whatever weight you can manage."

The tug captain's reply was devastating and simple. "Sorry Pilot, I was so excited, I came too far, and the boat is on the north side of the jetty. We have missed you, I cannot help."

"Great, the senior representative on the quay in a V. I. P. viewing spot, and I have nothing left to resort too. Too late for the anchors, bow thrust is full to starboard and the engines are on full astern, rats!" At that moment, totally unexpected and certainly not in the passage plan, there was a "thump" on the starboard quarter, at about the position I had hoped the assistance would come from the tug. It was the wooden jetty on the north side of the entrance approach, and in connecting gently with the quarter, and without

---

19 A method of reducing speed: by putting the rudder hard over, from one side to the other. Particularly useful on a large vessel.

damage, the force generated pushed the quarter further to port. Thus the turning moment pushed the bow those vital inches clear of the south side of the lock and the unforgiving stones as the vessel shot clear into Brombro' dock.

I stopped the engines as we whistled through the lock, soon after, ordering a double ring, "as much as you have got" astern, to bring her up in a flurry of whipped spray in the middle of the dock with a cloud of black smoke from the funnel engulfing the boatmen on the lock wall. The bottle had remained in place!

Elated, and safely alongside the allotted berth on the south side of the basin, we left the bridge and repaired to the captain's cabin to celebrate. Sipping a glass of whisky, I was disturbed by the arrival of the awkward dock-master, cap in hand. "Wonderful job Pilot, well done!"

The captain leapt to his feet demanding to know who the intruder was. Learning that it was indeed the dock-master, the captain ordered two burly sailors to escort the unfortunate, and unreasonable man from his ship, with the insistence that he was never to set foot on the vessel ever again so long as he, the dock-master, lived.

Once, in February 1973, I joined a Dutch coaster, the *Breevecht*, which was moored on that, same berth. She was port side to, bows west and had no bow thrusters to swing the bow. The captain was concerned that we did not have the room to make the hundred and eighty degrees turn necessary to approach the lock without tug assistance. Asking him to trust me, I brought the stern off the quay using a head spring, but then, knowing that the gate was closed on the lock, I correctly anticipated that the River Dibben's flow would catch the starboard bow and push it short round to port. It did. When I asked the captain to sign my bills, he asked what the "blank one" was for. I informed him that that was for the operation in the dock itself. I was delighted when he filled in the blank section with the words: "Artistry in Bromboro Dock without tugs." I still have a copy of that dock-pilotage note.

Liverpool 8 - 2 1973

CERTIFICATE

M/S BREEVECHT per GEORGE WILSON.

This is to certify that the following services have been rendered to the above vessel, viz:

Ardis Try in Bromboro Dock without tugs.	8	70
+ TAX b.	1	50
Master	10	20

Received .... : Pilot

Not quite so successful, was the Dutch coaster, whose master "knew how to handle his ship." I believe that I was a "shorthand" (not first class) pilot. We had docked at Brombro' on a big tide in the middle of the night. As soon as we were in the dock, and heading for the south side, the captain declared that he would manoeuvre the vessel alongside himself. I accepted the fact that it was his ship, and that the dock-pilotage was voluntary, but stated that I would now give a kick astern, for we had excessive speed.

There were no lights on the south side, and it was pitch black, as we sped across the darkness of the night. "I think half astern now would be prudent Captain," I ventured. The captain took no heed. "Full astern now Captain, we are closing rapidly."

"You were right pilot," came out of the darkness, as we picked ourselves up off the deck. There was a hole in the bow. It was only the size of a tennis ball, but the ship had been hurt unnecessarily, and that hurt me even though I was not in command of the manoeuvring.

A similar incident was to happen years later at Garston. A small ship carrying a heavy lift, a crane from the Mississippi, arrived at the Bar Pilot Station. I boarded and was told that the captain only wanted a pilot from the river to "show him where Garston was". I explained it was easier to be aboard out at sea, and chose not to become embroiled in the argument about compulsory pilotage, for the vessel was a compulsory ship.

A straightforward daytime passage brought us to a safe entry into Stalbridge Lock on the top of high water. Perfect, I thought, and then it all went horribly wrong. "I am taking her now Pilot, we are not involving ourselves in unnecessary expenses on this ship." If only he could have had a glimpse of the immediate future and the ultimate expense, which was to be involved.

"Fine," I replied "but tell me what you intend to do so that I may help if you wish and Captain we need to slow down now." Same as at Brombro', we sped across the dock with the captain trying to decide whether he was going to swing to port or to starboard. Then he tried both ways unsuccessfully before stemming the south side of the dock! The damage was somewhat bigger than a tennis ball sized hole in the bow in this case. "May I ask why you did that Captain?" I respectfully requested. "Well you see Pilot, I did the same in New Orleans some weeks ago, and I was determined to get it right this time." I made no further comment, and wished him good fortunes in his future as a captain, that is if he had a future as a captain. I left the ship totally bemused.

Docking on the flood at Stalbridge Lock Garston was a totally different matter from docking on the flood at Eastham Locks over to the west, across the river. When the North Dock had been open, during my apprenticeship, the coal boats used to run themselves aground on the mud and slide themselves up to the entrance, jockeying for position. Sometimes they would land the ship's mate at the Pierhead, possibly on the pilot's river launch, to take the bus up to Garston to sign the ship in before she docked.

At a forerunner of mid-apprenticeship release, I attended the old pilot office on the Canning Pierhead for verbal tuition from a retired pilot boat master by the name of Captain Jerry Pendleton. I remember him giving us a tip about resolving the problem if we were on board one of these coasters edging across the mud and became stuck in the mud. "You will note the water rising up the side of the ship," he said "This will indicate that the hull has stuck fast in the mud!" He advocated sending a man up each mast to hammer on the truck of the mast with sledgehammers, (that is if the ship were to be carrying sledgehammers) to break the suction. Fortunately, I never did have to try that one out, but I believed him.

Docking at Stalbridge was acceptable near the high water, when the tide was easing off. First lock was a dangerous proposition. Some of the smaller coal boats did occasionally dock but piloted ships tended not to. It was the day of the second Moon landing. I was aboard a small 'Danish Blue' coaster, which as most of the Danes were, was left-handed. That is to say that the propeller turned to the left, so that in going astern, the effect was to pull the stern to starboard, so that the bow went to port. Therefore, in going astern at Stalbridge, the bow of the ship would turn for the lock with an astern movement intended to slow the ship down.

I was young and interested in anything new, which seemed like a feasible proposition.

The captain and I listened to the Moon landing, which coincided for the last few metres with our own landing in the lock! Both went well, ours because the ship was left handed, as I had predicted. A left-handed propellered ship should swing bow to port when the engines are turned astern. It went so well, however, that I vowed never to try the manoeuvre again, and I never did.

A final story about these two fascinating and complicated entrances is the story of the Dutch coaster the *Hoop*, when we tided it round from Mostyn, the small port on the Welsh side of the River Dee.

I had been manned to board the ship at the Bar Light Vessel, for the agents did not want to pay the outport-pilotage involved in me going to Mostyn by land as we often did. Outward bound on the pilot launch, we received news that the tide was slow in making prediction, and as a result the ship was running late. We were cruising out slowly, with just myself on board. I began thinking, and took out the Bay Chart from my bag. As I have mentioned, the Rock Channel had been closed years earlier. That is to say that the buoys had been removed, but some form of natural channel remained, buoyed even by the local fishermen.

The adrenalin started flowing, as the old wish of the pilot came to the fore, that if it was at all possible, the object was to catch the tide. As the launch was not required for any other vessel for some time, I requested the pilot master, as the shore master was now called, that I take the pilot launch down to the Wirral Sewer Outfall Buoy to meet the ship. The request was granted and we headed south to rendezvous with the *Hoop*, which was on her way at last.

I boarded, explained the plan to the master and set a course to the east, vaguely in the line of the old Rock Channel. I received a V.H.F. call from the pilot master to tell me that a colleague, who lived in New Brighton, had heard of my intention. He wished to increase my confidence by informing me that he had been down to the promenade, at low water of the tide. He wished to indicate, where he believed that the deepest water was to be found, clear of the bones of the wrecks, which one can still see marked on the chart.

The ship rocketed into the main channel off New Brighton over the covered stones of the training wall on that sunny April day in 1984. I was so close in to the shore; I could even hear Bernie Trott, (for it was Bernie who had given the unexpected and welcome information to be passed on to me from the pilot master) cheering from the beach.

The *Hoop* crossed the sill at high water, and a not often possible passage had been completed. David Dodd, a now retired coxswain of the Hoylake Lifeboat and Rob Lydiate, another lifeboat crewmember, were both in the shore team on the lock, and we have often spoken of the day the *Hoop* tided it from Mostyn to Brombro'.

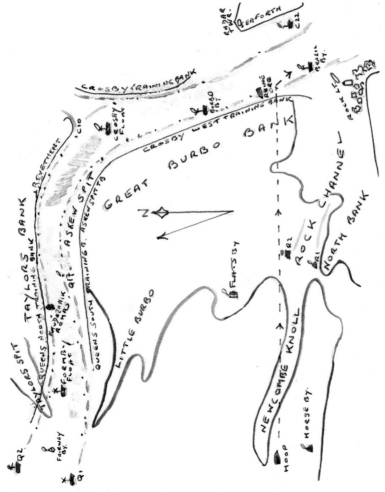

Rough map of Liverpool channel approaches, circa. 1967, showing approximate positions of *Rhine Ore* and *Khudozhnik Romas* when first 'motionless', and the course line of *Hoop*.

SLOP CHEST

There are many items, which were left on board ships in the past, and kept in a chest for others to use. The chapter title comes from its use in the nautical enthusiast's magazine *Sea Breezes*, which deals with readers' letters with items of interest. The stories told here are of the same nature, and are a mixture of themes thrown into a verbal slop chest.

Losses at sea are always a disaster. Just over one hundred years ago, a vessel belonging to the Isle of Man Steam Packet Company was lost during a northerly storm at the Mersey Bar. The *Ellan Vannin* was the ship's name and of many theories as to how she came to be lost, I am one who subscribes to the theory that the ship actually struck the seabed in the trough of a wave and subsequently broke in two, drifting out, away from the shallows on the ebb of the tide.

Whenever I was approaching the actual sand bar on a ship with not much clearance under the keel, I was always mindful of the tragedy, and would await more water from the flood of the tide to cross the Bar in a swell. On one occasion when I was inbound on a deep-drafted grain carrier, I called up the V.T.S. control to ask John Woodfine, retired pilot, then a V.T.S. operator, for a Hilbre guage reading to assess if the tide had made on prediction. I added the comment on the V.H.F. radio, that: "I did not want to do an *Ellan Vannin*."

The following day, John rang me to ask if I would be kind enough to get in touch with a certain Richard Stafford who was writing a history of the account of the loss of the S.S. *Ellan Vannin*. Speaking to Richard, it transpired that he was listening to my conversation with John on a V.H.F. scanner and wanted to ask me what I had meant by my comment.

I was to inform him, and it was to be included in the book. Sadly Richard has since died, but the book makes fascinating reading. Harry Edwards has since organised a magnificent centenary memorial service both in Liverpool and the Isle of Man to commemorate the tragedy's centenary.

This theory of striking the bottom, I believe may be applied to another unsolved disaster, which took place, far out in the Atlantic Ocean. On the night of the 12th/13th of December 1978, the Lash Carrier *München*, was lost, way out in the North Atlantic whilst on passage to the United States. She was an unusual ship in the fact that she carried a cargo of barges, which could be floated on and off the vessel. The idea was, and I have piloted other Lash carriers, that a cargo of empty barges are left at "each end" of the run, being discharged and then loaded again, whilst the ship is in transit between ports with her full cargo of the third set of barges on board.

München, a ship of around two hundred and fifty metres in length, was to vanish with all hands and left little trace. Several life rafts and beacons were basically all that were found over a wide area of the Atlantic before the search was called off.

There was a phenomenon called attenuation during the period of the search. This means that radio waves are "bent" on the earth's surface and calls can be heard over long distances. Those of us operating in Liverpool Bay were able to hear on the 2182 KHz. radio frequency, the vessels involved in the search calling to each other.

I was involved in two pieces of personal research during the period. There was a National Geographic Magazine map, which my parents possessed, showing the North Atlantic with the "plug pulled" out, as if the ocean was drained. It showed the volcanic ranges running down the centre of the ocean. The Azores, south of the last known position of the *München*, is a group of islands, which in effect are in this volcanic range, but are above the water. North of the Azores, where the ship was lost, there are soundings on the chart, which are not that far beneath the surface. So with the 'Caventsman,'[20] which is the main theory given for her loss,

---

20 German name for a huge wave with, importantly for my theory, its exceptionally deep, associated trough.

and the resulting trough from that wave, I believe that *München* could also have actually struck the bottom, in the same way as the *Ellan Vannin*.

A final spine chiller on this loss is something, which I never saw referred to in the subsequent reports regarding the·disaster, but which is an undeniable fact. On board a German coaster during the search period, the German mate and myself looked up the details of the vessel in the shipping lists. There she was with all her details, but what caught both our eyes were the signal letters, which all ships are allocated. *München's* were: D E A T, with the next capital letter in the line being H for Hapag!

"At once, take a taxi!" That order usually resulted from a ship finishing cargo unexpectedly on the ebb, but possibly still in time to catch the tide. Occasionally it came because the agent had forgotten to book a pilot. On the first occasion, which I will recount, the order heralded one of the most hilarious times that I ever spent at sea. I was to be aboard the tugboat *Trafalgar* and the wind was westerly storm ten.

It was late in June of 2006, and therefore late in my career. The Burbo Wind Farm was being constructed off New Brighton. Some time earlier, outward bound on an A.C.L. container vessel, I had reported two very strongly lit cardinal marks to the south of the Formby Channel. It was sometime in the middle of the night and no one in the Port of Liverpool had known of their existence. They had been laid for the wind farm construction, and there had been no consultation or notification, which was both unbelievable and totally out of order.

The Competent Harbour Authority, invested in the Mersey Docks and Harbour Company from the Pilotage Act of 1988, rightly took umbrage at this oversight in their district. They were to insist that all traffic involved in the construction took a pilot for safety, even though the distance into the actual area of the district was relatively short.

My orders were to proceed to Woodside Landing Stage, where I would be picked up by the Schmitt tug *Trafalgar*. We were to proceed to the *Jumping Jack* rig on the wind farm site, and tow her to the Wild Roads anchorage off the North Wales Coast. The wind was already westerly storm ten, so this was, I believed, an emergency.

In the event, I was there ahead of the *Trafalgar*, which was slightly delayed in her locking out of the Liverpool system. The rig was having problems with one of her telescopic legs, and required shelter for repairs to be effected. Once clear of the Rock Lighthouse and the shelter of the land off New Brighton, we were to feel the full effect of the seas as the banks to the west of the channel were covered, and the storm was in full blast.

The reason why the full thirteen hours, which this job was to take, turned out to be hilarious was because of the magnificent company, in which I found myself and the Liverpool sense of humour, which in adversity was side-splitting. I ached for hours after I had left them. The sense of humour was to add to my already existing admiration of their seamanship, tug handling, and professionalism every time I was in command of a vessel requiring tug assistance. Since I had been appropriated to A.C.L., I had come to know these men by name, and I knew that if it were possible, these professionals would do their best to help me to achieve a successful operation in all weathers.

There were two tug skippers on board, Alan Hodge who was the master, and Colin Puzzar, ably assisted by the mate, about to be made up to master, Brad Cummings. For the lay person, we are not talking about gentle breezes, but a full-blown storm, where trees can be ripped up from their roots, and bins and bin lids go hurtling down the streets in exposed places if the direction of the wind is not blocked by shelter. It was horrendous, but the *Trafalgar* was to make good progress to seawards, despite the heavy seas, which we were encountering. I had had the honour, when I was Chairman of the Pilots' Cooperative, to be invited to the naming ceremony of the *Trafalgar*. I knew what a magnificent vessel she was.

We reached the rig, which had not been, and was not ever to be described as a casualty. Already tears were streaming down my cheeks, and my sides ached as the Liverpool sense of humour counteracted the appalling conditions we found ourselves in and, indeed in its own comic way, raged against the elements.

There was an inexplicable delay before we were allowed to attempt to make fast, as a crew change was effected by another, smaller tug boat, which was also in attendance. When it came to the job in hand, against Alan's advice, the master of the rig wished us to use his towing rope. This was eventually to prove ineffectual and the tug's own wire was finally to be made fast. The tow took almost an hour to be secured safely, and I was to watch in awe as Alan manoeuvred *Trafalgar* within centimetres of the rig, never once making contact with her until at last the tow was finally declared to be made fast. My own contribution was minimal, watching the huge waves, rolling towards us from the west, and notifying Alan, who was looking astern at the job in hand, if there was a particularly big wave approaching, which he should look out for.

We set off at last to the west, with the intention of making it down to the Rhyl Buoy on the last of the flood tide, to make it back in through the Welsh Channel off the North Wales coast to the assigned anchorage. Alan was handling the surge of the tow magnificently, the rest of the crew were still out on deck, squaring off the towrope, and I sensed that we had a problem. I had looked at the G.P.S., whose display alerted my concern. "Excuse me for asking Alan, but at what speed do you expect to be able to tow the rig against the last of the flood tide?" Alan glanced at the G.P.S., he had just accomplished the almost impossible in making the tow fast against all odds, "At about three and a half knots[21], if the G.P.S. is anything to go by," he declared. "Alan that, if you look more closely, is minus three and a half knots." We were going astern!

---

21 Nautical measure of speed: one knot of speed being one nautical mile covered.

"****!" was the expletive, and the professional in him sorted out the revolutions, which were possible from the *Trafalgar*, to tow the rig with safety to the west, with as much an increase as was possible. We made about two knots forward over the ground. It was painful progress, but the humour and the hospitality never failed, and included a fantastic chilli, which materialised from nowhere for the evening meal.

We were forced to run the Mersey Gutter, a narrow but deep, buoyed, short cut to within half a mile of the proposed anchorage, where the rig was to put down its legs in the lee of the land of the Ormes Head down to the west. The ebb tide boiled away, an ebb, against which we could have made no progress if we had proceeded down to the entrance of the Welsh Channel. We left the rig and proceeded to Mostyn Harbour, where the tug was to shelter for the night, and from where I was to take a taxi home, still with my whole body aching from laughter at the humour of the situation as viewed by these professionals, in spite of the wild weather, which we had experienced.

Months later, I was to pilot the *Jumping Jack* herself from the west to the wind-farm. She was being towed by a Dutch tug on this occasion, and the captain gave me a C.D. of the action of the making fast, taken from the deck of the rig on the day. It makes both exciting, and unbelievable viewing.

Another storm of a different nature was the one created in the attempted sailings, and the final sailing of a ship by the name of the *Zamboanga*. The vessel carried fruit from the Pacific to the fruit berth in Hornby Dock in the North system. She was not a large ship, but she was normally allocated two tugboats for safety when manoeuvring.

It was at the end of March in 1979. I had been on leave, and somehow no one had informed me that there was a problem with the sailing, not even the shore master who had manned me at the five o'clock manning, the last manning of the day when pilots were allocated their ships. The problem that I was unaware of was that she had been unofficially "blacked" by workers in the port over some dispute, which was only vaguely related to the ship. The situation had been ongoing for almost a month. The pattern was that everybody concerned was booked for the sailing. A lock was ordered, tugs, boatmen and pilot were arranged, and all appeared to be in order.

What then transpired over several weeks is almost unbelievable. The pilot turned up as I did, to find, as expected, the two tugboats waiting to make fast. He was also to discover that, although they had been ordered, there were no boatmen. Unofficially, the boatmen were boycotting the ship because she had some connection with a dockers' dispute with the ship's agents regarding another ship.

I knocked on the door of the captain's cabin to find a delegation waiting for me. The captain himself looked exhausted. The dimly lit cabin was filled with smoke and the agent, who did the talking, explained the situation to me. Each time the pilot arrived, because of the lack of boatmen, the sailing was cancelled. Tide after tide it was the same, but this time they had mustered staff from the agent's offices to act as boatmen. The question was, would I sail?

The days of the mobile phone were still a long way off, but I had noticed that a landline phone had been installed in the cross-alleyway outside the captain's cabin, and that it was still connected. I excused myself from the meeting, and went to ring Joe Webber, the Senior Representative for legal advice. My concern was to know if I would be accused of breaking the law if I were to attempt to sail under these delicate, and unofficial circumstances. I was assured that the situation was a result of unofficial action, and further, if I believed that the sailing was a safe proposition, as a self-employed person, I was in my rights to continue to do my job and earn my living.

I went ashore to speak to the tug captains, and to request that if they would not make fast, that they would not in any way interfere with the safe passage of the ship. They accepted that I had the right to attempt to sail, and confirmed that they would neither make fast, nor hamper our departure.

Back on board, I gave orders to the agent as to how I wished his staff to be deployed and informed him of what ropes would be needed and where and when they were to be run. The night was clear with little wind, and the backing down the branch dock and ensuing swing into the Hornby/Alexander Dock Cut was achieved without any problems. As we began to move south through the cut, the agent shouted up to the bridge that Dock Company officials had told him that we had to stop because the lock gatemen at Langton would not accept us into the lock without official boatmen. I put out a back-spring forward from the port bow and stopped to give myself time to think. Something was wrong about the whole situation, and most important for me was the distressed state of the captain of the ship. The unfortunate man was exhausted, for the pressures on him were intense.

I made the decision, which was to please the captain, not to go back, but to request a lay-by berth, so that our efforts had not been in vain. It was not until we were safely alongside, starboard-side to on North-West Langton Dock that I realised that this decision had also pleased the Dock Company who wanted the working berth clear for the next vessel, which was waiting out at the Bar Anchorage. I had been used.

I attended the ship on the next two consecutive tides, always with the promise that she would sail, and on both occasions, no one would open the lock gates for her. I was not pleased to be deceived, and nor was I pleased to witness what was obviously a deterioration in the captain's health as he suffered from the frustration of the situation, which for him was intolerable. I even chased a high ranking Dock Company official and his wife through the dock system in my car on the Sunday morning, to insist that he return to the ship to inform the captain personally as to why he could not sail on the tide. The man had quite simply shouted up to the watchman at the head of the gangway to inform the master that he was not sailing, and had then driven off.

I was cancelled after the attendance on the Sunday night's tide, and manned on a coaster outward bound from Eastham Locks on the Monday morning's tide. With little sleep, I attended the following day's pilots' meeting to make the case that one of our numbers had been used. I was awakened that afternoon, my second eldest son's birthday, by a call to tell me that I was back as pilot on the *Zamboanga*, and that she would sail on the night's tide. The agents had taken the case to court, and an injunction had been served on the Dock Company for failing in their duty to ensure that their staff at Langton Lock obeyed lawful orders and opened the gates to allow the ship to sail.

Now I could not sleep, and I remember playing football at my son's birthday party that evening on the field close by my home, with tired feet and brain attempting to make the birthday memorable.

I left my home towards midnight with a police escort to take me through the dock system in case there were any problems. There were none, and we sailed with tugs and boatmen out into the darkness, the tired but thankful captain and not only his ship, but all the company's ships, leaving Liverpool for the last time. The regular run had ended to the detriment of Liverpool as a port, for the company would not risk such an expensive fiasco again. I believe it was after this experience that on my way home I first had the thought that: "Now then, there is one for the memoirs!"

As I am on the theme of strike action, either official or unofficial, the tale of the occasion that I was to take the captain's daughter home with me comes to mind. I was a young first class pilot and had been boarded down at Point Lynas, on, what to me then was an enormous Dutch container vessel, bound for Seaforth. The *Hollandia* arrived at the Pilot Station, and we all had the knowledge that strike action was possible in the near future, if not later that day. It was a bad year for Liverpool, for these threats were becoming more numerous, and it was the June of the same year as the saga of the *Zamboanga*.

We were to dock the following tide, strike action permitting. It was evening and my decision was to proceed in towards the Bar, whatever transpired. Just short of the main channel entrance, before we were to commence the inward passage, we were informed that we were not to dock on the tide, but we were to await the news of the situation the following morning.

I swung the ship around, and proceeded to the northwest of the Bar Light Vessel to a safe anchorage. Once anchored the captain showed me to the luxurious suite of rooms, which was allocated for the pilot. He suggested that I might like to take a shower and freshen up. I was to join him, his wife, daughter and the ship's officers for aperitifs in the ship's bar before the evening meal. It was on occasions like this that life really did seem somewhat of a dream.

After, a superb meal, we all repaired to the officers' mess, where we played games such as a sophisticated version of shove ha'penny, and I ended up serenading the gathering with songs such as the *Leaving of Liverpool* on the boatswain's guitar.

The following morning was one of disappointment. The risk of a strike was too great and the ship had been diverted away from Liverpool. We were not to dock. The captain's daughter burst into tears. She was inconsolable, for she was to have left the ship in Liverpool and gone to meet friends. They were to work on a strawberry farm in mid-Cheshire, both to earn money and to improve their English.

I too was disappointed that I was not to dock this splendid ship, but I saw a way that I could help the captain's daughter. "Captain, the pilot-launch will soon come to take me off, but you are waiting for a tug, which is outward-bound to bring you mail and stores. If you can arrange with the agent that your daughter may be taken ashore on the tug, I will promise to meet her at the landing stage; I will take her home to meet my wife and family. She may sleep at our home, and tomorrow, we will take her out to the farm."

This was arranged and a very happy young Dutch girl was to give the Liverpool Pilot a big kiss before he was to leave the ship.

Taking people home was not a regular occurrence, but as I have described with reference to Boris Revunenkov, it was a possibility on occasions if the time and tide were right. Earlier in the strike year, I had taken the Cuban captain of a grain ship named the *XIII Congresso*, which I had docked in Birkenhead home for a meal. He was a charming man who had been a bank manager before the days of Fidel Castro. He was entranced with my family, and was to refer to my youngest son, Nathan, as his "little man!"

Another Christmas when the children were young, a large bulk carrier with a cargo of grain was in port for a month. The cargo was being sold in parcels, and each time a "parcel" was discharged, she had to shift off the berth to allow other vessels to discharge their cargoes. I shifted the ship several times and got to both know and like the captain whose name was Ho.

The ship was what we referred to then as "Red" (Communist) Chinese, as opposed to "Hong Kong" (British) Chinese. We would discuss the Tiananmen Square massacre, which had only recently taken place. Ho described a very poor, low paid job. He and his wife had opted to have two children, a girl and a boy, so he was paid mate's wages instead of full captain's wages. The family could not afford a car, but all four had bicycles.

I shifted the ship again near Christmas Day, and suddenly, because the opportunity had presented itself, decided to invite Ho home for Christmas dinner with my family. He was delighted to accept, but like the Russian captain should have been, he had to be accompanied by a political commissar. Ho chose a man who could not speak English.

The meal and the evening were a great success. When faced with soup for the first course, both of the Chinese guests lifted up their bowls and started to drink the liquid. My wife and children looked at me horrified, until I swiftly lifted my bowl and began to drink my soup too. The mirth at the table was unbounded as the whole family began to slurp their soup from the bowl. The evening was off to a resounding international start. Ho was to write to me several times over the years but, so far, we have not been able to meet since. Ships, which pass in the night!

A story of ships that pass in the mystery of night is the story of the ship, which "had no name." It is a tale combining elements of the *Flying Dutchman*, espionage, silence, drama and darkness, mixed with a certain wry humour.

It was in the early days of the shipping of bulk genetically modified grain. Greenpeace had been targeting such vessels and there had been a tip off that a particular vessel was next. I was manned off and told that my ship was to be referred to as: the "ship, which had no name." We were to maintain radio silence and only communicate by mobile telephone.

I proceeded to Point Lynas with a police escort both on shore and aboard the pilot launch. On the drive down the North Wales Coast, we passed two Greenpeace rhibs[22] being trailed to the east, towards Liverpool. Once aboard the large bulk carrier, which did in fact bear the name *M.V. Polska Walczaca*, we set off on the passage plan for a normal docking.

A police helicopter passed over us from time to time as the darkness closed in. The passage was uneventful until we were proceeding up the Formby Strait, when I noticed two very fast targets proceeding outward bound towards me on the radar, visually they carried no lights. I entered into the spirit of the operation by reporting, on my mobile phone to the V.T.S. that I had sighted two possible bandits outward bound in the Crosby Strait. Moments later, blue flashing lights appeared on the targets. They were police rhibs identifying themselves.

Simultaneously, a ferry asked for our name from V.T.S. The operator replied that he was unable to give it for the ship on the

---

22 RHIB: rigid hull, inflatable boat.

Crosby Bend "had no name". The ferry then called up: "The ship, which has no name...!" Well, I thought, if Greenpeace did not know where this huge panamax bulk carrier was before, they do now!

We docked, not without incident, whilst a Cunard Liner, which took the "limelight," was berthing at the old Liverpool Landing Stage. As I approached the lock in strong westerly gale force winds, the lockmaster advised me against docking, but I reasoned that, as the conditions did not seem "that bad" from the bridge of the ship, we would "take a look at it.'" Conditions were indeed bad, but all was well as the bulk of the ship calmed the horrendous swell off the lock, and soon we were safely in with the master and myself relieved that we would not have to go through the same clandestine passage on the following day.

In the lock, we were boarded by twelve police constables and a sergeant, who were all amazed at the view from the bulker's bridge. (It is impressive!) I had to ask the sergeant to order his men back from the front wheelhouse windows so that I could see where we were going in the docks!

Greenpeace left us alone, possibly lulling the authorities into a false sense of security for they were to "hit" the next one. She, for some reason, best known to the captain, dropped anchor at Point Lynas, to wait only for half an hour or so for the pilot. Greenpeace arrived with two rhibs; climbers scaled the anchor cable and set up a bivouac close to the hawse pipe, preventing the anchor from being heaved back aboard. From this position they were able to make their protest.

"THE SHIP WHICH HAS NO NAME"

LIVERPOOL PILOTAGE SERVICES LIMITED		
M/V POLSKA WALCZACA		
PASSAGE PLAN		
P.S. (FOR DOCKING WIND: NW 36-40K)!		
DATE 8.12.99 for 9.12.99		
TIDE 0013 10.12.99 HT. 8.9 M.		
M.V. POLSKA WALCZACA		
DRAFT	F.	A. 11.45 M.
TUGS 3		TIME 2215
MIN UNDERKEEL .6		
PLACE @ BK. approx	TIME 2130	
1) FORMBY < 1H(+) 2130 2130		
2) CROSBY < ..(+) 2200 2200		
3) LOCK .(++) 2300 <		
4)		
5)		
NORTON, YEW, WILLOW.		
CIRCUMSTANCES MAY RENDER THIS PLAN LIABLE TO CHANGE		

POSITION	PLANTIME	ACTUAL TIME
400-05.5	1500 1961.	1500
LYNAS	1700	1700
BAR	2100	2100
FORMBY	2130	2130
CROSBY	2155	2200
BRAZIL	2230	2230
LOCK/BERTH	DOCK. 11.5 (TIDE 0013 8.9.)	
	CLEARANCE 06 L.D. 6.8	
	TOTAL 12.1 5.3 =3HRS	
	L.D. 6.8 REQUIRED, =12.1 =2113	
	5.3 2300	
	0030	
NOTES: CLARKSON'S.		
IAN GIBSON 666 1575		
07899 067547		
JOHN CLAY — .. — 9		
"BRAVO" ?		
B.D. FROM HARBOUR (SOYA S.M.)		
FULL POLICE: AIR, SEALAND COVER		
MASTERS SIGNATURE		

"*The ship, which had no name.*"

The final tale in this "slop chest" is the story of the *Texaco Stockholm*, then in the late winter of 1978, a brand new Norwegian ship, and one of the first vessels to be fitted with computerised systems, both for navigation, and for the engine room.

I was boarded down at Point Lynas, and the first question, which the captain asked me, was: "May we proceed by computer Pilot?" It was morning, around breakfast time, and we were to dock on the afternoon's tide. The passage from Point Lynas to the Bar is basically an open sea passage of some thirty-five miles. "Please Captain, inform me what that entails, and would we have immediate access to bring the controls back to manual?"

I was assured that this was the case and, off we set, with what was basically a crude, and early form of navigational electronic charts, which were just about to be born. These were computers linked to both navigational instruments and to the engine room machinery. The whole system was manufactured by Norcontrol, which is a company based in Norway. The system was impressive, and heralded major developments in the technological advances in the science of navigation.

Once up to full speed and on course, I was to question the captain in depth about the system, which I found fascinating, but naturally could not be expected to trust, particularly in the fast flowing waters of the Mersey. Upon approaching the Bar Light Vessel, I insisted that the vessel was returned to manual, and we proceeded inwards for a successful docking at the Q.E.II. Dock, with the captain insisting that he believed the computer could have coped with the correct information having been fed into it. He was wrong, as the system was in its infancy, and linked satellite navigation and electronic charts were still systems of the future.

Only weeks later, I was to attend the Third World Symposium for Vessel Traffic Systems, which was held in Liverpool. A French pilot, giving a paper, which was basically expressing the concern of pilots for the safe inshore-water navigation of vessels, which were to rely on computers in the future, had asked for an interpreter. As a Liverpool Pilot, with A Level French, I fitted the bill. During the conference, I was to be introduced, by my radar lecturer in previous studies, to representatives from Norcontrol. I had told the lecturer, Alan Bole, about my experience on board *Texaco*

Stockholm, and he believed that Norcontrol would be interested to meet a young pilot who had recently experienced their products on board ship in the course of his duties.

They were, and after discussing my views of their equipment over coffee, I was astonished to be invited, at their expense, over to Norway for further discussions as soon as I was able to make the journey.

The meeting had been on the last day of the conference, so the next morning, after talking it over with Gill, I rang Norway to say that I was available to travel the first day of my next leave, which was to commence in a few days time. The following day, an envelope dropped through my letter box with train tickets from Liverpool to Felixstowe, first class accommodation and tickets for a crossing with Tor Line to Gothenburg, and train tickets from Gothenburg to Moss, which is on the east side of the Oslo Fjord.

I was to cross the North Sea with the Tor Line, for their larger passenger ferries were fitted with Norcontrol systems, and the captain and officers of the ferry had been instructed to brief me on the system's operation and inform me of their opinions of them. I was to leave the following day.

I made the crossing, and then the train journey north to Moss. When I arrived at the station at Moss, I was to cross by ferry to Horten, where Norcontrol was based. Alighting from the train, and walking to the ferry, in the darkness, I felt like a war-time agent behind enemy lines possibly would have felt, not so long before in the great scheme of things, and it was exciting.

I arrived at Horten and there my instructions ended. A taxi was waiting for me, however, and took me to the door of the Hotel Klubben in Kristiansand. I presented myself at the reception desk, and yes they were expecting me, the representative from Norcontrol would be with me after breakfast the following day. Meantime I was to make myself comfortable and a table was booked for me in the restaurant. I found the whole experience hard to believe, for at that time the Liverpool Pilots were not on those kind of wages, and I had a young family, which was a great expense. I sat in the dining room, after the meal, sipping a brandy, and listened to a female singer, who sang the then topical song *We Are Sailing* particularly well.

For the next few days, I was to discuss with Norcontrol the pilotage at Liverpool, and was to discover that my concerns regarding computerised navigation in both tidal and restricted channels was justified. A possibility at that time was a fixed beacon on a bend, around which a vessel could navigate, keeping set distances off. The sophistication of Satellite Navigation with the Global Positioning System, (G.P.S.) and electronic charts, have now been developed, but I like to think that my small involvement was a contributory factor in the race in their development to today's standards.

I was asked what I would like to visit on my way home in Oslo, for I was booked on an evening flight from Oslo to Manchester. I tossed up between Thor Heyerdahl's *Kon Tiki* raft, and the Edvard Munch Museum. The latter won. I made the train journey north on the west side of the Fjord, took a taxi to the art gallery to discover that I was not to be allowed in. I asked why not, to be told that I had to wait for half an hour or so for the King of Norway was showing round an ambassador from China!

I was eventually allowed in, and to my surprise found myself following closely behind the King's official party. I was asked to keep only a few metres behind the group, and was actually looking at the painting of the *Scream* at the same time as they were.

I flew home, and was asked to write a paper, which was published by the Transport and General Worker's Union, on the subject of 'Computerised Navigation in Coastal Waters.' Both the knowledge and the development of computerised systems have moved on so far since that time. Despite, the cyber-world, in which we now live, however, no system, has to date, replaced the pilot's eye, and his personal judgement when it comes to handling ships in close quarters situations.

'PULL FOR THE SHORE BOYS, PULL FOR THE SHORE...'[23]

No account of my life would be complete without a reference to the Royal National Lifeboat Institution.

I first made up my mind to become a lifeboat man whilst I was a boathand, serving as Second Lad on Number 3. Pilot Boat. Captain Littler had sent off Bob Swift, the Senior Lad, for the day on a leadsman, so I was, in effect Senior Lad on board at the time of our docking.

It was late November of 1966 and the *Arnet Robinson* was the Point Lynas Station Boat. The weather was appalling. The wind was what is known as catabatic, that is moving constantly round the points of the compass, at times reaching hurricane force.

Being the Western Station Boat, we had shelter from the westerly blows in Moelfre Bay, but north of northwest we had to make our way up to the Isle of Man for shelter. When the wind shifted to the east, we made it in to the North-West Light Float, some seven miles to the west-northwest of the Bar Light Ship. Southerly round to the northwest it was back to Moelfre Bay. I forget, just how many times we made the passage to each of the shelters, only to find that the wind had altered and we were on a lee shore, and we were off again!

The Greek cargo vessel, *Nafsiporos* was out there with us, and every time the wind shifted, the vessel called for advice, and every time the vessel arrived in a place of suggested safety, the wind shifted, and advice was asked for again. The pilot boat was faster than the *Nafsiporos*, but more or less in the same predicament.

Thursday of the cruise arrived, and our docking day came. When the other pilot boat had relieved us we made it in towards the Bar. The wind was northwest when we reached the channel entrance,

23 The first line of the R.N.L.I. Lifeboat Hymn.

and Captain Littler, called for his most experienced helmsman, who happened to be me, to take the wheel.

Captain Littler took the boat up to the northwest of the Queen's Channel before turning to run before the storm. The seas were horrendous, but he kept his nerve and ran down the face of the waves until he reached a point where he could turn for the channel, gaining some shelter from the exposed banks to the north of the channel. Wow, did we roll, but we made it. Captain Littler was to go that evening to the Liverpool Pilots' Hotpot (Annual Dinner) where he was to receive a well-deserved standing ovation from the assembled gathering.,

When I arrived home, because so often it had been me who had relayed Captain Littler's advice to the *Nafsiporos*, during the week, I tuned in to my father's radio set, which had marine band. I had picked up on the fact that the *Nafsiporos*, on the night we made it into shelter, had been caught on a lee shore off the North Coast of Anglesey. Both Holyhead and Moelfre Lifeboats were launched, the former being badly damaged before being forced back to Holyhead.

Moelfre Lifeboat managed to stay the course, with Coxswain Dick Evans making numerous passes at the stricken ship, taking members of the crew aboard the lifeboat. On his last pass, the lifeboat was swept onto the decks of the casualty, and then swept back off again by the next breaking wave. For this rescue, Dick Evans was awarded the R.N.L.I's Gold Medal.

Several weeks later, the *Sunday Times* Newspaper, in one of its first ever supplements, I believe, featured a double page of all those organisations involved in the rescue of the ship and her crew. (The *Nafsiporos* was in fact saved, and eventually towed into Liverpool, dead ship, that is, without power, with a young pilot, Bruce Fulton on board.)

The double page of the supplement featured photographs of coastguards, ambulance units, R.A.F. helicopter crews from Valley

Air Base, mountain rescue units and members of the R.N.L.I. crews, to mention most, but not all involved. Staring at this double page in admiration, I swore that if ever I lived near a lifeboat station, I would offer my services and contribute my seafaring knowledge to the endeavours made in saving life at sea.

When I became a second-class pilot, in 1970, Gill and I moved to West Kirby, minutes from the West Kirby Inshore Lifeboat Station. A week or so after the move, I was in the front garden when the single maroon was fired, calling out the I.L.B. I jumped into my car and drove at speed down to the lifeboat station. Harry Jones, boatman at the West Kirby Sailing Club, and the leading figure at that time in the newly established Lifeboat Operation at West Kirby, and only one other crew member were there, ready to save an angler, cut off by the tide on Bird Island, off Red Rocks, on the North Wirral Coastline. I drove the Land Rover, towing the I.L.B to the launch site, whilst the other two went in the boat. I had become a lifeboat man.

I mention the "minutes", which I live from the lifeboat station; it was just under two actually, as I was to prove, some years later. I had returned home on a Sunday morning from sea, and had just parked the car on the front drive, when a maroon was fired. West Kirby fired only one for a "shout"' (Call Out) so I was back in the car, answering the call with all speed possible but not so fast as to be a danger to other traffic and pedestrians.

I leapt out at the station, and was about to bring the rig out onto the promenade, (that is the Landrover hooked up to the I.L.B. on her trailer) wondering where everyone else was, when another maroon was fired. Whoops! I looked at my wristwatch, it was two minutes past eleven: Armistice Sunday! West Kirby had not been tasked at all. I retraced my steps home, somewhat more slowly, and did not mention the incident for some years!

On my twenty-year service certificate, it states that during my time with West Kirby, the lifeboat saved one hundred and nine lives. I know that I was not involved in all the rescues, but I do know that a good number of people lived to fight another day because I was with the others at the station.

When I think of the dramatic rescues that one reads about regarding the R.N.L.I., and I was involved in a good number in hard weather conditions, my personal most dramatic rescue was quite different. One never knows the moment.

West Kirby had spent several hours with a shore-based district inspector's visit. We had been checking equipment, which included the mechanism of the outboard motor, and verbally going through regular drills. The district inspector at the time was George Cooper, who was later to become the chief of operations for the R.N.L.I.

"Well lads, that's it. Oh, I have forgotten to ask about mouth-to-mouth resuscitation but I take it you are all up to date with that?"

One of the crew, Rob Lydiate, expressed his wish to go through the drill. This, as events unfolded, turned out to be both fortuitous and somewhat uncanny. We put the youngest on the ground and went through the motions. Obviously, in the absence of a dummy, we could not go through the procedure fully, but we were able to refresh our memories of recent First Aid courses.

We then adjourned to the West Kirby Sailing Club for lunch. It was late March, and a beautiful winter's day. Sunshine and clear blue skies, not a breath of wind and the spring tide's ebb was away.

We were down to three left at the bar, and just about to leave, when a telephone call came from Hilbre Island, seconds later we were launching the lifeboat. Twelve minutes after the telephone call, we were approaching the casualty, slightly to the east of a line between the Middle Island, and Hilbre Island itself.

Observers on Hilbre Island were firing white, parachute flares with amazing accuracy, for, even though only the person's head was visible in the water, it was ringed with the drifting parachutes. Ron 'Taffy' Jones was on the helm, Rob Lydiate, 'Robbie,' was mid-ships, and I was forward with the radio. Taffy cut the outboard as we came alongside the man in the water. Robbie and myself grabbed him and attempted to pull him aboard. Now pulling a person on board a boat from the water is a difficult thing to do at the best of times, but even though the casualty was in an advanced state of hypothermia, he was particularly heavy.

Then we realised that there was another man, wrapped around the first man's waist with a bird netting, mist net. Taffy took the strain with the two of us and we all heaved. After a great deal of effort, up they both came. The first fell on top of me in the forepart of the boat, the second fell on top of Robbie, and this man was literally blue in the face and he was not breathing. He was apparently dead.

I wrapped the first in a tinfoil blanket and set to rub life into his hands and feet, Taffy waited to re-start the outboard, and Robbie set to giving mouth-to-mouth resuscitation, this time for real.

The time seemed endless with Robbie working away on the casualty, and then miraculously, the blue face puckered and the mouth began uttering gurgling sounds before the man was violently sick, and started to breathe again. It had worked. The man had been brought back to life. The vomit pouring from that once dead mouth was one of the most beautiful sights, which I have ever seen in my life.

Taffy gunned up the outboard and we sped to the sailing club slip and a waiting ambulance. With the bit between his teeth, Taffy hit the slip at speed, lifting the outboard at exactly the right moment, so that the craft hurtled up the slip, almost shooting into the back of the ambulance itself!

Both men however, were not in a fit state to be transferred to hospital, and spent several hours in the paramedic's care in the warmth of the sailing club. Both men survived.

The events leading up to the near tragedy were explained to us later. The custodian of Hilbre Island, Tim Cleeves, was expecting a bird-watching friend and licensed bird-ringer, to join him on

Hilbre for lunch, and stay over the tide, mist-netting and ringing migrating birds.

The friend, David Cross, was running late, and wisely opted to stay on Middle Island. The custodian, having made lunch, chose to paddle a double kayak over to the north end of Middle Island to collect David, who did remonstrate with him over the foolishness of his actions before boarding the craft.

On the passage back to Hilbre, they both told the same story that the kayak did not capsize, but rather was it "sucked" from beneath them by the treacherous crosscurrents flowing between the islands

The three of us, who were the crew that day, received letters of thanks from the R.N.L.I. for our swift response.

I was with West Kirby for over twenty years and was allowed three extra years over the age of forty-five with medicals, before the R.N.L.I. lowered the maximum age limit rules for manning an I.L.B.

At the same time, Hoylake All-Weather Lifeboat (A.L.B.) Station, were requiring a Deputy Launching Authority, (D.L.A.) and I was offered the job. At the time of writing, I have been with Hoylake a further twenty years. Ten of these years have been spent as D.L.A., and ten as, first of all, Honorary Secretary, although soon after my appointment, the Hon. Sec's. title was changed to Lifeboat Operations Manager. (L.O.M.)

At Hoylake I have launched the lifeboat to all manner of casualties, day and night, but perhaps the most unusual, and probably unique launch, was the occasion when I launched the lifeboat to my own ship.

The practice of the Liverpool Pilots has always been to man off square-riggers and sail-training ships from volunteers from the holiday, or leave men. On one such occasion I had volunteered for the Sail Training Association Vessel: *Malcolm Miller*.

Hoylake Lifeboat, 'Lady of Hilbre,' with her coxswain and crews

The vessel was due in time to dock on the day tide at Alfred Lock on the 21st of April 1994. She was crewed by a mixed-sex group of Birkenhead youth. I awoke earlier than my expected call-out, before breakfast, and rang the pilot office to ascertain if there was any news of the schooner's arrival. Michael Wright, now retired pilot, who was a watch-keeper in the radar tower, answered my call and, in reply to my query, excitedly replied with concern, that she was some ten miles north of the Bar Light ship, and had just that minute called in to inform the coastguard that they had a "Man Overboard."

I broke off our conversation, replaced the phone, then redialled and gave the order to fire the maroons to launch the lifeboat to my own ship! Later, the *Malcolm Miller* was called away from the search area to dock with a traumatised crew, and I boarded her, taking with me a counsellor from the S.T.A. on the pilot launch.

When we were safely off the berth, with ropes out, but still a distance off being "alongside," I noticed that the captain still had his pyjamas on under his sailing gear.

"Captain, looking at this crowd of anxious parents, along with both plain and uniformed police amassed here on the quayside, I believe you would probably feel better to cope with all the demands, which are now going to be made on you, if you were to have a shower and have a change of clothes?"

"Certainly Pilot, but there is obviously no time, we are almost alongside."

"Captain, in my opinion," I replied, "a man of my experience could take at least as long as it takes for you to freshen up to get this ship alongside, please be my guest."

Hugh O'Neill dashed off, to reappear some fifteen minutes later, spruced up and wearing his full uniform, ready to face the necessary questions. I had simply ordered the crew to stop heaving on the mooring ropes, so that we lay safely off the quay to give Hugh, what I believed was necessary time.

Sadly, the young man who had fallen overboard on that spring morning was not to be found alive, despite a long and intensive search. His body was to be washed ashore in the River Ribble, some months later.

I have enjoyed my time in every position I have held with the R.N.L.I., giving back to society in some small way something of what society gave me in my pilotage training.

I have been fortunate at Hoylake to have been part of the movement to ensure the building of a brand new, state of the art lifeboat station, and will, I hope, still be in tenure, when the replacement for our present Mersey Class Lifeboat, the much loved *Lady of Hilbre*, arrives on station. The Mersey Class boat will be replaced with a much faster craft, the Fast Carriage Boat Two (F.C.B.II), now known as the *Shannon Class* Lifeboat.

The increase in speed between the old and the new is planned to be around nine knots, (sixteen to twenty five knots to be exact.) which will enable the Hoylake crews to reach "that hand above the wave" that much faster before it were to disappear for ever, and enable Hoylake to be both faster and more versatile in the saving of lives at sea.

I managed to organise a passage, inward-bound, so that the present coxswain of the Hoylake Life-boat, David Whiteley, accompanied me on board the *Atlantic Companion*, from Point Lynas to Seaforth Dock.

David has two sons in the lifeboat crew, James and Daniel. This is a continuation of the traditions of the Lifeboat Service. The Dodd family, for example, has David Dodd as the present head-launcher, David having also served as coxswain of the boat. Andy Dodd, his son, is the present full-time second-coxswain mechanic at the Station. David's grandfather, Thomas Dodd, was coxswain at the Station in the early part of the 20th century, being awarded a silver medal in 1902 for the rescue of the crew in from a Russian barquentine, *Matador* registered in Riga.

The Armitages, Birds and so many other local families, still have links dating back from the establishment of the lifeboat at Hoylake by the Trustees of the Liverpool Docks, over two hundred years ago.

On the 22nd of December 2010, a memorial was unveiled to the memory of eight crewmembers of the Hoylake Lifeboat, who lost their lives attempting to save the lives of others, on that day, two hundred years earlier. The coxswain of the boat, who survived the disaster, was a retired Liverpool Pilot, one, Joseph Bennett.

I have only the highest praise for the coxswain, crews and committees of the Hoylake Lifeboat Station, with whom I am privileged to serve.

TALES FROM THE 'PIT'

Eastham Locks are situated in the River Mersey on the Cheshire Bank, and are the first, and entrance locks, of five, which make up the Manchester Ship Canal lock complex. From Eastham Locks to Manchester is a distance of approximately thirty six miles. The canal was built towards the end of the nineteenth century, so that ocean going ships could take their cargoes directly to the City of Manchester.

Initially Liverpool Pilots piloted the ships, but I can imagine my forbears thinking, "Lynas to Manchester, blow that!" (or words to that effect) and although a few were to remain piloting in the canal, a new service was formed to handle what became a large volume of traffic. Several times in my career attempts were made to amalgamate the two Services, but to date none has been successful. Since the average size of ocean-going ships has risen, traffic in the canal above Stanlow Oil Terminal has diminished, and few ships now make the passage to Manchester, whose docks have largely been refurbished tastefully into modern facilities with waterfront sites.

Marsh Lock was a smaller entrance lock, further up the Mersey, and some small coasters, in my early years as a pilot, went up to this lock, before a dispensation was allowed for these vessels to enter the canal at Eastham. Eventually the lock fell into disuse for commercial traffic, but is still in use for pleasure craft.

In the days of my apprenticeship, and in the early days of my being a licensed pilot, the Eastham Ferry Hotel, situated near the Eastham Locks, and originally built to offer lodgings to travellers from the south, awaiting a ferry over to Liverpool, housed a splendid collection of nautical memorabilia. Of particular interest was a Luftwaffe, wartime, and aerial photograph of Eastham Locks. A red circle had been stamped over the locks themselves by the German authorities. The old pilots, (younger than I am now) used to say that the orders, which went with the red circle, were that it was imperative that bombs were not to be dropped within the circle's limits. The logic for these orders was that, if left unscathed, the locks would cause more trouble for the allies than if they were to be destroyed.

It was often said that if a pilot were given a shilling for every minute that he spent waiting for a lock in the Eastham Channel, he would be a rich man at the end of his career. There were many hours spent chatting with the masters of ships, waiting a turn. I learned a lot of facts about other countries, politics, customs, and added to my growing collection of tales of the sea.

The Norwegian captain who came up with the tale of *The Clockwork Ship* whilst dodging off E6, the last red buoy before the lock, may well have begun it with Jean Graf's preface: "and this is no shit!"

A French port and a French pilot booked to take a Greek vessel out to sea. The pilot arrives at the berth at the appointed hour to discover to his dismay the proverbial, red-rusting, floating wreck. Upon arriving on the bridge, and wishing to perform his duty, which would rid the French shores of this particular pestilent Greek, he demands assurance with regard to the ship's main engines. For, which he receives the confident reply:

"Mister Pilot, my engines, zey are like clockwork."

Reassured, the pilot makes the tugs fast and proceeds "dead ship" (without using the ship's engines) to the lock where he finds that the vessel is going too fast. He orders his engines astern, and when nothing happens, and the tugs are not arresting the speed, he orders a "double ring," (maximum revolutions.) astern. Still no engines, and the ship speeds silently and swiftly onwards, colliding first with the head tug and then with the outer gate of the lock, causing immense damage.

When both the pilot and the captain have picked themselves up off the deck, the pilot demands an explanation:

"Captain, vat about yoorr engines, zat are like clockwork?"

The Greek replies with great aplomb in his weak defence by posing the question:.

"Mr Pilot, 'ave you a clock, zat goes backwards?"

I wrote a poem about the incident.

Few agents paid the "voluntary dock pilotage monies," which were earned by the individual pilot in the Liverpool, Birkenhead, Garston and Brombro' systems, up at Eastham Locks. It is true also that, generally speaking, handling a ship in the dock systems was more satisfying than just ending the passage in a lock. Thus when asked where he was bound with his ship, the pilot would often reply glumly: "Last on the right," or, quite simply: "the Pit."

The amount of traffic handled on a tide, both in and out, in the busy post-war years, was astonishing. The tide began as soon as the vessels had water to float outside the locks, and four coasters in and four coasters out at the four hours to high water was invariably the start of the tidal movements. The "tide" finished only when the ships had no water to float in the channel, and were consequently forced to await the next tide.

Initially in my career, there were four lockmasters only. Their names as I recall were: Joe Booth, Abe Cook, Ernie Lacey and Ernie Smith. They would remain unruffled, no matter what was going on. On one occasion, a young pilot, Ronnie Bradford, licensed a year or so before I was, had left slowing down too late on the flood of the tide. As the bridge of the ship hurtled passed Joe Booth, before colliding with a Harker's oil-barge in the top right–hand corner of the lock, on the same level as the pilot's height of eye, hands in pockets, Joe was heard to inquire nonchalantly of the young and inexperienced pilot, "Are you stopping, they usually do?"

My first three ships were outward bound from Eastham Locks, but a great many of my ships, particularly in the early days were both to and from Eastham. On one occasion in the aftermath of a northerly gale, which was still blowing hard out at sea, I was manned on a ship by the name of *Aegean Sky*. With a name like that there were only two possibilities: a superb modern vessel or a heap of floating rubbish. In this instance the coaster fell into the latter category.

She was waiting for me, run down to river level in the small lock. As I walked over to the lock I was gravely concerned, for I noticed that her derricks were rigged and that her hatches were open. The ship was in ballast.[24] I introduced myself to the captain, and asked him where he was bound.

"We go only to the Tees, is not far, we go north about to make it quick, Mister Pilot," was the reply. I asked him if he had a chart available so that I could point out the perils of his passage in a northerly gale. The captain produced a road atlas, claiming that the charts were too expensive in England. He showed surprise, total shock even, when I told him that we would not be sailing until the weather moderated, and that he must lower his derricks and close the hatches before the next sailing time.

I left the ship and walked over to the pilots' rooms, where I received a telephone call from the harbour master who wished me to present myself in his office to explain my decision. I duly arrived in the office to be told that I had to sail the ship. I, in turn, asked the harbour master, as a fellow mariner, would he sail the ship in the prevailing conditions, in ballast with the derricks rigged and the hatches open. I also asked him why he had allowed the vessel into the lock without consultation with the Liverpool Pilot? He had no answer to that, but realised that a mistake had been made in allowing the ship into the lock.

"Will you take her out into the river, swing her and bring her back into the big lock?" His inquiry was prompted because of the fact that the Manchester Pilots would not back her astern into the canal. I readily agreed, for this was a safe proposition, and with the named agents came dock-pilotage, both in and out. It was a fine afternoon, and we had shelter from the strength of the wind.

---

24 The term for a ship, which is empty, having no cargo on board.

The job was done and that meant that I was no longer responsible for the ship.

I reported her to my office for I was genuinely concerned about the vessel and her captain. The ship was to sink in the English Channel some three months later in bad weather, and I was not surprised.

Pilots are above all individuals, some are, as in all professions, better than others, some are slow and some are fast operators. Upon arriving on the Bar Pilot Boat on one occasion, early in my career as a first-class pilot, I was told that I was manned on the *Regent Falcon*, second ship of three for Eastham with three tugs. The locks could cope with around four "Big Lock Jobs"[25] inwards on any given tide, before there was insufficient water for a big ship to float in the channel. They were allocated positions for docking with the deepest drafted ship taking the first slot.

I was initially delighted, but then I asked who the pilots were for the other two ships. I was horrified. Both men were dear to me as friends, but the one on the first ship was renowned for being slow, and the one on the third ship was renowned for being very fast. We proceeded up the Eastham Channel like a railway train, almost hooked together.

The first, slow ship's stern tug almost sitting on my head tug, and the third ship's head tug pushing on my stern tug. I learned a lot, but I was exhausted by the time I left the bridge, when the ship was safely in the lock, and my neck ached from twisting to look ahead, and then astern, and back again.

Another near drama on a big ship for Eastham was aboard a Greek tanker by the name of *Pytheus*, inward bound, a few days before Christmas of the first year of my being a first-class pilot. It was a daytime tide and all was progressing smoothly until we passed abeam of the Rock Light and entered the river. I was on time, and had reduced to dead slow ahead to keep to my schedule

25 Ships, which can only fit, by virtue of their size, in the bigger of the two locks available at Eastham.

of what we now refer to as 'The Passage Plan.' The engine room telephone rang, and the captain answered it. From being a pleasant companion, chatting about the 'Five Hundred Spartans' at Thermopylae, Odysseus, (my hero) and other Greek histories and myths, he turned into a raving monster. "It is all over, it is all over." He screamed, flailing the wheelhouse air with his worry beads, "It is all over." He repeated over and over again, and then began screaming: "We must go anchor, we must go anchor."

I have never known whether I had been taught not to panic as a pilot, or whether I had picked the capability up from the observation of more experienced colleagues, or whether it just came naturally. Whatever the reason, I noted that we were on schedule and in the position, which we were supposed to be in, and that we were clear of all other traffic. Perhaps, as it turned out to be the most important factor, I noted that we still had revolutions for dead slow ahead on the main engines.

"Captain, please calm down," I entreated, "Please tell me what 'is all over', and why you think that this is the case?" Still agitated, he informed me that a cylinder con-rod had snapped, and that once we stopped the engine, we would not be able to start it again for fear the con-rod would penetrate the engine casing. "But Captain, I do not want to stop the engine." He was shocked to silence. "I propose that we keep going on dead-slow, and although we will be a few minutes late, we will keep the engine running, turning ahead until just before the lock, where we will, after ordering an extra tug, make two fast aft, one ahead with the pusher on the port side, I will stop the main engine, and I will dock her "Dead-Ship.""[26]

This I did and the Manchester Pilot was to take her dead-ship to the crane berth in the canal, where repairs were carried out, and the ship proceeded to Stanlow with only a minimum delay. I recall that the agents actually sent me a Christmas card thanking me for the safe docking.

---

26 That is with no main engine power from the ship herself, using only the tug's power for propulsion.

During the lead up to 1986, and the Pilotage Act, I remember the occasion when I was boarded late for the tide, inward-bound as first ship for the Canal, on a Polish sulphur tanker, called the *Tarno Brezeg*. She was one of four on the run. They had all been fast ships, but they were getting old and had lost speed in age. I respectfully asked the pilot master to send me out an hour earlier than usual to make allowances for the speed deficit. For some reason, he chose not to listen, and sent me out at the normal time, that is, to be on board to be passing the Bar Light Ship at approximately two hours and ten minutes before high water of the tide at Liverpool. I knew on the landing stage, before I had even set foot on the outward-bound pilot launch, that I was already running late. I had no idea however, of the drama, which was to take place, before I would dock safely at Eastham.

I boarded the ship late as I had feared, and was disheartened to find that she was slower than even I had believed. We set off as fast we were able. Normally, the pilot tends to think of his colleagues and their ships, but when the chips are down, the necessity to think only of the safety and furthering of his own ship takes precedence. That was the situation here, and we were running for the tide.

All went well until the ship crossed the bar at the Eastham Channel entrance, and thus passed the point of not necessarily no return, but certainly, with a ship of her size, of difficult return. I had been allocated two tugs and the ship had a weak, but serviceable bow-thrust. I reduced speed on crossing the bar, and we were going to make the tide, albeit, about an hour late. It was time to make the tugs fast. It was at this point that it all began to go wrong.

We were supposedly on slow speed ahead, but the ship's head was paying off to starboard, heading for the shallows to the west of the channel. The helm indicator was hard to port, but it was having no effect. "Bow-thrust full to port, please Captain," I ordered, intending to push the bow back into the line of the channel. The situation was to deteriorate further as the stern boat then called up and told me that his engines had jammed on half-speed ahead. As he was unable to slow down to make fast, we would have to dock without him.

"Come aft," was my order to the head boat, "we will dock with the bow thrust forward and yourself aft." I then noticed that the rev counter had stopped. The engine-room called up to confirm my worst fears, the engine had blacked out and the steering had failed, as had the bow thrust. We were dead ship, and as the old 'Nelsonian' expression has it, we were, quite literally "Up the creek without a paddle!"

Great! It flashed into my mind that Margaret Thatcher's government was about to stab pilots in the back because there were too many of them, which was true, but all those concerned who thought pilots were a necessary financial evil, were attempting to eliminate us altogether.

My orders to the head-boat now were: "Slide down the port side and attempt to push on the port quarter to bring us into the channel, where we will attempt to anchor, to wait until we can muster further tug assistance." I was aware that time was running out, and we would be aground as the tide ebbed before too long, but we had to try.

All looked grim, and then as the tug pushed successfully on the stern, the news came that we had both engines and steering restored, but no bow thrust. The situation was looking brighter particularly when the stern tug called to say that he had sorted out his engines. From imminent disaster we were saved, and went on to dock without further problems.

MORE TALES FROM THE 'PIT'

River Morning

Dawn ran like cold grey fingers
Across the black back of night,
Which retreated westwards
Over the lingering hills of darkness.

"I will return," said the night
Forever hunted in the eternal chase.
The river murmured
And:
Gently tugged at the seaweed, contraceptives and plastic cups,
Which lay amongst the mud and stones
On the banks of shadows.

"I will return," said the night,
The river murmured.

Early on in my career, as a third class pilot, I was presented with a situation, which had been caused by other's misunderstandings. Such incidents occur when two characters have had a misunderstanding, or possibly, one or both parties, have been unreasonable.

The time was late morning on the day of a spring tide. In those days, with a tide in excess of somewhere around the nine metres mark, the canal was level with the river. As the gates opened inwards, when the canal was level with the river, it was, and still is, impossible to hold the mitre of the gates. The gates on Eastham Locks open to make the canal level with the river as far up as the second lock situated at Latchford. Since the early nineties, storm gates, which have the opposite mitre, have been fitted, and these may be closed to avoid a level and bring about what is referred to as a "Storm Gate Tide," where the canal is, in effect, closed off until the river level falls back on the ebb of the tide.

Naturally the tide builds up, to pass through Eastham Locks at speed. It was considered difficult, but safe, to dock on the level up to about twenty minutes after the level had been made, so the entrance to the lock is a flood tide docking with the tide behind the ship. After the twenty minutes, the tide raced through the locks, and it was considered unsafe to enter the lock, for it was virtually impossible to bring the ship up in the lock with the full force of the tide behind her. I have mentioned docking at the first lock, or four hours to high water. After the three hours, it was considered that the tide swept across the entrance at too great a speed to dock safely, until it slackened off at around the hour to high water. In the pilot's oral exams, the examinee had to say that he would never dock on the flood of the tide at Eastham, but it was accepted, paradoxically, that if ships did not dock on the flood, then the canal could not cope with the volume of traffic to be handled.

On the day-tide in question, which was over thirty feet, or in excess of ten metres as we now operate in metres, I was to join the pilot launch at Woodside Landing Stage at approximately half an hour to high water. I always found it difficult to come to terms with having point six of a metre, for safety, under my keel, anywhere, when I was always happy with two feet under the keel. To have less than two feet under the keel, which on rare occasions did happen, was referred to by the old pilots as "Being in danger of putting a stripe through the flatfish!"

The old Danish master had passed the Bar and the station pilot boat, having had an exchange of words with the pilot boat captain. The ship had requested a pilot, and one had been ordered, but unfortunately the pilot boat was awaiting a fresh complement of men to arrive, which included myself.

The captain was informed that he might wait for the pilot launch, which would mean, as his was a slow ship, she would miss the tide, or being under the tonnage for compulsory pilotage, he could proceed up into the river to meet the pilot on the outward-bound launch.

By the time the ship had made the passage into the river, the captain had decided against taking a pilot at all. Unfortunately for him, we had manned a pilot off to cover his original request, and our launch was more than twice his speed, so we had no trouble catching him, and I was able to vault over the gunwale and onto the main deck.

Upon reaching the bridge, I was met with a tirade of abuse. "Oh dear," I thought, "Just how am I going to cope with this one?"

"Where are you bound to Captain?" Was the question, I chose for my opening gambit. "Runcorn Salt Works, and without your interference," was the gruff reply.

"And when will you be docking into the Eastham Lock?" I inquired.

"On arrival of course, I have no time to lose."

"Ah Captain, that is fine, but it is not as simple as that I am afraid. Have you ever been to Eastham before Captain, and are you aware of the "level?"

No he had not been to Eastham before, and what was this "level?"

I explained to him about the gates being in the "off," position" and about the resulting run of tide, adding that at high water, when we would be arriving, the run would be at its strongest. We looked at each other warily, and then he laughed, and proffered his hand.

"You will take me Pilot."

I too laughed, with relief, and then said that it was not possible because we had to stop in the lock to pick up a Manchester pilot, and with the tide behind us we would risk serious damage in the attempt.

"I do not take a Manchester pilot, the ship is too small." (That is, under the required tonnage, as it was at that time.)

"But you must stop for the customs, as you are inward from a foreign port."

"They will board at Runcorn," he countered.

"But you must stop to allow me to leave the ship Captain," was my last possible reason against not docking "on arrival."

"You will come with me to Runcorn Pilot, and I will pay for your taxi back to Eastham."

I had no further arguments, but certainly I still had both my concerns and reservations about such a proposition. I called the Eastham Control on the V.H.F. to explain the situation and to request permission for the vessel to enter the canal on the top of high water.

The request was granted. The controller omitted to inform us of the fact that a fairly large ship was making the outward-bound passage, and that we were to meet her in the final strait on the inside of the lock. With the Danish vessel, being only a small coaster, the confrontation was easily overcome because there was room to pass but, momentarily, upon sighting the outward ship, there was cause for concern.

I was also to emphasise that once the ship had crossed the outer sill of the lock, I would be having no further part in the navigation, for it is out of the question, ethically, that any pilot should operate as a pilot in another pilotage district.

We hurtled up the Eastham Channel, with the last of the tide behind us, and I eased back on the engines as much as I could to bring down the speed for manoeuvring. When the bow was between the pier-heads of the big lock, however, I was forced to increase to full speed ahead in order to maintain steerageway, and we hurtled through the middle of the lock. Ship's full speed was seven knots, which we had plus, maybe, four from the tidal run. It was very fast indeed, just like shooting the rapids in a canoe, but we were in. The captain "missed" the outward vessel, and we docked at Runcorn Salt Works from where I returned to my own district by taxi, paid for as promised, by the captain of the ship. I remember that his final words of both thanks and farewell included the positive declaration that he would never do that again.

The only other occasion when I handled a craft in the canal was when I skippered the Wincham Trust's historic craft *Wincham* on passage from Ellesmere Port Boat Museum to Canning Dock. That also was an exiting passage with myself alone on the bridge and twenty turns of the wheel from hard over to hard over, if I remember correctly. Sadly, through lack of funds, *Wincham* was broken up on the banks of the Mersey some years ago.

During the second Icelandic Cod War in 1973, I was boarded at the Bar Lightship, on an Icelandic coaster bound for the Canal. The ship had been to the Canal on many occasions for she was a regular runner, and we had plenty of time for the tide. As I made my way up from the main deck to the bridge, I noticed that the ship was turning hard to port and increasing revolutions to full speed ahead, away from the main channel. Upon arriving on the bridge I found an excellent captain with a great sense of humour based on sincerity and belief in his country and its prosperity.

We shook hands as he gave a course to the north. I waited, knowing that we had plenty of time. After a few minutes he asked me if I was interested in where we were going. "Naturally," I replied, "but no doubt you will soon tell me."

The captain explained that as we were "at war," he had been sent to capture a "naval expert." "You will do." He said, unable to stop himself from laughing. Soon after he stopped playing games of pretended espionage as we turned for the channel and the scheduled docking at Eastham. During the whole passage, he bombarded me with valid reasons why cod fishing in Icelandic waters should be under the jurisdiction of the Icelanders. Shortly before we were to enter the Eastham Channel, the captain left the bridge to return with a frozen Icelandic cod, weighing about five pounds. He solemnly presented the fish to me as 'a sympathiser with the cause' explaining sadly, and all too truthfully, that the fish was one of the few left in Icelandic waters.

I left the ship with the fish head and tail protruding from my bag. There is a rider to this tale (no pun initially intended) for I had to go to Liverpool on my way home. By the time I had finished my business in Liverpool, and was in the lift at James Street Station, the ice was melting and the fish was beginning to smell strongly. Heads were turned, and noses wrinkled. We ate the fish that evening, it was delicious.

Another "wartime," or rather "cold wartime" diplomatic situation connected with Eastham occurred when, for whatever reason, I found myself as a passenger on a Polish vessel by the name of the *Wrozka*, inbound for Eastham. Possibly the launch had broken down, and it was the quickest way to be back ashore for an outward bound pilot, or possibly, I had left my car at Eastham and was returning to collect it. Whatever the reason, I was there, and once on board the ship, I was shown to the saloon and was told to help myself to coffee from the coffee machine.

Soon after, a man in a shore-side suit joined me, poured himself a coffee and we started to chat. It turned out that he was a Polish physicist by the name of Josef Namylowski. Although we were still deep in the Cold War, Josef was on board with not only his wife, but also with his two children. The family had most unusually been allowed out of the country in order that Josef might work at the University of Manchester for an academic year, and his wife, a consultant, was to work at Prestwich Hospital.

We became firm friends and subsequently, Josef was to come over to West Kirby with his family. On one occasion Josef and his wife came to dinner with an international group, which included a Chilean couple, Hernan and Vivienna Rozenkranz, who had been forced to flee Chile following the Allende coup.

At the end of the year, we were invited to Prestwich for a farewell dinner for all the friends whom the family had made during their time in England. Josef's mother had been allowed to come over to help officiate and to cook the thirteen course banquet. I particularly mention the number of courses for, as we sat at table for the first one, our glasses were filled with Polish vodka. Josef raised his glass and proposed a toast to his British friends insisting that we all, of all ages, drank the liquid in one gulp. This we all managed to do, but were then horrified to find that the glasses were filled up immediately and a second toast was made. This ceremony was re-enacted between each course. The British backed off and indulged in sipping the liquid, and insisting that there were no refills. Josef seemed to be unaware of this fact, for he carried on, proposing toasts and throwing back the glasses of vodka, two between each course.

The meal was delicious, each course a work of Polish art, accompanied with glasses of Polish wine, but the last we were to see of Josef was his recumbent form, slumbering peacefully under the table, which had been laid for some thirty guests. Gill and I corresponded with Josef for many years, particularly at Christmas, but it is some years since the last exchange.

Eastham and the fog were not pleasant. The channel is narrow, and the tide mostly fast flowing across the main part of it. Proceeding at slow speed was dangerous, but possible. After several days of one of the "old pea-soupers," I found myself inbound aboard a Fisher boat, which was under the command of a Hoylake man, Captain Tom Tyson. Tom's wife, Betty, was at that time the landlord of the *Plasterer's Arms*, a public house in Hoylake.

On the previous day tide, a colleague had brought a large tanker up into the river and had moored her safely alongside one of the Tranmere Oil Jetties. A superb act of pilotage, in my opinion, but an act, for which he was sadly to get into trouble soon after. My policy in fog was, first of all, to assess the efficiency of the ship's radars, and then to assess the possible traffic movements to be encountered. If both were favourable, I believed that it was safe to make an attempt to dock safely. Safety was all, and any doubts meant turning the movement down. As my father used to say: "It takes a good man to say no." That principle was to apply to me in strong winds, as well as in the fog.

The Fisher boat's radars were both excellent, and there were no other traffic movements. Most had opted for the safety the clearance would bring and had anchored. The clearance would also bring an increase in the traffic bound both to and from the port as the backlog was cleared. Captain Tyson was with me in my suggestion that we were to proceed as far as we considered it safe.

We proceeded through the main channels and the river without incident, passing many anchored ships awaiting the clearance. Our propeller churned the grey, unseen darkness of the night, the engines thumped, muffled in the eerie silence of the hidden waters.

Approaching the Eastham channel we became aware of a large target on the radar, about which we had not been informed. The target was that of a Gorthon Boat, which had been forced to anchor on the previous tide. The vessel's anchored position, forced me to go to starboard, close to the Bromboro' Buoy. It disappeared as a target on the radar. All hands were on deck as lookouts, and all eyes were staring out into the fog to sight the buoy. "Forget it, it's here." I called, having been looking directly down at the water from the bridge. There beneath me in the silence of the fog, was the buoy, gently sliding down the starboard side of the ship. It was to vanish, flashing its ghostly light into the white, swirling mists astern.

Being with such an experienced and competent captain as Tom was a pleasure in such conditions. Soon after "finding" the buoy, with only two and a half miles to go, Eastham Control called us up to inform us that the canal was closed, and that they would not consider us docking on that tide.

We were both disappointed having come so far. We anchored and docked the following day, fighting with many other vessels, each jostling for a docking turn on the tide. Tom and I were to meet the evening the day after our docking day, for we had arranged to discuss the passage in the *Plasterers* over a pint, as Tom was going on leave. I arrived with the news that on the next day's tide, outward from Eastham, I had sighted an undamaged Brombro' Buoy, and verified its position. There was no need for a report. We had a second pint on the house.

On one occasion, proceeding up to the QE II Oil Dock on board the *Cableman*, which was under the command of the legendary Captain David 'Daisy' Andrews, I found myself being polite to a female officer, when for her further education, I believe in retrospect, that I should have adopted a firmer approach.

We were approaching the vicinity of the lock in a misty dawn. The visibility was about three-quarters of a mile and it was just after the top of the predicted high water. I went out onto the port wing of the bridge with a pair of binoculars to sight the flow, if any, of water on the last port hand buoy, ostensibly to see if the ebb tide was 'away.'

Staring intently at the buoy, I heard a polite cough and the words: "Excuse me Sir, but I think that it is E6. (buoy)." My reaction, and definitely because she was female, was to politely thank her for this information, rather than to possibly make some sarcastic comment, which I was more likely to have done in reply to a male officer.

Subsequently, I have envisaged the young lady telling the story at dinner parties of the time when she was with a Liverpool Pilot, (and his ship so close to land) who was searching for the name on a buoy to find out where he was.

A final "windy'" tale to round off this chapter is the one of the Finnish coaster, which I foolishly succumbed to sailing in a storm. The previous day a large Shell tanker had been blown off the Tranmere Oil stage, had run aground mid-river, and had demolished the Esso mooring buoys, which were never to be replaced for the pipeline from the buoys to the Dingle Oil Terminal, was also wrecked.

The Finnish coaster was in the big lock at Eastham, ready to sail. The winds were still westerly force nine to ten out at the Bar Light Vessel and my advice to the captain was that we did not sail on the tide, but that we waited until we had a moderation.

The captain looked at me with scorn as he announced his belief that: "You Englishmen, when it comes to sailing in bad weather, you are like rabbits!" "Let go all ropes, engines slow ahead" was my foolish response, and we sailed out into the storm. We took well over an hour to sail down the last two miles of the Queen's Channel to gain the open sea.   During this hour, the captain realised "our folly" and apologised profusely. He then made an offer to appease me, an offer that was only made to me once in my career.

"Pilot, when we are clear of the channel. I will send the girl to your cabin." I was happily married and was embarrassed by the offer, an offer, which I would not accept, but I also did not wish to offend the captain for refusing "his generosity"!

"Captain," I began diplomatically, "I must stay on the bridge until we are clear of the pilotage district, which is almost forty miles to the west. At this speed, by the time we get there, I believe that I will be too tired and will be in need of sleep." No more was said of the matter, but next morning I was served breakfast by a very attractive, young, blonde, Finnish girl. Ah well!

A further comment on this adventure is that I battered my way to Swansea. That day, five pilots were "carried away" from the port. Two went on the same tanker to Bilbao, one went on a Shell tanker to Rotterdam, and one went on a Monte boat to the Canary Islands. With the passage to Swansea on a slow ship, and the interminable, though picturesque train journey back through central Wales, I was the last of the five to report back for duty!

'LIVERPOOL, I SEE YOU LIVERPOOL, HELD IN THE GRIP OF THE POWERING TIDE'

As I was to state in the film *Passport to Liverpool*, (Bright Moon Films 2008) made in Liverpool's year as Europe's Capital of Culture, after having swung an A.C.L. ship off Gladstone Lock in the darkness of the night for the cameras: "A magical place to come into... Liverpool."

The wonder and mystery of the port both lie in the relentless and constant movements of the tides. No matter what happens in the daily life of the human race, for examples political squabbles, the ups and downs of family relationships, international conflict, success and failure of any individual, the birth of a child, there will always be a tide flowing, whether it be on the ebb, or whether it be on the flood, and there will always be another tide.

This fascination in the movement of water, governed by the celestial movements of the moon in relation to the sun, so far away from the Earth, yet "standing still," (both before and after Galileo's discovery) which causes the tidal cycles, is created by the very existence of the universe itself. All is shrouded in the mists of time, and our knowledge of the tides, and of how craft may move both on and in their waters, has been built up over the centuries since primeval man, or maybe it was a primeval woman, who found themselves to be the first to be afloat on a drifting log.

I have made reference to the pilot's ship-handling skills being classified as an art with the story of the coaster departing from Brombro'. A story of a near gale docking into Gladstone Lock in the early seventies emphasises the importance of the arts for some pilots, myself included.

During this period, Great Britain was involved with the 'Troubles' in Northern Ireland, and five troop carrier/landing craft of the R.F.A. 'Round Table' Class were running troops and supplies between Liverpool and Belfast, at one point with a frequency greater than the passenger ferries running between the two ports.

They required pilots, both inward and outward bound. I piloted all five of them many times, and they were all difficult to handle, in particular because of the very thin nature of the materials used in building their hulls. Liverpool Pilots devised a safe method of tying these vessels up in Gladstone Lock, by mooring them in the middle of the lock, with ropes out from both bows and from both quarters, so that at no time should the thin hulls land on the hard stone of the lock.

Sir Galahad arrived one early morning at the Bar Light Vessel, and I was boarded for a straight run up to dock on arrival at Gladstone in the dawn light, with the help of two tugs, her own twin screws and her own bow thrust. Conditions were not too bad, but the westerly, force six wind which was blowing would not make it easy to escape damage.

As the daylight strengthened, so did the wind, but all went well both in the lock mooring and on the approach to the north end of S6, our berth. Another vessel was lying on the south end of the berth so that there was a 'shoe-horn' job required to bring the vessel in safely to tie up starboard side to. The bow was nearly there, and the stern was clear of the ship astern, so I ordered that the head tug should let go so that I may thrust the bow gently alongside. The head tug was of the old style, single screw variety, and in manoeuvring himself clear over to port, he put weight on the tow-rope, pulling the bow out, over to the west and the stern fell down to the east towards the flair of the bow of the ship astern. We moved from being "nearly there" to an emergency. I split the ship's twin screws, the port engine ahead and the starboard engine astern with the bow-thruster to starboard, and as a result, serious damage was avoided.

Alongside, the captain with a mixture of both relief and disappointment indicated that we had to retire to his cabin to make out the damage report, with its many associated forms.

"Damage Captain, I was not aware that we had done any damage, although we did come very close to the other ship's bow."

The captain explained that, although the vessel's hulls had not made contact, a bottle-screw[27] on a safety net on our flight deck had caught the bow of the other ship and one end of it had sheared off! (We were that close!) I observed the troops leaving the vessel through the bow-door ramp in armoured vehicles.

"Has the vessel a Land Rover on board, which I might borrow with a driver for a short while?" I enquired.

"Yes, but why should you want to borrow a vehicle Pilot?"

I explained that the bottle-screw, although not my fault, was such a minor damage, which did not, in my opinion warrant all the form filling in (which he was dreading), that I would drive over to the nearest ship's chandler in Liverpool and buy him a replacement. He saw my point, and we abandoned the report.

This "damage" was proven to be particularly trivial, in later years, when the ship was bombed with the loss of so many lives of both sailors of the Merchant Navy, and of soldiers of the Welsh Guards in Port Pleasant, off Fitzroy, during the Falklands War.

I came ashore to find that a boatman by the name of Jacky had waited for me in his car, which was a very kind act on his part.

"That was a tough one Pilot," he sympathised, "I thought that you might like the offer of a lift to the Pierhead." I gratefully accepted the offer. As we set off he was riffling through a bank of tapes.

"I believe that I have just the thing for you Pilot."

It turned out that Jacky loved classical music. These were the early days of quadraphonic sound in motor cars, and Jacky had a system installed with a comprehensive selection of classical music tapes, which he would listen to whilst sitting on locks, and on dock walls waiting for ships at all times of the day and night.

---

27 A device for securing wires and ropes, which may be tightened with the use of a twist lock at each end.

He selected a tape and further selected a movement, which he believed was what was required to relax me after the demands of the successful docking of the ship. Jacky chose the fifth movement from Beethoven's sixth symphony, the *Pastorale*. The joyful and thankful feelings after the storm! The music flowed both over me and through me. It was a life-changing experience. I sat on the Pierhead until the shops opened at 0900 hrs. before going up to Rushworth and Dreaper's music shop in Whitechapel to buy the L.P. with Herbert von Karajan conducting the work with the Berliner Philharmoniker.

From that day on, I returned home, whether by day or night after an exacting job and listened to the movement. (In my drinking days with a large scotch in my hand!) I am eternally grateful to Jacky and his kindness, which went far beyond what he had originally offered to a young pilot, with what was initially, simply a generous lift to the Pierhead on that gale-torn, grey morning.

There are two heavy-weather dockings of Nigerian National Line ships, which are both worthy of mention. The first was the *River Jimini*, which took place in the March of 1982. I had passed my good friend and colleague, Bill 'Tizzy' Owen at the top of the Lynas Jetty at breakfast time on a stormy morning with a strong westerly gale blowing.

"Forget it," was Bill's advice, which I respected and was based on the latest forecast, which gave no sign of moderation for the next twenty-four hours. I boarded the vessel and proceeded up to the Bar Light Vessel to "have a look at it" and show willing in case there was to be an unexpected moderation, but I was not hopeful.

As I passed the lightship, preparing to swing back outwards to proceed back to the west, I was waiting for a colleague who was in the radar tower at the time, to assess the situation off Gladstone Lock by asking the Gladstone dock-master for his assessment of the sea state and conditions off the Lock.

There was a delay in the reply being transmitted, and with wind and tide behind me, I was rapidly approaching the channel entrance. I was not concerned, however, for there was no other traffic about as it was early on the day-tide.

The vessel was up to the Q1 buoy before the reply came.

"Dock-master says that it is not too bad but if I were you John, I would not look at it." Now a colleague's advice is the best you may have from an experienced man who is on scene, miles ahead of your position, as it were.

"Right Captain, we are calling it off for this tide but as we are entering the channel, I will require half-astern on the main engine to start the turn back to the west." This was one of the few occasions where I asked for an astern movement to start to turn a ship in similar circumstances.

No engines came and we drifted further into the channel. Both anchors were ready but as the chief engineer wrestled with what turned out to be the impossible, to turn the engines astern, I requested that he try them ahead. They turned, and we shot past the point of no return for a biggish ship at that state of tide. I reassured the captain that we would make fast a tug and swing in the river, after all we were underway and there was to be shelter further up the river from the westerly gale.

Now 1982 was the year of the arrival of the Voigt Schneider tugs on the river, the first being the tug *Canada*, and she had been booked for the *River Jimini*. I passed Gladstone Lock, for the river was already like a maelstrom off the lock, and the spring tide carried me onwards to the south, as I would not risk an astern movement.

I noticed that conditions were not too bad off Langton where the tug *Canada* began making fast. Off Alfred Lock, I abandoned a starboard swing, for the engines would not go astern, and I rudder-cycled[28] towards mid-river, south of Woodside Landing

---

28 A series of consecutive rudder movements from one side to the other, which helps slow the passage of a ship through the water.

Stage, where I intended to attempt a swing using the ebb-set off the Sloyne and the tug. Round we came with such speed and certainty that I was astonished by the capability of this new tug.

"Captain," I asked on the V.H.F. tug channel, "If you were made fast aft, do you think that you could keep my stern off the wall at Langton if I can arrange a docking there?"

I had thought of requesting a berth on the Rock Ferry Tank Cleaning Jetty for necessary repairs, but to be safely in dock would be much preferable for everyone concerned.

"Pilot, if I am made fast aft on this ship in these conditions, I will keep your stern off the wall at Langton," came the confident and welcome reply. The docking was re-arranged, a conventional tug made fast forward, and the *Canada*, as good as his word, kept my stern off the wall and the ship was, almost by default, safely in.

This was my first of many exciting experiences with the Voigt Schneider tugs of the "North-Enders." The company changed names and owners several times in my career, but the men who manned them were the same, and they were excellent in every way, right up to my retirement passage, years later after many operations with big ships, particularly the A.C.L. vessels. A much used and less powerful tug *Canada*, was actually still operational on many a successful A.C.L. passage.

In the January of 1984, aboard the *River Rima*, I was to experience another bad weather docking with a Nigerian National Line vessel in strong westerly winds. This time I had been boarded the previous evening down at Point Lynas in moderate conditions with a westerly gale forecast for the following day.

Following the old adage: "Get as far as you can when you can," I opted to proceed into the river and anchor on the ebb of the tide prior to the one, on which I was scheduled to dock. With this move, I was able to find shelter in the river before the wind strengthened and also, by anchoring on the ebb of the tide, the turn of the tide would swing the ship in readiness for docking.

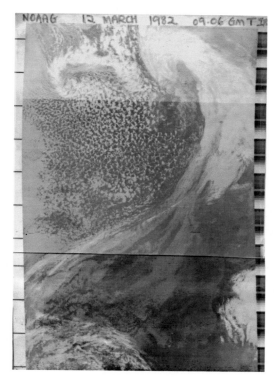

NOAAG   12 MARCH 1982   09.06 GMT

Spot the 'River Jimini!'

I anchored the ship late in the evening, river north, shortly before the high water of a spring tide and shortly before the wind strengthened.   At the turn of the tide the wind swung to the west and blew up to storm force.   The whole river was heaving, water crashing everywhere on every side, waves breaking as if an invisible giant was bathing, and had taken it upon himself to splash about like a child in a bathtub.

The ship leaped about in an alarming fashion, moving on the sloping waters, as the massive waves rose and fell into their gaping troughs.   These filled with pouring streams of water from the next swell able to reach the depths first, from whichever confused direction it was coming.

The anchor held, but I did not sleep much that night, choosing rather to grasp the porthole in my cabin, through which I was to observe and marvel at, yet again, the wonders of the deep moving according to Poseidon's wrath.

Dawn brought a minor moderation down to gale force, which with our docking time being before the three hours to the high water meant, that we could dock, combating the wind, but without the swell as the still uncovered Burbo Bank acted as a break water. I attempted to make the third tug fast on the port shoulder, so that she could pull off to the west, and help to keep the ship off the unforgiving stones of Gladstone Lock.

This attempt to make the third tug fast was a failure, for the big and very strong Nigerian sailor detailed off to throw the heaving line down to the tug from the main deck, was unable to do so. The strong man's efforts attracted my attention, as he hurled the coiled heaving line downwards, possibly half a dozen times. On each occasion the wind hurled it back at him as if it were a gossamer thread.

Unfortunately for the sailor, a monkey's first knot, possibly filled with lead, had been tied on to the end of the rope. Each time the rope came back; the fist hit the sailor on the forehead with accurate positioning. The sailor finally staggered to the hatch combing, where he sat down, bemused and totally exhausted, and possibly suffering from a mild concussion.

I opted to continue the docking without the third tug being fast, and we made it safely with a lot of effort on the two tugs' part, which were both made fast, and with the use of the ship's main engines and rudder.

Safely alongside, sipping a beer in the ship's saloon, I was to witness a major drugs' haul, when customs' officers discovered the cache hidden beneath the opening windows in the forepart of the ship's saloon.

There was one other vessel of the same company, which I attended, but did not sail for various reasons. This was the *King Jaja*, during the December of 1974. The vessel had been laid up for some time in the northwest corner of Sandon Dock. Each time I attended the vessel over a period of five or six tides, either gale to storm force winds were blowing, or the vessel had an engine problem. The master of the *King Jaja* was an older British captain, and a Captain Jonas, a very tall Nigerian, was the superintendent of the company based in Liverpool. We had numerous telephone calls and meetings on board the vessel deliberating on her future,

Eventually, I was to go on leave and handed the responsibility over to another colleague, who eventually sailed her and had a complexity of problems, which were the result of a mixture of strong winds and engine failures, before she was clear and away from the port. Other involvement piloting vessels of the same company was not so remarkable.

I have mentioned piloting the ships of Clan Line, my 'cadet' company. I was also fortunate, before the demise of the company, to pilot all the ships of the Booker Line, my 'Third Officer' company. Further, I piloted the captains, other than Captain Armitage who had retired by then, with whom I had sailed as third mate, as master in Ted Jones' case, mate in Bob Machechnie's case, and second mate and mate in Eddie Puddifer's case. The latter was captain aboard the last British Booker Line vessel to leave Liverpool, and I was the pilot of that vessel, the *Booker Crusader* in May 1982.

Eddie was not a happy man when I met him on the bridge and he informed me that he believed that the company would fold before the ship reached South America. He was right for both cheaper and faster German vessels would take over the run before containerisation would also replace these German general cargo vessels.

When I think of the "old general cargo trade" of the big British companies coming to an end, one story, which is always there in the forefront of change is the tale of the Ellerman 'Market' Boat the *Darinian*. The class were third-class vessels, but with bridge amidships and full British crew, piloting one of them gave the young pilot the sense that he had made it, as it was almost like being on a big ship.

I was boarded at Point Lynas, delighted to have been manned on the vessel, for they, although small ships, were normally covered by Ellerman appropriated pilots. We docked into Liverpool without incident.

About one week later, when I had changed from "sea-turns" (bringing them in) to "long-shore" (taking them out), I was manned on the Greek owned vessel *Konstansis Photinis*.

"By the way John," said the shore-master, who gave me the orders to shift the vessel from Liverpool to Eastham Locks on the day tide, "Until this morning she was the *Darinian!*"

That information was both well intended and well received. I went down early to discover that I had at my disposal the chief and first engineers from Ellerman's, who were making a 'handover' trip. I also had the new owner, who would not admit to any qualifications, a Greek second-officer and two Greek seamen. The rest of the crew, including the captain, had been delayed on the flight to Manchester from Athens.

"We must sail and make the tide into the Canal," insisted the owner, "or I will be ruined before I start," he continued. "You will be captain," he declared, pleading with me rather than ordering me.

I explained that it was not that simple but I would do what I could. It was in the days long before mobile telephones, so I had to dash ashore to the nearest telephone box to ring the senior representative of the pilots for advice. As always it was sound. Basically, I could do as I believed was fitting, but I must not make mistakes or I might be in trouble.

With this in mind, I returned to the bridge and took command. I smiled when I compared this sailing to the vessel's docking when we had the first officer with three gold stripes and his crew on the foredeck, the second officer with his two gold stripes and his crew on the afterdeck, and the third officer, with his single stripe swinging the bridge engine-room telegraph on the bridge with the captain with his four gold stripes and myself, the pilot.

Here we had the two Ellerman engineers down below so I was assured of the competence of the engine-room, one sailor forward and one sailor aft, the owner doing as he was told on the wheel, and myself swinging the telegraph.

There was no wind and I swung the telegraph with glee as the 'Market' Boat, from a class renowned for their good handling, made the passage safely to being moored in Langton Lock. Here a coach arrived with the remaining missing crew, so we were able to sail to catch the tide up at Eastham with a full complement.

I was not exactly relieved of my command, however, for the captain, dressed in an immaculately tailored, mustard coloured suit, chose to sit on the bridge seat with his "dolly-bird" (I believe that that was the term we were using for mini-skirted, good-looking young ladies during the sixties and seventies) wife or girlfriend, I never found out which, sitting on his knee throughout the passage up to Eastham!

Another shift around that time on a similar sized ship from Liverpool to Birkenhead but requiring two tug-boats, first gave rise to a thought of mine regarding the pilot's relationship with the tugs, with which he was operating.

The ship was Egyptian, the *Ben Ha*, around about the 2000 tons mark. Unusually for me, I decided to go down early to sleep for a few hours on board before the early morning start. I was shown to the pilot's cabin, which appeared on the initial inspection to be old but clean, the bunk being made up with fresh linen.

I stripped off and turned in. I lay staring at the deck-head with an increasing sense of unease. After some minutes I began to think of the Sunday mornings on board the Clan Line ships and the captain's weekend inspection of the crew's quarters. The captain would be accompanied by a cadet brandishing a carton of D.D.T. powder, which was shaken into the corners of the sailor's bunks to deter unwanted and unhealthy guests.

I leaped from my bunk, switched on the cabin light and lifted the iron mattress-support. There beneath, disturbed by my action was a veritable menagerie of creepy-crawlies of all descriptions, all running and wriggling in every direction.

I swiftly dressed and escaped to the bridge, where I settled uncomfortably in the bridge chair where I dozed fitfully until sailing time.

The passage was made to Birkenhead, without incident. When the Alfred Basin was level with the system, I manoeuvred the ship through into the East Float, where I was to swing through one hundred and eighty degrees and back stern-first to the berth. It was when I had given the orders on the relatively new hand-held V.H.F. sets now used by pilots to command the movements of tugs, that I first had a revelation with regard to the comparison of a pilot with the conductor of an orchestra.

The conductor raises his baton; the orchestra waits for the initial signal from the waved baton, which will instruct the start of the playing of the piece. I stood there, on the wing of the bridge, on my dais, having 'waved my baton' by having ordered the head tug to pull broad off to port, and the stern tug to pull broad off to starboard, when he had room to do so. The "movement" was in motion. I realised that if I did not continue to 'beat time' with a vocalised waving of the baton, (my V.H.F. set) the orchestra, (the tugs) could lose the rhythm and the whole operation, the "movement" of the ship herself, would very soon be out of both tune and harmony. Only the pilot has the overall view of the operation from the bridge, "the conductor's podium."

I have used this comparison often when instructing young pilots who were with me in later years on training trips. We were in the transition period from whistle signals to the use of V.H.F. radios. In the days prior to this, a 'pea whistle' (usually an Acme Thunderer) was used to blow set signals to the head tug, and the ship's whistle, to blow set signals to the stern tug.

As the ships grew in size, it was often necessary to swop over the whistle used, for it was possible in a gale that on a long ship with the bridge and funnel aft, the head tug would not hear the pea-whistle, particularly in strong winds. I am indebted, as all pilots are, to the young pilot, (or was it a tug captain?) who brought in the now obvious "percentage power" orders, which made the operation with tugs on a ship so much more precise and refined. So, for example, rather than "Weight on the port bow please," followed by "and a touch more on the port bow," we now have the more precise: "Twenty percent power on the port bow please," followed by "and take her up to fifty percent."

Good jobs became even better, and a sense of delicacy could be discovered, even on the largest of ships in the extremes of weather.

I remember on one occasion, docking at Birkenhead, later in my career, when the stern tug called me up on the V.H.F. radio to tell me that we had a problem, for the head tug's V.H.F. had failed. In my own relaxed style, looking for the next step, I simply assured them not to be worried for I would use the ship's whistle to pass the order to the head tug. There was no answer initially, and in the noticeable silence I realised that there could be a problem with the young skippers on the tugs not having been about in the days of whistle signals! The V.H.F. eventually crackled into life, with the message that the head tug had managed to "fire up" another set!

On another occasion when I went down to sleep on board a vessel before an early morning departure, I came across a problem of another kind. The ship was an American general cargo ship, the *Trans Columbia*, of about fifteen thousand tons, berthed on the then security berth in Gladstone Dock. It is strange to use the

Greek term "Spartan" for an American ship, but American cargo ships were spartan! They generally had no carpets in the alleyways and the doors to the cabins were metal, and there was little sign of comfort of any kind.

When I arrived on the main deck, a young officer wearing baseball boots met me. When I explained that I had come down to sleep on board, he was thrown into consternation. "We have a problem, for we have no pilot's cabin Pilot," was his answer to my request to be shown to that room, which by the laws of the sea, every vessel must have for the eventuality of a pilot having to sleep on board. The officer explained to me that a lady passenger was to make the passage to Londonderry and that the cabin had been commandeered for her use.

I requested that I might be taken to the captain, so that he might resolve the problem for the lady was not yet on board. I was taken to this 'tin door' on the captain's deck, where the young man showed concern that the captain might be sleeping. Knowing that the captain would have a better deal if his pilot had been able to have some sleep, I knocked loudly on the door. The young man was right about the captain being asleep, for after several knocks, the door flew open to reveal the spectre of a very large American dressed in a vest and shorts, and with "dog-tags"[29] round his neck, he looked like a character out of a Second World War movie!

"Who the hell are you?" he rasped angrily.

"I'm the Liverpool Pilot," I ventured, believing that this proclamation would impress. It did not, however, by any means.

"I don't need no god-dammed pilot," was the abrupt reply, and the tin door slammed in my face.

O.K! I had to take control of the situation, and having established that the lady was not on board, I ordered the officer to take me to the cabin where, I would sort out the problem if the lady was to arrive and contest the right to the pilot's bunk.

---

29 Colloquial term for identification discs worn around the neck by soldiers.

I remember that the pilot's cabin was basically all shiny and filled with plastic-imitation leather furniture. I did not sleep too well even though the lady failed to arrive. I also remember lying awake near the time when I was to rise and prepare myself for the sailing. I was waiting, in the interests of all pilots worldwide, for the knock on my door. It came:

"Who's that?" I called out.

"It's the captain," came the expected reply.

"I don't need no god-dammed captain," I pronounced delightedly in a loud voice.

"Aw gee, come on now Pilot, get me outa' here!"

Naturally, I obliged as I was always going to, and we struck up a good working relationship. I finally helped him out for his future, realising that someone on board was lacking in the knowledge of Ireland's important socio-geographical matters. As I shook hands with him and was about to leave the bridge to disembark at the Bar Pilot Station, I asked a question, which was prompted by an earlier sighting of an ensign placed in readiness for hoisting on arrival at his next port.

"Captain, would you confirm that your next port of call is in fact Londonderry?"

"Sure thing Pilot, Londonderry in the good old Emerald Isle."

"Then Captain, may I recommend that, for your own good, you hoist the red ensign as your courtesy flag at the fore, as you did in Liverpool, and certainly not the tricolour that someone has put out in readiness on top of the flag locker."

I left him pondering on that one!

Arriving on the bridge of another ship, the *Ibn Hazam*, outward bound from Liverpool, I first received an apology, and then an invitation. The apology was from the young ex-Blue Funnel Line officer who was the captain who apologised for inviting me down an hour and a half before the sailing time because he had learned that the "ladies of the night" (prostitutes) who were on board, led by the legendary 'Glasgow Lil' refused to even start leaving the ship until the pilot was on board. The invitation was for dinner in the saloon, which turned out to be roast duckling, and which was rather good.

The other memorable event, which took place on my disembarkation down at the Western Station towards midnight, hours later concerned my briefcase and a sailor whom I was to describe in a poem later, as possibly being a better camel driver.

The wind was south-southeast, force six, almost the limit of working the Point Lynas pilot station. I climbed down the pilot ladder onto the deck of the pilot launch and looked back up to sight my briefcase, not made fast to the heaving line, but rather with a loop passed round it, but not passed through the handle of the bag. Half way down the side of the ship, the bag tipped and dropped between the side of the ship and the launch.

As the captain spotted the loss, he stopped the engines and the propeller turning, for the bag was floating down the side of the ship towards the stern. This it did, passing over the propeller blades, which, as the vessel was fairly light, were almost on the surface as the waves broke over them. The launch crew and myself pursued the bag round the Irish Sea, the bag itself held in the grip of a searchlight beam. I, myself, lying prostrate on the bow of the launch, gripping the deck with the toes of my shoes, managed to grasp the underside of the bag as it rose upwards on a wave-crest. The A.B. on deck grasped my shirt collar and heaved, as I had instructed him to do. The bag, attached to my finger-nailed, "tallon'd grip", was plucked from the clutches of the sea.

Back, alone up in the pilot's rooms, I surveyed a heap of paper-pulp poems, a wreck of a ruined radio, along with other damp items, and a shirt with a torn-off collar, not to mention a pair of shoes with no soles. The following afternoon, I emptied the contents of the bag on the agent's desk up in Liverpool. I received an apology and a substantial amount of money to replace the damaged items. I wrote a poem about that one too!

Years later, not far from this position, whilst boarding a chemical tanker of about five thousand tons, which had been anchored in Moelfre Bay awaiting the tide and had fouled her anchor on another ship's lost anchor cable, I was to become "married to the sea."

The captain of the ship had managed to make a lee by using the bow-thruster, whilst the crew struggled successfully to clear the unwanted cable. The lee was not perfect, but reasonable, and as the launch rose on a wave-crest, I timed my jump onto the pilot-ladder, a jump honed in its execution through a lifetime of practice, my left hand, however, clouting the sailor/coxswain, Geoff, on the head as I did so.

Upon reaching the main deck safely, I realised that something was not quite right. My left hand felt strange, naked almost. When I had caught Geoff on the head as he helped to steady the ladder, I had caught him with my wedding ring, and it had been torn off my finger. I made a note of the position from the G.P.S., for the ring was not on the deck of the launch. For any helpful, and interested scuba-divers reading this account, the ring lies in position: Lat. 53° 23' 30" N. Long. 04° 13' 20" W.

Another story of my being master in command, is the story of the shift from Liverpool to Birkenhead of the "American chartered" vessel the *Sir Thomas Brocklebank*. This vessel was the ex. No.1 Liverpool Pilot Boat, which was being looked at, with a view to being bought by an American firm. The agency was the same as the agency were to be for the *Zamboanga*, and the shift was necessitated by the Americans' wish to have a complete dry-dock survey before completing the sale. In the event the sale did not go through.

The tide was early afternoon, so the sailing from Liverpool through the Langton system was around breakfast-time. We were to lock in on the level at Birkenhead on the day's tide, so it was going to be a long day. Now, we must remember that I had been booked as the pilot, and that was what I was being paid for. So it was with interest that I boarded her in the dock, waiting to find out what crew I would be working with.

The then superintendent of pilotage met me on the bridge, and explained that we were under our own power with Dock Company marine engineers on board and the ropes were to be handled by a shore-gang group of sailors employed by the Dock Company.

"I take it then that you are the captain?" I enquired of the superintendent.

"Certainly not," was the reply, "I have to be back at the office, you are the captain."

The superintendent had not thought it through, for aboard the operational pilot cutters a pilot was employed as captain by the Mersey Docks and Harbour Company, and before that by the Board, and was paid for the responsibility accordingly. But in this case, I was a licensed pilot simply manned off from the working list of pilots to pilot the vessel.

Off to the shore phone in order to telephone the agents to explain the position, and to offer my services as captain, providing that I was to "sign on"[30] in that official capacity. This was agreed to, and I thoroughly enjoyed my day out. Sending a sailor over to the nearby pub when the vessel was safely moored in Alfred Lock to buy a bottle of beer and sandwiches for my lunch solved the lack of rations problem.

Once, the *Sir Thomas Brocklebank* was safely moored in the dry dock chosen for her in the West Float, I left, as we pilots often did, in a cage swung over from a crane operating on the dry-dock side.

"Lucky to get here pilot," commented the foreman in charge of positioning.

---

30 To become legally part of the crew of a ship.

When asked to explain, he pointed to the large mooring rope, which somewhere on the passage had been picked up by the propeller.

"At least I have brought her safely into a dry dock where you will be able to clear it!" was my both measured and philosophical response.

I docked with the then young James Smart, son of my dear friend and retired colleague Roger Smart, as leadsman, into Birkenhead shortly after the twelfth day of Christmas in 2008. This timing is important because of what unfolded in the sequence of what should have been a straightforward docking in a light southerly wind.

I had been allocated one tug to back the vessel, a small tanker, astern up to the East Lewis's Quay in the West Float, (opposite the old dry-docks, in which I had left the *Sir Thomas Brocklebank* those many years ago).

As we manoeuvred the vessel into a position for the swing in Stavanger Bay, I noticed a Christmas tree in the waters of the dock, and then another and another. My concern was for the bow thrust, and I endeavoured to stop the thrust if I sighted a tree anywhere near the bow. I had swung the ship and was proceeding slowly, stern-first, behind a large cargo vessel, which was ahead of me in the line, waiting for the Duke Street Bridge to swing for us to enter the West Float.

The ship was holding well with the tug aft and the bow thrust forward, even though I had to push the whole unit south from time to time in the wait, as the light southerly breeze was affecting us. Then at least one Christmas tree, which must have been below the surface, was sucked into the thruster and it ceased to function.

The "unit," which the tug and the ship composed, drifted north at an angle, across the float towards the *Landfall*, once a club ship moored in Duke's Dock, Liverpool. *Landfall* although now not much more than a floating wreck, has a much more important claim to fame than having been a club-ship, for she is the last remaining landing-craft still afloat of those which hit the Normandy Beaches on D-Day!

I had no wish to be the one who would finally end her career, although for a brief period it looked as if this was going to be the case. We drifted, gaining speed laterally towards the frail shell of the *Landfall* moored on the north side of the float. I conversed with the tug captain aft, explaining that I was going to need a series of short, sharp pulls up on the starboard quarter to straighten the ship. These would be in conjunction with a kick or two on the main engine to brake the lateral speed, as I positioned the vessel alongside *Landfall* as gently as I could.

Somehow, I achieved the main aim, although the skipper of a small fishing craft moored ahead of *Landfall* claimed, a day or so later, that the flair of the bow of our ship had bent his top-mast, slightly. Someone bought him a new one, but no one had reported the contact officially to the bridge.

We were to wait for a tug leaving the large vessel ahead of us so that we were able to reach our berth safely, without too much of a delay.

The Mersey Docks and Harbour Company, the Competent Harbour Authority of the Port, were to send directives to the owners and tenants of the newly converted flats in the old Spiller's Mill, forbidding them to dump their Christmas trees in the Float ever again!

BIRKENHEAD

'But nothing changes,
Save for the seasonal, human leaf-fall
From this world's tree...'

In October 1980, I sat on a large bulk-carrier, large that is for being able to dock into the Birkenhead Dock System, and mused upon my professional life in relation to my predecessors, in particular to the working life of my father, as a pilot before me. I wrote a poem, of which the last three lines are the title of this chapter.

Alfred Locks, the entrance to the Birkenhead System on the Wirral Bank of the Mersey, have always been notorious for catching the newly licensed, and later, the newly authorised pilots unawares.

The locks were built at the mouth of a natural inlet where the River Birkett flowed into the Mersey. The southerly lock, which was excellent for small ships to dock into on the ebb of the tide, was closed about halfway through my career to save on manpower in the manning of the locks. When I first sailed for sea on the T.S.S. *Clan Brodie* the two locks and the Alfred Basin, positioned between the locks and the system, could handle seven "large" ships out, and seven of the same size back in on the same tide. "Large" here refers to the Blue Funnel, Clan Line size of conventional cargo ships of the time.

It was all precision ship handling and exciting stuff! The outward traffic commenced undocking from a "levelling" (or "run down") tide, as running the basin down to river level is called, at around the two hours to high water. The inward ships were already waiting to the south of the locks for their inward passage. I remember that there were often times, which were fraught to say the least, when a late inward bounder, for example, would arrive with six other tug jobs waiting to the south of the locks, and when the outward traffic was already backing out into the river.

The existence of a counter current off the locks, explains why Alfred Locks presented a problem, and explains why the outward ships were to enter the river stern-first. This counter current, runs outward bound off the entrance for most of the tide, strengthening noticeably before three hours to high water.

The old pilot's adage for Alfred Locks was quite simply "Bags of no way!" Meaning: no speed over the ground. The secret for success at Alfred is to bring the vessel being piloted, up abeam of the North Lock, stemming the flood tide to the east of the ebb set. That is to roughly have the head tug and the bow of the ship at right angles to the north side of the lock, and the face of the Seacombe Ferry Landing Stage 'open' on the ship's port bow. When the lock is ready to accept the vessel, she is swung to port, wheeling in to the lock across the ebb set.

In the days of conventional tugs, before the advent of azipods and Voigt-Schneider, and other such versatile power units, which make modern tugs so much more manoeuvrable, the conventional tug's single propeller made life difficult and emphasised the effect of the ebb-set off the locks.

To understand the difficulties off the locks, the knowledge of what happens to a ship manoeuvring with conventional tugs, has always assisted me in my approach to the entrance, no matter the size of the ship.

Following the order being given to the head tug to commence the swing, this tug immediately gave the ship headway. The pushing tug, positioned on the south side, to keep the vessel's port side from coming into contact with the south side of the lock entrance, also gave the vessel headway when power was applied to achieve that tug's objective. Finally, the stern tug, in conventional tug days, was made fast on his towing rope aft, but was lying alongside the ship on the vessel's starboard side, heading in the same direction of the ship. When the turning motion was commenced, this tug would peel off, into the flood tide to assist the turning motion, but in the lever effect produced for the turn, this tug would also be giving the vessel headway.

There was in my early days as a pilot, a copingstone to the north of the lock, painted in fluorescent orange. This marked the spot where the inward bound vessels would be likely to make contact if the pilot got it wrong!

My first inward bounder with three tugs was the iron-ore carrier *Sheaf Wear* in the December of 1973, and is a fine example of what I have explained, and a story of how I very nearly got it wrong on my first "big ship" into Alfred.

We were the only tug-job docking on the tide, and I was in good time, standing off the lock awaiting the docking-signal. Inadvertently, I let the ship, with all three tugs in position, drift too far, both to the west and to the south, so when the signal came for us to make the approach, I was already in the ebb-set. I started the turn, the vessel already creeping north. I remembered the adage, "Bags of no way," and ordered dead slow astern. The head tug wheeled for the lock, the stern-tug began his swing, and being to the south, the pushing-tug was already pushing. We began to move rapidly north. "Slow Astern." The lights of the land were moving astern faster than I would have liked so I ordered "Half Astern", swiftly followed by "Full Astern."

Seconds later the nonchalant voice of the tug-master on the head boat came over the ship's V.H.F. radio: "I would give her a touch astern now if I were you Pilot." "Oh dear!" With disaster looming, I gave the order, which I was to give very few times in my career: "Double-ring Full Astern Captain."[31]

The vessel shuddered and juddered, the wash swirled in the darkness. The bow of the *Sheaf Wear* cleared the north side of the lock by a hair's breadth, the stern lifted and she was in.

When we had moored in the basin, the captain, who was much older than myself, and remarkably smaller than I (as I stand at five foot four inches so that takes some doing) invited me down to his cabin for a beer. We sat and I, trying to sound casual, remarked

---

31 Emergency order meaning: maximum possible power astern.

that I was pleased with the job so far, and, as to the entrance into the lock (knowing that we had not touched) nonchalantly stated that: "If we have touched it was only a brush!"

The captain looked at me sternly and spoke in his Geordie accent: "Pilot, I know that that was your first tug job into Birkenhead, and I also know that we did not touch. You got away with it. I will insist that never again will you be light-hearted about such matters. The last time we "brushed the bow" of this vessel, it cost ten thousand pounds to put the bristles back in!"

I heeded this advice, and never again made light of such serious matters. I took both my error in starting the turn from the wrong position, and my frivolous remark about the brush, as part of the steep learning curve, upon which I was embarked, in my chosen career.

Years later, I was to take a young colleague who had done damage at Alfred, on a small ship with me on a coaster, shifting from Liverpool to Birkenhead. The coaster had a bow thrust, but the exercise, explained to the captain, was not to use it. I got away with that one too!

Shifting the other way on a small coaster, after berthing successfully in Liverpool, I was stopped homeward-bound in my taxi by the Port Police at the dock gate. I was instructed to take a call from a superintendent of police from Birkenhead. I was accused of stealing the ship. I got to the bottom of the matter after explaining that I had followed my orders, and having docked the ship into Birkenhead in the first place, I was satisfied that the orders were followed to the letter. Further, the captain of that ship was the same man who was still in command of the ship, and was pleased to be further progressed on his voyage.

It turned out, (after I had told the superintendent that I believed that he was being very silly) that the captain of another small coaster, who was taking wine in the dock-side pub known as the 'Blazing Stump,' (so nick-named after the landlord who had a wooden leg had fallen asleep too close to his hearth-fire after closing time! The real name of the pub was *The Swan*) had seen us going past. In his alcoholic haze, he had mistaken us for what he thought to be his own ship!

In the December of 1979, I was to pilot a German 'Tribal' tanker, (Tribal because all the ships were named after American Indian tribes) the M.T. *Toltek*, in for East Lewis's Quay in the West Float. The ship was early, and we were able to proceed upriver and anchor safely in the Sloyne Anchorage, south of Woodside Landing Stage.

I was able to negotiate an early locking in, working on the principle mentioned elsewhere of: "Getting as far as you can when you can!" I was actually in trouble from the agent over this because it did not suit them, but it certainly suited the captain and crew for we were to dock in the evening, rather than the early hours of the following morning.

There was still time, however, to go ashore and move my car up to the berth. I was to land in the pilot launch. I noticed a sack on the after deck of the launch, which was wriggling. After inquiring as to what it was, I was to be told that it was a seal pup, which had been recovered from the mud up at Garston by the R.S.P.C.A. The pilot launch had been requested to take the creature back out to sea.

For my part, I reasoned that it might be better to release the pup out on the West Hoyle Bank in the River Dee, where there is a grey seal colony. Consequently, I loaded the sack into my V.W. camper wagon and took it home to West Kirby. Here my young family were able to see it before the then Coxswain of the Hoylake Lifeboat, Harry Jones, was to run it out to the water's edge, close to the bank and the seal colony. I myself returned to dock the ship safely.

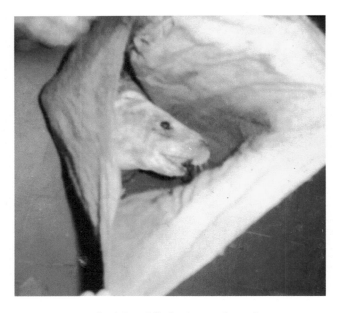

Seal cub hopefully "on his way home!"

Now, as the poem indicates, nothing changes "save for the leaves falling from this World's tree." Things do change, however, and with regards to Alfred Locks, it fell to me to implement change. Throughout my career, outward bound from Alfred on a large vessel was a set manoeuvre. From the safety of the lock, the ship was manoeuvred, stern first, as swiftly as possible out into the tide with both head, and stern tugs fast. As the stern of the ship was caught by the flood tide, the stern tug was to try to hold the stern up to the tide until the head tug was clear of the lock and able to swing the vessel's head to starboard.

There were a few moments always of concern where, in waiting for the stern tug to be let go aft, the main engines had to be stopped so that there was no risk of picking up the loosed tug's wire. Then it was ahead on the ship's main engines, helm hard to starboard to assist the head tug's efforts to bring the ship head to tide so that she may proceed safely to sea. With the advent of the building of the Twelve Quays Terminal, south of the entrance, there was an extra risk of the outward ship being carried down onto the new terminal, which lay to the north of the position of the old Wallasey Cattle Stage site.

Towards the end of July 2001, I was given a consultation for a large vessel for Birkenhead, a bulk carrier, which had a very wide bridge. The consultation was concerning the checking of measurements to ensure that the *Elver* would pass through the bridge-way from the basin safely into the East Float.

I deemed that she would pass safely and docked her on the day tide. I mused upon such a vessel clearing the lock safely outward bound, as some smaller ships had experienced problems, even though the Twelve Quays works were not completed at this time. I worked in my mind on the concept of "rewinding" the film of how I had just docked the vessel safely, and believed that it was possible to exit the lock into the river slowly, by "playing back" the operation in reverse.

I passed this information to the agent at Cory Brothers, and expressed my concern about the vessel's departure if the tried and previously tested operation was to be employed. The agent asked if it was possible for me to pilot the vessel outward bound. I explained that I did not think that it would be possible, but he could try asking the pilot booking office to see if he could be allowed to extend the original consultation.

The following day I had taken the opportunity of some hours between ships to drive down to the Clwyd River to fish for sea trout. I was wading in the middle of the stream when my mobile phone rang. It was the superintendent of pilotage, Captain Steve Knuckey. Steve explained that he had had a request from the agent of the *Elver* for me to take the ship out, would I accept? I was delighted to accept the booking.

On the night's tide of the sailing, I was taken up to the ship by car by the latest pilot about to be made up to first class. He was to have his examination the following day. Chris Booker was at the pilot's office at Birkenhead, Woodside, completing his studying for the next day. Chris, intrigued with the proposed operation actually, unbeknown to me until after we were safely clear, hitched a ride on the stern tug to witness the operation for himself.

Out we crept stern first, "playing the film backwards" until she lay, "Head North," and all stopped in the water. "Before we move ahead Gentlemen," I asked of the three tug captains involved, "I would appreciate a comment on the manoeuvring into the river, in particular, I would like your agreement that we are both safe, and in a position to return into the lock if we so wished?" All three agreed with me on the unqualified success of the undocking, and so the safe "Rewind" at Alfred was born.

As I write, Peel Holdings, the present owners of the Port, have plans to turn the Birkenhead Docks into a new precinct of shopping malls and flat dwellings to bring new life to what is now, because of the increase in the size of ships, almost an obsolete port. The new buds of that tree, however, have yet to burst.

R.F.A. Orange Leaf docking at Alfred North Lock,
Birkenhead with me as pilot
Photo: Peter Langley.

'O CAPTAIN, MY CAPTAIN...'[32]

"The Director of Companies was our captain and our host. We four affectionately watched his back as he stood in the bows looking to seaward. On the whole river there was nothing that looked so nautical. He resembled a pilot, which to a seaman is trust-worthiness personified."[33]

"To be sure Pilot, it is a bit of a windy day!"
It was late morning on the last of the flood tide and I was standing on the bridge of a small Irish coaster lying in Garston's North Dock. The name of the coaster was something like the *Irish Rover* from the song of that name. The captain had the appearance of a leprechaun, (or rather the appearance of what I envisage that a leprechaun looks like) and he was wearing a trilby hat. I believe that the story is the more amusing, if it is read to yourself, or out loud, in a Southern Irish accent, when the captain is speaking.

I was fairly certain that he was the same captain on the same ship, which I had once sailed on a New Year's Eve, many years before. On that occasion the crew were so drunk that they were not able to heave the ropes in from forward or aft after they had managed to cast them off. "Take her Pilot, take her, let the ropes run over the side. I'll pick them up next time that we are here, and I'll have these bastards tomorrow when they are sober. Never argue with a drunken man Pilot!"

The "bit of a windy day" to which he was referring was a full-blown westerly gale, and I had not expected to sail on that tide. We were to shift from Garston to Eastham Locks on the tide and the captain was undaunted.

"To be sure, we will have the shelter of the land, when we are up at Eastham Pilot."

---

32 Poem by Walt Whitman.
33"Heart of Darkness." Conrad. J. p. 3.

He was right of course on that point and somehow we extricated ourselves from Garston and reached the shelter and a safe docking. On the way over the river he recounted an incident from the previous trip, which he wanted me to share with him. The incident took place on another "windy day" (strong, westerly gale force nine) after his previous visit up to Garston.

"It was like this Pilot, we were outward bound from "the Garston" and we were abeam of Point Lynas in the forenoon, and I said to the mate, Mate keep her going Mate. I went below and turned in, returning before the "dog-watch" (the evening six to eight watch).

We were still abeam of Point Lynas Pilot, so I said to the mate, "Mate we might as well be anchored, hard to port and we will anchor in the shelter of Moelfre Bay. And do you know what Pilot, we were anchored!"

Somehow, the motion of the ship had loosened the brake in the swell, and the whole chain on the port anchor had paid out, unnoticed to those on board.

"How was the anchor when you had heaved it back aboard Captain," I asked with interest.

"Polished silver, Pilot, polished silver!"

I, like most, thought that it would be impossible for such a thing to happen on board a ship with efficient and conscientious officers, let alone on one where I myself was the pilot! Years later, however, it did happen to me outward bound in the Crosby and the Queens Channels, on a coaster by the name of the *Hoo Fort*. (The captain was a cockney and came up with the question: "Hoo Fort" ov that one Pilot?)

We had sailed from Birkenhead in the early hours of the day out into strong westerly winds, and heavy weather, so we were making slow progress down the Crosby Channel. A dredger, outward bound, astern of me suddenly "caught up" and sheered off to port, missing us with a profound apology on the V.H.F. radio, for giving us a fright.

Soon after this, another colleague repeated the first episode including the apology. The second time I really was concerned, and somewhat bewildered that two competent navigators could each make such a mistake.

The ship, now in deeper water, moved into the Crosby Bend, making slow but steady progress until, coming out of the bend, and thus into shallower water, she sheered off to port, and I stopped the engines before we hit one of the starboard-hand buoys.

The captain muttered something about steering failure, and dashed off down to the steering flat. I observed the vessel carefully, watching as she came head to wind and steadied, all stopped in the water of the flowing tide. I ordered the sailor who was with me on the bridge to go down aft and fetch the captain. I added: "Tell him to go forward and heave up the port anchor, and this time to make sure that it is well secured in the pipe!"

When we were underway again, I was further amazed when the captain told me that the same thing had happened the month before when the vessel was leaving New Orleans!

As the basic qualification in most ports for pilots now is a class one certificate, with command experience, I believe a comparison to the medical profession is valid. The captain, or master is the equivalent to a G.P and the pilot, with his knowledge of the local conditions of the river and the port is equivalent to a specialist.

My good friend, fishing companion and colleague, Alan Davis, better known as Yak, suggested that there are three kinds of captain for the pilot. There is the old school German coaster captain with his pronouncement: "I take her now pilot," off the lock. Now this man might know his ship better than the pilot, but unless he is a regular (in which case we would expect him to have taken a pilotage exemption certificate) he will not necessarily know the tidal sets and other problems, which are going to affect his ship. The pilot watches closely until, inevitably the moment comes when: "If you do not," (which indicates necessary avoiding action) "there will be damage on..."

This is best illustrated with a story told against himself by a German captain approaching a lock with Duncan Mackenzie, then a very new pilot on the river, and it must be said, a young man armed with the latest jargon.

The approach was not going well and damage was likely when Duncan could be silent no longer and came out with the gem: "Captain, if you don't give her a "tonk" ahead, and a "wang" to port, we are going to "twat" the starboard side."

When translated into good English and the orders carried out, the captain acknowledged that Duncan was absolutely spot on, and damage on the ship was saved.

The second kind of captain in Yak's opinion is possibly the most difficult to cope with.

"I know my ship pilot, you know the tides, and so we will do this together." The pilot then spends a nerve-racking docking watching to see if the captain has given him what he has asked for. Sometimes in this arrangement for examples: "Slow ahead," asked for produces only dead slow on the engines. "Starboard twenty" (degrees of helm) produces starboard ten (only ten degrees of helm). The pilot is then faced with risking asking for more than he actually needs to achieve what he has in mind. The risk being that the captain might give him what he has asked for, which is too much, and which could end in a disaster!

The last and best captain for the pilot Yak reckons is the old Greek on the ancient, heavy bulk-carrier, who if asked "to unbolt the funnel and throw it over the side," would do so, without question.

Language difficulties can be a problem, although English is the international language of the sea. One docking, which started with me being extremely concerned with the situation, ended with me docking the ship in uncontrollable fits of laughter so intense that I believe that I almost died laughing.

The ship was a Sicilian registered tanker, the *Isola Delsa*. The wind during the previous night had been catabatic (that is swinging round to all points of the compass). For several hours the wind blew strongly from the west, then it would swing through one hundred and eighty degrees and blow strongly from the east. My colleague in the V.T.S. that night, John Woodfine, was uncertain where to send the pilot for the ship.

If he sent him to the Bar Light Vessel Station, it could be impossible to board the ship in time for the day tide if the wind was from the west. If he sent the pilot to Point Lynas the same could happen there if the wind swung to the east.

John wisely hedged his bets and ordered the ship to anchor at Point Lynas upon his arrival there as he was passing, the ship having come from the south. John would make his final decision later. Unfortunately, as I was soon to learn, this was the first sign of the fact that the captain's understanding of the English language left a lot to be desired, for he ignored the order and proceeded into the Bar Light Vessel.

Upon his arrival there, he was turned back to Point Lynas. This entailed some seventy miles of extra passage time and the extra fuel burned would have been both expensive and unnecessary. This, I was to find out, eventually, was the cause of the captain's anger, for angry he was.

I, blissfully unaware of this drama, travelled with Alan Lindfield down to Point Lynas by taxi, as ordered. We were there in time to enjoy toasted bacon and egg sandwiches, which had been left for us by Monie, a valued member of the staff at Lynas hostel.

The sun was shining, the wind was blowing strongly from the west, but we had good shelter down in Moelfre Bay, and all was well with the world. That was, until I reached the bridge. There I found a very angry man. I could not, however, understand a word he was saying, but in screaming at me in an unintelligible language, he did give the impression that if I was not diplomatic in handling the situation "heads were going to roll."

I was the representative of the Port. This so well put in the anonymous six liner:

The Pilot

"The first to say good morrow,
The last to say goodbye,
Whatever port they hail from,
Whatever flag they fly,
He leaves them in the offing,
Their distant coasts to win,
He meets them on the high-road
And brings them safely in."
Anon.

I became both concerned and extremely serious in my approach. The important matter in my mind was to take command.

"Captain steer 075 degrees and give full speed ahead on the ship's engines." This stopped the unintelligible tirade, momentarily, and I was able to add: "Captain, calm down, I am going to hang my coat in the chart room. When I return to the bridge we will discuss your grievance."

Hanging up my coat, I took several deep breaths before returning to the bridge: "Now Captain, please, slowly, tell me what has caused you to be so angry."

Over some twenty minutes or so I gleaned with difficulty that the facts of the case were that he had not understood the order to anchor at Point Lynas, for the wind had been from the east when he had arrived there. The resulting extra steaming time and the cost of the fuel were not acceptable to him.

I then, slowly and laboriously endeavoured to explain to him on the chart the problem, which I had now understood that John Woodfine had been faced with. Pointing at the chart with its open sea and landmasses, whilst indicating the different wind directions were to no avail. The captain stared at me blankly. "Right, time for some art-work," I decided, and chose a sheet of paper, (which

I still have) and a pencil. I drew the Bar Light vessel on the right hand side of the paper, and Lynas Point on the left. The captain watched intently. I then drew on the two wind directions and the state of the sea at each location depending on the direction of the wind. This was accompanied, depending on where I was pointing to with: "No good Captain," or: "Now good Captain."

Time was passing, and I, frustrated, was running out of ideas, when I realised that he had understood something, for he was staring ahead. I looked through the bridge window following his disbelieving stare to observe the wind was now again blowing at gale-force from the east!

In whatever language, it could be argued that I had been speaking a load of the proverbial. I was mortified until, moments later a most unusually dressed character presented himself in the chart room doorway. The nearest character whom I can liken his appearance to, is the extrovert painter Salvador Dali. He had dirty, long, thin, streaky, black hair and a Dali moustache. He was dressed in a filthy, threadbare evening suit, dirty white evening shirt, complete with black bow tie. Over his right arm was a folded, heavily food-stained tea towel.

As I took all this in, the character, a caricature from a play, who I realised must be the chief steward, addressed me, his eyes lighting up as he asked me the simple, and unexpected question (it was nine o'clock on a Sunday morning): "Mister Pilot, You wanna pizza?" For some reason, this struck me as so funny following a time of concern, that after having declined politely the offer of the pizza, I started to laugh. I could not stop laughing for hours. I entered the QE II Lock at Eastham, hanging over the bridge wing with my sides aching and tears flowing down my cheeks.

On the same tide, ahead of us, the obsolete tug *Nelson* was to sink, off the Garston Bar whilst being towed upriver to be scrapped. This was a sad end for a magnificent tugboat with such an iconic name.

I shifted an Everard tanker from Birkenhead to Liverpool with another Cockney captain on board. He was a young man and he was charming. That kind of passage, if locking out, rather than levelling at Birkenhead, would take three to four hours, during which period there is time for a lot of conversation. On this occasion, I could only say that the young captain was a pleasure to be with. He indicated that we should meet again soon as he was only just starting his tour of duty.

A few weeks later, I was manned on the same ship and was surprised to discover our old Everard friend, Captain 'Poxy' Donnel in command. Poxy because for many years everything was poxy: A poxy time of night, a poxy lock, and a poxy whatever he was not pleased with! Only for a short time when he was given command of a "magic" seventeen knot ship did everything become "magic." All was to return to normal, however, after a "magical" summer's night docking at Langton Lock, where the pilot's "magic" spin went wrong, and only a "magic" whisker averted a poxy disaster!

I inquired as to where the captain, whom I had met on the previous occasion, was.

"Ah now Pilot, there lies a tale!" (Another tale where the Southern Irish accent is recommended!)

"He fell out with Dame Ethel (Dame Ethel Everard) Pilot."

"Oh and how was that Captain, he seemed such a charming man?"

"He was indeed Pilot, he was indeed, but he chose to take "the" wife on a trip from the Thames over to the continent for a weekend, Pilot, and Dame Ethel found out."

"Dismissal seems a bit harsh for such an infringement Captain, don't you think?"

"I would Pilot, I would, except that it wasn't his wife!"

The husband had found out and rung Dame Ethel herself at Green Hythe to complain, and Dame Ethel had reacted accordingly.

Ingenuity is often the secret behind successful piloting, which can be further illustrated more than it has been so far in the pages of this book by the simple story of the use of someone else's bow-thrust to manoeuvre my own charge.

I was ordered to tie up, second off to a Stolt tanker, which had an operational bow-thrust, whilst I was on board a coaster not fitted with a bow thrust. We tied up, as ordered, in Alfred Basin to await the run-down of the tide before we were to be able to sail.

When the basin was level with the river, because the southerly wind had strengthened to near gale force, I found that my ship was pinned on the side of the Stolt tanker. With the overhanging accommodation on both ships, an attempt to leave at an angle would have meant serious damage to both ships. I called my colleague on the other vessel and requested that he operate his bow-thrust to port when I requested him to do so. The colleague agreed, and with our helm hard to port, our engines dead slow ahead, together with the Stolt tanker's thrust to port, the ship was able to sail safely, being "blown" clear of the other ship by her own bow thrust's wash up against the wind. We were to sail unscathed.

Another colleague, Jim Pauling, when faced with a language problem regarding, which way he wanted the captain to operate the bow-thrust, came up with an ingenious and foolproof way to ensure that there were going to be no misunderstandings.

"Captain, when I want the bow to go to starboard. I will order "bubbles to port," and when I want the bow to go to port, I will order, "bubbles to starboard!" When I want the bow to stay steady, I will order, "stop the bubbles." It worked and the vessel was to dock without problems but with lots of bubbles from the thrust! (I had requested "bubbles to starboard" in effect from the Stolt boat in the previous story!)

There are times when a ship will "follow the helm" when the engines are put astern. That is on a ship whose propeller is turning to the right when going ahead, when going astern the left-handed turning effect of transverse-thrust will pull the stern to port and the head will go to starboard. The opposite should be the effect with a left-handed turning ahead propeller. This is not always the case, as is best illustrated by the Greek captain who, when asked to tell me what happened when his engines were put astern, replied:

"Mr. Pilot, when my ship's engines go astern, my ship always turns to starboard."

In the lock, I went astern and the ship's head went to port. I looked questioningly at the captain. He shrugged his shoulders and replied:

Mr. Pilot, she is like a woman, sometime she goes to port!"

This turning motion can depend on many variables beyond the pilot's control. Wind possibly on the accommodation, current in a tideway, the trim of the vessel, the actual power of the engine movement given, and so on. All that can be done is to see what happens on the occasion, and correct the effect by trying something else if it is not the one, which you had hoped for.

Once, when docking with our good friend, Captain Robin Ray, he with the deep voice, on-board the *Robert M*, we were just short of the small lock entrance at Eastham on the ebb of the tide, when the outer west gate failed and started to close on us. "What now?" was the question, and there seemed only one answer to me initially, and that was to go astern on the engines with enough power to arrest the headway and hopefully avoid the starboard sheer. I ordered "Half-Astern," and the vessel not only brought up, but also backed off in a totally unexpected straight line to a safe position to await developments. When Robin asked me how I had managed to accomplish this manoeuvre, I answered honestly, with one word: "Luck!"

Captains are not always as pleasant as Robin undoubtedly was. During my career I believe that I had serious disagreements with captains on only very few occasions. I always believed that I was a guest on board the ship, and that it was for me to establish the level, or stage on which we as actors in our profession could produce a successful play.

One near disaster came about when I disagreed with the captain on a Weston 'Biscuit' boat, the *Gretchen Weston*. The owner of Weston Biscuits had a large number of mainly female grandchildren, and had determined that each would have a coaster of the fleet named after her. The fleet was engaged in the carriage of bulk grain destined for biscuit making.

It was necessary for us to anchor the vessel in the 'Middle-Deep' anchorage off the Eastham Channel Bar to await the tide into the Manchester Ship Canal. "Come down and join us for the evening meal Pilot," was the kind invitation. I accepted and added that the mate must keep a close watch on the anchor bearings, and that ship's engines must be left running for it was the flood of a big spring tide.

"This is my ship, I give the orders here," was the sadly ignorant reply.

We ate the meal and then I counted the small crew who were watching the television in the mess-room. They were all there. The reply to the question as to who was on the bridge was simply the repeat of "This is my ship."

I excused myself and said that I would go back onto the bridge and read my book. Within ten minutes, I felt the slight shudder beneath my feet, which indicated that the anchor was failing to hold and that we were beginning to drag. Astern of us was a dredger. "Captain we are dragging anchor,[34] get yourself back on the bridge, and order the chief engineer to start the engines." I shouted this desperate order down to the mess-room.

The engines were fired up in the nick of time with our stern close to the dredger's anchor chain. We heaved up our own anchor and remained under-way until we finally docked. Apart from orders concerned with the safe docking of the ship, we never spoke again.

---

34 The term applies when an anchor has lost its holding power and the ship is in effect, drifting with the current.

On another occasion, on board a Dutch coaster, sailing from Huskisson dock in the North Liverpool System, I was to find the wind strength increasing from virtually flat calm to a storm, which had been forecast but for twelve hours later.

I reached the Langton Lock, having pulled out all the stops and was pleased with myself for having done so. The captain, against my advice, opted to sail the ship expressing his opinion that I had done the difficult bit!

We made it to just west of the Bar Light Vessel, where, my advice to "tack downwind" and inshore for shelter from the westerly wind, not having been taken by the captain, the ebb tide turned and the flood held us. At times we were going backwards. I sat miserably on the bridge chair, clutching my brief case, wondering if a helicopter or a lifeboat managed to reach us, would I be allowed to take my briefcase with me when rescued.

The tide turned, and the wind abated sufficiently, hours later for us to finally make Point Lynas and a successful disembarkation. The captain did apologise on that occasion, but I was only too pleased that I lived to tell the tale.

A humorous event, and with only a slight splintering of wood on Alfred lock gates, fortunately only classified as light damage, came after running for a day tide on board an admiralty survey vessel, H.M.S. *Fox*, in June 1985. I chose to come in on the starboard helm against the ebb-set and achieved success at the entry, as we aimed between the pier-heads of the lock. Time to slow down, but no, as so often with the captain, "who knows his ship," "I'll take her now Pilot," came the order, and it was from a naval commander who did not need to take a pilot Bye-Law.

"Right Captain, but do start to take the way off her, we are running out of space."

I was aware of the speed and also of another, what turned out to be an influencing, factor. This was a white Triumph Spitfire sports car on the north side of the lock. Leaning against the car was a young couple, watching with interest our both late and swift arrival.

"Both engines full speed astern now Captain!" I advised with the utmost concern in my voice. This order was followed, but the effect required was not quite in time. The ship's bow just caught and slightly splintered the wood of the gate.

Why, was my question, which was answered by a simple and honest answer. This response was not an excuse but an explanation. The young man was the first lieutenant of the vessel and the young lady was his fiancée. "I was trying to impress Pilot." This received the reply "And you certainly did Captain!"

This incident also reminds me of an occasion when dining out at a neighbour's house, my good friend, the late Geoff Sample, then naval liaison officer for the North West of England. Another of the guests at table was the commander of a nuclear powered submarine visiting Liverpool. The latter was to make a comment beginning with: "The trouble with pilots, bless them…!" I gritted my teeth and was not drawn.

These stories bring me to the unresolved "grey-area" question as to who is in command of the ship. When I went away to sea as a cadet on the bridge of a Clan Boat, the pilot boarded and into the bridge order book went the statement: "Vessel proceeding to master's orders and pilot's advice." This indicated that the final decision, and therefore any possible blame, lay with the master.

The Law, however, has classified pilots in the United Kingdom, as "Men of Straw." That, as I have always understood it, is that the damages likely to be sustained on a ship would be at too great a cost for the individual to bear, and therefore this cost to the individual was limited, and covered in full by insurance. Hence the nautical expression: "A1 at Lloyds." Further, Liverpool Pilots, under the 1913 Act, as my father pointed out, were, 'Bye-Law' (a serious matter this) in command of the manoeuvring of the vessel once he had boarded, and presented himself to the captain on the bridge.

Sadly, the 1988 Pilotage Act did not clarify this point as the earlier Act had done, and so the controversy rumbles on. In a recent nautical journal, I have read further discussions, which arise from, and deal with, matters resulting from recent accidents such as the *Cosco Busan* in San Francisco Harbour in 2007. This large vessel, under pilot's command, hit one of the San Francisco bridges in dense fog. Jail sentences for pilots are becoming more likely as the courts change their opinions. I, however, throughout my forty-one years as a pilot, always believed that I would, and should be to blame if I did make an error of judgement.

I have always reverted to the 1913 Pilotage Act in my mind, even when it was replaced. This is of course in keeping with the French Code de l'Environment, which considers, rightly so in my opinion, that the pilot has the actual control of the navigation of the ship and is therefore liable to blame. This logic would imply that the pilot be subject to criminal sanctions if the incident has been caused by the pilot's error of judgement. Surely here, as in all walks of life, the individual must be responsible for his actions?

Now retired, I may simply have my opinion, and finish this musing with the story of the sailing of one of 'Macbrayne's Steamers' the old *Claymore*. She was in fact a motor ship, but Macbraynes still spring to mind as a "steam-ship" company.

I was at the end of my tour of duty one summer, I had been told that I was not required for another vessel and that I was on leave. That was as it stood when I reported in from the bridge of my last ship, an inward bound A.C.L. container ship. I arrived home and within a few minutes the telephone rang. It was the office. "Sorry, got it wrong John." Another "Hurry up" job had come on. The vessel could just make the tide out of Birkenhead if the pilot was able to reach her "at once." "Best Endeavours" was what we called such requests, and I was on my way.

Arriving at Vittoria Dock some twenty minutes later, I boarded the vessel, which was lying bows west, so she needed to be swung one hundred and eighty degrees before proceeding outward-bound for the lock. I ran up to the steps to the bridge-deck and sighted a figure, in uniform with four stripes. He was on the mobile telephone, and I assumed that he was the captain. I waved and indicated that I would head for the V.H.F. to arrange the sailing with the lockmaster. "Take your time Captain," I called out, "I'll get things moving." The figure acknowledged my words with a wave of his hand.

I found my way into the wheelhouse, however blocked by a large figure of a man dressed in tweed plus fours. "I am the captain, not him Pilot." The words were pronounced in a strong Scottish accent and seemed to fit the bill of what I had expected of a captain on a Macbrayne's of the Highlands ferry.

"Take no notice of them Pilot, for I am the captain," came from a third figure who was standing behind the chart table. The man on the wing of the bridge, finished his call, and shouted, "No Pilot, I am the captain." I realised that all three were serious and watched and listened as a dreadful clamour erupted when the argument broke out between them. Now, as always I worked on the bottom line that I had a job to do, and that the ship had to sail and we were desperately short of time.

"Stop, stop, stop," I shouted, one of you tell me what the problem is and maybe I can sort it out for you." The Scot explained in temper that he was the Macbrayne's master and that it was "his ship." The character on the wing of the bridge was a master from the Faroe Islands who were taking the ship over on charter. The third character was a master from the Isle of Man Steam-packet Company who was handling the charter handover.

I realised that this was one big legal mess, in which I wished to play no part or even attempt to judge, but as both a responsible and an experienced pilot, I did have an answer. "Right Gentlemen, we have somewhat of a mess here, but I have a suggestion, for if we do not sail soon, we will miss the tide, and no one is going to be pleased with any of us if that happens, so let us all agree, whilst I am on board that I will be the captain!" With muttering all round, they all reluctantly agreed in the interests of the ship.

Having "taken command" I now had to organise my officers. I ordered the Macbrayne's man to stay on the bridge with me as I reasoned he knew the ship best of all of us. I ordered the Isle of Man Steam-Packet man to go on the after deck because we had to pick up some oil drums on the stern ramp, and he would not be wanting any delays. I ordered the Faroese master in the uniform to take the wheel. Here I reasoned that from that position he would learn the most about the command, which was about to be his on the charter.

They are wonderful, handy little ships to manoeuvre and it was fun to take her at speed to the lock in time to catch the tide. Once in the river, and heading north, with all three captains on the bridge with me, I took their compliments for having resolved the situation.

Then I said: "Gentlemen, as I see it we are safely away, but we still have one major problem." They questioned me with great concern as to what the problem was now that we were on our way. They then all agreed that we had, not one, but four captains on the bridge. So my question, with all these high-ranking commanders standing together was "Who the hell is going to make the tea?"

THE 'UNOFFICIAL LEADSMAN'

I was Chairman of the Liverpool Pilots when the first non-pilot apprentice pilot was taken "on board." Alastair Singleton was the man and he has become a very good friend over the years. Whilst returning on the launch in the early hours, soon after he had become an authorised pilot, Alastair, myself and another pilot were "swinging the lamp."[35]

When I arrived home, I realised that Alastair knew nothing of the background to some of the stories, which we had been telling. I mused on the fact that we still had the old pilot cutter: *Edmund Gardener*, in the Canning Dry Dock, as part of the Maritime Museum. I had been partially responsible for her being there.

The late Richard Foster was then the Director of Liverpool Museums, and a friend. The next day I was to call Richard, and ask permission to take Alastair on what has become known as 'The Unofficial Leadsman.' I requested unhindered access to the boat, a request, which was granted. I was part of a "living history," and Richard saw the point of me sharing my knowledge of history with the new recruit.

I was to take Alastair on board the *Edmund Gardener*, starting "down aft" in the Boathand's accommodation, and conduct him through a thorough tour of the boat. The next recruit requested that he came with me after he was authorised, and so the Unofficial Leadsman was born. I have taken every single new man to date on this: 'Leadsman into all our Histories.'

I took a photograph of each one as a memento, and overleaf is one, which one of them took of me.

One evening, whilst dining with younger colleagues in the Isle of Man, (all our inward ships had gone back a tide because of bad weather) they were all asking me what I was going to do in my new life of retirement. I answered with a great many hopes, which

---

35 A term used when tales are being told amongst seafarers.

I had for the future, including the writing of this book. I then turned the tables and asked them what they intended to do to safeguard the standing of a Liverpool Pilot. The following poem was the result of the conversation, and was penned the following day on the bridge of my inward bound Independent Container Line ship; somewhere out in the middle of the Irish Sea:

Changing the Watch

A pilot may not fight the tide.
Better were it the case
He respect both it
And the mysterious ways
The water moves, relentlessly.

A pilot may, however,
Fight for his right
To sail on that tide.
His struggle
Is against accountants,
Whose financial aim
Is to rule the waves.

'Without the sap rising,
The old tree withers and dies.'
This is your future,
But you have no right
To spoil futures
For those who follow,
And for those who follow,
Not yet born,
And for those who follow them.

Set a course,
Which will clear the shallows,
Not yet visible
In other lifetimes.

218

THE JEWEL IN THE CROWN

Myself piloting the inward bound A.C.L., about to commence: 'The Waltz'

I had, following my father's beliefs before me, not believed in appropriation. That is individual pilots being "selected," "chosen," "appointed," however attached to an individual company. My father believed that he was a 'First-Class Pilot' in the Port of Liverpool, and that therefore he was licensed to pilot any type or size of ship within his district. He also was the advocate correctly of the sound advice that all ships need looking after. The small vessel could sink the large vessel.

Companies of course were prepared to pay extra monies for a known pilot who would be allocated to their ships. For most of my early years in the Service the appointments were known to be not necessarily fair, for some appointments were made along one line or another of the 'Old Boy Network.'

It was a complicated business, and it was only with the threat of the Pilotage Act, implemented in September 1988, that I began to consider the simple fact that, if I were to be appropriated, I may be kept on if jobs were to be lost as a result of the Act.

In the summer of 1985 I stood on the bridge of a Gracechurch charter ship in Garston North Dock, the *Sabine D*. She was a German vessel with a charming captain whom I met when I arrived on the bridge. Also on the bridge was an equally charming, softly spoken Irishman, Peter Dobbs, who turned out to be the then managing director of the Gracechurch Line.

The managing director was busy on his mobile telephone. It turned out that he was dealing with "late-arrival" containers. "Just two more now Captain… we have found another one. Four more at the gate on lorries…" and so on. I watched the German captain as he was transformed from a calm, polite gentleman into a very anxious and unhappy person. The wind was strong westerly, and although feasible conditions to operate in for the undocking, we were running out of time for the tide.

I had always considered it part of my duty as a pilot to look after the welfare of the captains of my ships if it was at all possible. Having not interfered until it was necessary, I finally addressed the managing director, interrupting him on yet another of his phone calls:

"Excuse the interruption," I began: "but I can stand here no longer without becoming involved. It is going to take me between forty-five minutes and one hour to pilot this ship safely from the berth to the lock in these weather conditions. I have watched the captain of the ship become increasingly uneasy as a result of these late acceptances of containers, so I have an ultimatum as we are running out of time. I give you five more minutes to leave the ship, or I leave. The ship will then miss the tide, and I will not return until one and a half hours before high water on tomorrow morning's tide." We sailed!

Soon after I had a phone call from the managing director of Gracechurch to thank me for my professionalism, and with the request that I became the Gracechurch appropriated pilot.

I was both flattered and interested because of the political situation. I replied in that vein adding that there were two important issues, which needed to be brought to Peter Dobb's attention. One was that under the old rule, I would not be eligible for appropriation until the August of that year, and the other was that I wished to speak to my father about this important step, which was one, which he had not taken.

Peter accepted the delayed start, and my father, now on his deathbed, said, without hesitation: "Take the job son."

Having "sold myself to the devil" of appropriation, I embarked upon my new role with enthusiasm. I saw that, with me being so young, Gracechurch might well be a steppingstone to bigger things. I was wrong. With the change of status brought about by the Act, my own colleagues initially caught me in the system when the service went into the employ of the Mersey Docks and Harbour Company as the 'Competent Harbour Authority.'

It was to be many years later before I broke the bonds, which were imposed on me, and thanks to many factors including the kindness of my good friend, and then my Vice-Chairman of the Liverpool Pilots, David Cockram, I was to be appointed to the appropriations of "big ship" appropriations, which David had collected. (By this time most pilots were appropriated to at least six companies in the new era.) David's appropriations, were Backhouse Blore, (grain-ships) E.M.R., (European Metal Recycling, scrap ships, mostly Panamax bulkers) Northwest Trading, (tankers and bulk-carriers) and the best appropriation on the river, in my opinion, Atlantic Container Lines, (Container/Ro Ro.) which has been the company described as 'The Jewel in Liverpool's Crown.'

I added these to the two, which I already held, both container companies; Gracechurch, (later to become Borchard Lines) and I.C.L. (International Container Lines). These new appointments meant that my last decade as a pilot were to be amongst the happiest and most demanding of my career.

I was fortunate to still be a pilot at all for, with a great many contributory factors including the frustration of being employed, I had drunk more than was good for my health over a period of years. I was in short fortunate to be given what was in effect a final, final, final warning. As a result of the efforts of my colleagues, pilot's representatives of the time and Len Schofield, a councellor, I was to experience one of the two miracles of my working life. After a serious battle, and with much help and support from Bernie Dabner, David Cockram and Gill in particular, I was able to abstain from alcohol all together.

I believe in the former years, which were undoubtedly to change after the *Exxon Valdez* disaster in Canada, that alcohol was the cause of an industrial disease amongst seafarers. Availability was the reason for the cause of many early deaths, which were alcohol related.

I have an amusing story to tell with regard to what I believe constituted my own start down the slippery slope to destruction, from which I was thankfully rescued. I had battled my way through a storm as a second-class pilot from Point Lynas to West Langton Dock. I was pilot of a second-class, Greek cargo ship with the bridge amidships. Having made two tugboats fast in the river, I finally ended an all night out passage; by having fought the vessel against the elements to a safe berth around 0600 hrs. I was exhausted and was ready only for my own bed.

"Mr. Pilot, zat was a splendid job, you must come to my cabin and av a drink."

As always, I did not wish to offend the captain, and with my Gemini guile, I thought that I had come up with a polite way to refuse the unwanted offer and go straight home to bed.

"Captain, we have a saying in the Royal Navy that we never have a drink until the sun is over the yardarm, so I must refuse your kind offer."

The Greek captain looked at me aghast before producing the argument, which was I believe, contributory in leading to my near downfall:

"Mr. Pilot, we are seafarers, ze sun is over the yardarm somewhere in the world, and you WILL av a drink!"

The second miracle was experienced, when, after an accident on the riverbank of the Dee at Rhagatt Hall, fishing for salmon, I was to have both hips replaced. Adam Hoad-Reddick, son of my former Professor of German, was the orthopaedic surgeon with the magical touch. I returned to full operations for the best part of the final year of my career, to pilot over a further one hundred and seventy ships. This bringing my total of vessels piloted during my career to around six thousand.

Practice on a pilot ladder hung on my back garden wall!

I lay in intensive care as a flight took off from Liverpool to the Isle of Man with two of my colleagues on board. The younger one who had "googled" hip replacements that morning before the flight, declared to the pilot who had been our best man at the wedding, Bob Swift, that I was finished. Bob simply smiled and retorted that the younger man did not know John Curry!

I returned, twelve weeks later to full duties as Adam had predicted. My first ship was as a volunteer "leave man" aboard the Tall Ships. Gary Woodall, the then senior representative, had believed in me, and kept the draw for these vessels out of the hat until my return was confirmed. I am indebted to Gary for his support during this time and for his unswerving belief in his colleague. The poem: 'Changing the Watch,' is dedicated to him.

I was fortunate to win one of the five 'A' class vessels, a three-masted barquentine; the Norwegian registered *Stadtsrad Lehmkuhl*. As we sailed south from Langton Lock to join the assembled fleet in the Middle Deep off Bromborough, both my eyes and heart were full, so proud was I to be back on the river, which means so much to me, which I know so well, and on which I had spent my entire working life.

Stadtsrad Lehmkuhl

The last decade of my career was to prove to be the most enjoyable for me. I have explained how I was caught by the system, and how David Cockram had helped me to beat it! I have also explained how I had successfully beaten the dangers of alcohol. I had enjoyed my career, including my ability to be the 'Fighting Chairman' in the battle against the Dock Company, and all the other aspects of my life, which included my family and my studies, but until the last decade of my career, consistently handling big ships had eluded me. Yes, I had handled a great many, and I had enjoyed and learned so much from my association with Gracechurch, but constantly to be manned on large vessels was something that appropriation made inconsistent for those who were not "big ship" appropriated pilots.

With Gracechurch, at first there was my good friend, the agent Dave Davies. When Dave was to leave Gracechurch, he was to be replaced by Clive Schofield, who was to work so well with both myself and with the other Gracechurch pilots. I achieved manoeuvres with these handy ships, which I had never before believed possible, and it was fun! Dark and stormy nights did have their moments, but overall, the lasting memory is of the fun combined with an immense job satisfaction, which came from either leaving the ship safely moored on her berth, or watching her from the launch, disappearing over the horizon safely on her way to her next port.

One prestigious manning, which in effect was a "pinch job," (that is one, which should have been manned with another appropriated pilot, from a newly appointed pod of pilots) was the piloting of the *Seven Seas Voyager*. She was the passenger cruise liner booked to "open" the new Liverpool Passenger Terminal. The old problem of who would be tasked with, what, certainly I believed were prestigious acts of piloting, such as the *Q.E.2*, the Royal Yacht *Britannia*, and other such rare visitors, has never been satisfactorily resolved by the service. The senior man of my early days was, at one time, to be replaced by the Chairman, only to be replaced by the senior man again in latter years as the pilot chosen for high profile jobs.

Then the new era of pilots decided on, what initially seemed fair, and what was the establishment of a named pod of pilots to cover the new landing stage's visitors. Not being appointed to that pod, I was to be excluded from a part of the river for, which, as I have always maintained, I held a first-class licence. That was the same argument, which my father had used with regard to any appropriation: he was licensed for all ships to all parts of the district.

The members of the new pod were sent to a simulator course at the John Moores' simulator at Lairdside, Birkenhead. I had been to the old landing stages many times and the river had not changed that much in that area for an experienced man.

Then there came a stroke of luck for me. The old system of manning the senior man had not been altered in writing at the office, and the booking clerk, (bless him) rang me in my leave to man me on the Monday of my return to work. I accepted the vessel, which in piloting is sacrosanct. It was now "my ship." Ten minutes later the clerk rang again to give me the second one on to the stages, the morning after mine departed. With this one, I reasoned that the next senior man on the list should have a turn and passed the vessel on to my good friend Barry Littler.

Sadly, it was the day of Muriel Jones, my mother-in-law's funeral, which turned out to be a blessing in disguise for the manning. Whilst I was at the wake, my mobile rang. It was a call from one of the representatives who was also a member of the new pod.

I was able to say that before he was about to upset me with any matter, I was at the funeral of a loved one. The representative backed off and it was my honour to "open the new landing stage." An honour, which I was to fulfil successfully without simulation!

The vessel was arriving from Dublin, so my advice to the agent of the vessel was to send me to Dublin to avoid any risk of delays with the north westerly winds forecast and the fact that the Lynas Jetty was inoperable, bringing restrictions to the boarding at Point

Lynas. This was agreed to, as it was such a prestigious event for both the Port of Liverpool and the Liverpool City Council whose joint venture the terminal was and it was appreciated that I was eliminating risks, so far as it was possible, of any problems, which we may have encountered.

I arrived on board on the Sunday afternoon and was welcomed on the bridge by the chief officer to await the captain. Dag Dvergastein, the master of the vessel, arrived on the bridge. He was an ex-Oslo pilot, and was not initially enamoured to see me. "I should pick you up at the Bar Pilot Station," was his opening, and not friendly gambit. I explained about the possible problems of weather restrictions and moved on to the fact that I had ordered two tugboats, searching for the "level," on which we would work.

"This ship does not need tugs," was the reply. "Well Captain," I countered, "With the tide being in excess of nine metres, and with the current flowing in excess of four and a half knots, and a swing of one hundred and eighty degrees in the narrowest point of the river…" "Nine metres and a swing, we will need three tugs…" Got him!

"Right Captain, may I put my bag down and possibly a seat and a cup of tea would be more than welcome, whilst we sit and discuss the safe passage-plan, which I have made out for this auspicious opening of the new river-berth in the River Mersey?"

Dag and I were to get on with each other famously. He ordered the state cabin next to his own to be prepared for me. It was a straightforward job for me in the event, but I did pride myself on the fact that the ship "kissed" the stage, spot on the marks, on the minute of our expected arrival time, a fact, which was noted by the media. The riverbanks were thronged with crowds of people to witness the event in the morning sunshine. The two tug boats escorted us upriver from New Brighton with fire-hoses playing, and the huge white cruise liner, two hundred and fifty metres long, made a fine sight as she gently made her way into the Mersey. We sailed on the flood of the evening tide of the same day. History had been made and had been well documented.

Seven Seas Voyager

As appropriation did exist, and I had been unable to bring about its demise, the appointment to the "big ship" companies was to bring more pleasure. I am able to say, for whatever the reasons were, that I saved the best 'til the last. I was required to make six leadsmans with the other four A.C.L. pilots, before David retired and I took his place. I made three with David and one with each of the other three. This experience proved to me, what I had already known with regard to ship handling, and that is that there are more ways than one to skin the proverbial cat!

Each of my colleagues piloted the vessels with their own particular expertise, and I was suitably impressed. The ships were designed to be the largest, which would fit safely into the Gladstone Lock. They were designed, as I understand it, by a female designer, assisted by her husband. Both of them worked in the Swedish University System. The G3's, as they were classified, are certainly the finest ships, which I ever handled.

"Handled" being the operative verb. The Swedish masters of these five vessels, running a "conveyor-belt" of trade from the continent, via Liverpool to the United States and back during a five week cruise, all became my friends. They were more than capable of handling their commands, but when it came to Liverpool, it was the accepted procedure, both inward bound, and outward bound, that the pilot would take command of both the navigation and of the ship handling of the vessel both from, and to the Bar Light Vessel. I repeat, the secret of success with handling any ship, no matter what the size, but a secret, which is even more significant on a big ship, is to be in the right place at the right time, going at the right speed. Forward planning is all. However, if things go wrong, and they do sometimes, horribly, the good pilot is the pilot who can make things right again.

Two A.C.Ls moving on the same tide made life really exciting. If they were to pass in the dock system, the move, which I came to refer to as the 'A.C.L. Waltz.' had been perfected. The outward bounder left the berth and hung to the west of Seaforth Dock, whilst the inward bounder came through, swung bow west, and backed up to the berth. The outward bounder moved for the Seaforth Cut as soon as the way was clear. On many occasions the job was done so smoothly, that neither vessel came to a stop, hence the gliding movement of the waterborne 'Waltz.'

My first "solo" A.C.L. was the *Atlantic Cartier*, which for one reason or another arrived an hour late on her E.T.A. I knew that "the Port" would be watching me, so I had to pull out all the stops, and with a little good fortune I crossed the outer sill of the lock right on time one fine March morning. When I dismissed the tugs on the berth, my voice was to crack with the emotion, which welled up within me as I thanked Mick McCartney, skipper of the tug *Waterloo*, for his assistance on the day.

I revelled in this new responsibility, as I applied all the knowledge hitherto gained from other vessels to those of A.C.L. There were to be many straightforward passages and many which needed careful planning and execution in adverse conditions, which included both strong winds and fog.

There were a number of occasions when no tugs were to arrive on time due to a general lack of availability of tugs in latter years, and

The A.C.L. Waltz
Photo: Philip M. Parker

I was able to dock or undock without them, weather permitting, because of the power and manoeuvrability of these fine ships. There is one comparison, which I have often been pleased to make, and that is that the pilot on an A.C.L. drives them with a two thousand H.P. bow thrust forward, a two thousand five hundred H.P. stern thrust aft, the main engine up to seventeen knots, and the tiller, all in his sole control on the instrument panel, just as a driver would drive a motor car. I always made the taxi drivers smile when I then added: "It is not that different from driving a motor car, except that there are two main additional complications: One is that the road is moving and two: you have no brakes!"

These superb vessels were, so far as possible, booked in to dock in the lock, based on the time which they could cross the shallows in the Formby Strait. This was worked out taking into account the draft of the inward bound ship and then by adding two feet to the draft for under keel clearance. I was always happy if I had "two feet" under my ship, providing that she was travelling at a slow speed over the ground. Point six of a metre never seemed as much to me, one who had not been schooled with the metric system! As I have mentioned earlier, less than this under keel clearance meant that the pilot was in danger of "putting a stripe through the flatfish!"

My memories of my A.C.L. exploits are many. Fog, mist, falling snow, and any other conditions, including many gales from all points of the compass, tug breakdowns, lock breakdowns, all made the manoeuvring of an A.C.L. interesting and possibly dangerous.

Only once was I unable to dock because of adverse weather conditions on an A.C.L. This was on the occasion of a westerly storm. I was aboard the *Atlantic Cartier* and the storm forecast strengthened to the storm force in reality as we approached the Bar Light Vessel. I had been told by my peers, that up to thirty to thirty five knots, with two tugs and the thrusters, manoeuvring in the close vicinity to dock walls was a feasible proposition. Above this strength, depending on wind direction the risk of damage was too great. Northwesterly winds, once the vessel was round in the river, brought the wind towards the bow and therefore on the nose. But there were other problems to be faced before being rounded up and end on, as we shall learn.

On board the *Atlantic Cartier*, the storm force winds were in excess of sixty knots from the west to the north-northwest and there was no question of a docking attempt. The captain, Anders Barersjo, and myself, opted to proceed north towards the Isle of Man, even though the wind was westerly at the onset of the storm. The forecast was for the wind to swing to the north of northwest, which would make a Moelfre anchorage untenable. Anders chose to "steam" (keep motoring underway) back and forth between the Isle of Man and the mainland, whilst we rode out the storm. We were to miss both the day tide and the following night tide, before docking safely on the following day tide as the fury of the storm subsided.

During that night, the ro-ro ferry *River Dance* was wrecked on the Lancashire Coast, fortunately with no loss of life, although the ship was lost. Anders and I were to smile at the master of the *River Dance*'s comment that he: "was hit by a freak wave." This was reported in the following day's newspapers. Anders and I both agreed that, as we were only some twelve miles distant from the wreck site: the "whole of the Irish Sea" was covered in nothing but freak waves at the time the vessel grounded!

On another strong wind occasion, one of three such occasions, I had boarded the *Atlantic Conveyor* in the Isle of Man, and with Matts Olsen as captain, we ran before the wind to the Bar Light Vessel. There we turned to the west to await the promised moderation. It came, but not in a straightforward manner. In our position the wind moderated to twenty-five to thirty knots. The Hoylake Lifeboat was out on exercise in the River Dee, and the Coxswain David Whitely, reported a moderation down to twenty knots, whilst the Radar Tower, V.T.S anemometer was showing only ten knots!

We turned for the channel in good time for our docking with all the signs of the forecast moderation proving to be verified. "What do you think of the idea that we put the thrusters on standby as we enter the channel?" Matts' question, which I readily agreed to, almost certainly saved the ship on that occasion.

Steering in twenty to thirty knots of wind from any direction is no problem for an A.C.L. and we had an experienced man on the helm, but as we approached the bend, where the vessel must slowly make a starboard-hand or right turn from the Formby Channel to the Crosby Channel, with the helm hard over to starboard and the engines on full speed ahead, the vessel began, slowly, but inexorably to pay off, (turn) to port.

The red buoys on the port-hand side of the channel were coming closer and the vessel was creeping to a northerly heading, which development I believed would be exacerbated if we were to reduce the speed. Behind, and close to the red buoys, is the training wall of stone and certain disaster. The channel is narrow at this point and we are talking minutes between safety and the unthinkable. The controls were put over to the port side and I first activated the bow thruster up to full power to starboard.

Now thrusters do not normally come into use over four to five knots of speed, by which time the ship is usually clear and away from danger. I believe that, from this experience, there is a speed, at which the power becomes effective again, for at the seventeen knots, at which we were then travelling, the port swing stopped and the ship steadied with the application of close on two thousand horse-powers of bow thrust to starboard. This success was immediately followed by the application of close on two thousand, five hundred-horse powers on the stern thrust to port, and the vessel commenced a turn to starboard and the safety of the deep-water of the channel.

The wind had reached in excess of fifty-five knots from the north, which would indicate to me that as the other reports remained the same, a "corridor" of wind flowing down that line into which we sailed on the bend of the channel, was literally the "tail" of the storm.

Fortunately, I had instructed two small, outward-bound ships to reduce speed to pass the A.C.L. in the wider Crosby Strait, or we would have met them on the wrong side of the channel. When the concerned voice of the V.T.S. Operator, John Whitley, having watched in horror at the track of the A.C.L. on their radar screens, called to ask me on the V.H.F., if we were alright on board the *Atlantic Conveyor*, I was able to reply "nonchalantly" that we were, and that I had simply taken a "wide-swinging" turn through the bend! We were to dock within the hour with the wind, as reported earlier, at ten knots!

I was to have the thrusters ready for operation, on two subsequent occasions in similar conditions, both with successful results. Although successful, I would not have wished for any of these experiences.

My father had had an idea for his retirement. During the period, in which he was to retire, there were two "reefer," (refrigerator) vessels running between Liverpool and the West Indies carrying bananas, discharging their cargoes in Hornby Dock. One of them, as I recall was the vessel *Brunsdal*. It was my father's idea to sail, outward-bound on one of these vessels on his final act of pilotage and disappear into the setting sun to the West Indies. Instead, he was to end up, where he began on the *Gracehill* all those years ago at Garston, but this time, inward-bound on the *Saint Bridget*. I actually vacated the berth he was bound to, shifting a Manx Ben boat, which had anchor problems. Sadly, it was in the days before mobile phones and better communications, for I was to leave the dock area, only an hour or so before he was to arrive. Would that I could have known, and waited to greet him on the berth!

My father's idea was always with me, and I determined my own retirement passage as a result.

I believed that I had given good service to A.C.L., and had met Bob Moore, the then Managing Director of A.C.L., who was based in New York, at a simulator exercise connected with the proposed new build, the G.4's, at the John Moores' University Lairdside simulator in Birkenhead. I had expressed a wish to him, and was both delighted and privileged that my wish was to be granted.

It transpired quite simply that I was to dock the *Atlantic Compass* on the Friday evening's tide before my 65th birthday. On the Saturday afternoon, my good friend Brian McShane and his wife Pat, were kind enough to take my wife Gill and myself over to Seaforth, where we were to board the *Atlantic Compass* under the command of Ulf Olofsson, but shadowing a new captain, Jesper Klingsell, who was to take over complete command in New York.

Gill and I settled ourselves in to the pilot's cabin abaft the bridge. At sailing time, as usual, I took command and sailed the ship on a beautiful, late spring evening. Almost without incident, we sailed outward-bound. In truth, the stern tug's winch failed as we brought up in the lock, and there were a few anxious moments whilst I brought the ship up safely on the marks with the use of the ship's main engines. I believed after this minor drama, that it did illustrate to Gill that my job was not always as straightforward as it might have appeared to her to be up to this point!

We cleared the main channel at midnight. I reported the fact that the *Atlantic Compass* was now abeam of the Q2 Buoy, clear of the main channel with hazardous cargo and was closing down on channel twelve. The two masters (both in full uniform), and Gill, toasted my future retirement in sparkling water in the darkness of the wheelhouse, and I literally sailed off into the west and retirement.

After a memorable Atlantic crossing, where the crew were to make us so very welcome, Bob Moore and other A.C.L. office-personnel, dined us both out at the Boathouse Restaurant in Central Park, New York. We were to fly home, setting a course, (roughly east-a-half south!) into another life.

There are so many more stories, but the ones, which I have chosen, I hope, will illustrate a working life, which was both loved and treasured by one who can only see himself as a very fortunate man, and one who continually attempted to strive towards being, quite simply: "A true, 'bag-carrying' Liverpool Pilot."

"Q2. and clear"
Photo: Gill Curry

Even now, I remember the women you loved.
The late nights when you came home,
Alone, from your fateful affair with the sea.
How you never fully came back...
A part of you was always out there,
Drifting on the midnight tide...
At ease with the wind and the waves.

From: Even Now, Nathan Curry

GLOSSARY

The following glossary is by no means intended to be comprehensive, but it is intended to assist those not familiar with nautical terminology to understand some of the terms, which have been used in the text.

A

Abaft. Behind.

Abeam. At right angles to the position, at which the navigator is standing when looking forward towards the bow of the ship.

Aboard. On board or physically present on a ship.

Adrift. A vessel not made fast and drifting at the mercy of wind and tide.

Aft. Referring to the stern or back of a ship.

Aground. When a vessel has run out of water to float in, and is ashore on the seabed.

"All Hands." An expression, which encompasses every person present on board a ship.

Ahead. In front of a ship, or with reference to engines meaning that they are turning forward.

Aloft. Above or overhead.

Amidships. In the middle of a ship.

Anchorage. An area where it is considered safe for a vessel to anchor.

Ashore. Aground on land.

Astern. Behind a ship or with reference to engines meaning that they are turning in reverse.

Authorisation. That, which is bestowed upon an individual who has been examined by the Competent Harbour Authority to pilot ships in a port in the United Kingdom.

Awash. Almost submerged.

B

Back. Word used in the expression: "to back," relating to the direction of the wind altering in an anti-clockwise direction.

Barge. A small craft for transporting small parcels of cargo, sometimes a dummy barge without engines needing to be towed by a tug. Also, a slightly derogatory pilotage term for a small ship, which requires a pilot.

Batten Down. The securing of hatches, vents and other openings to prevent the ingress of water.

Ballast. Additional weight carried for stability. Water ballast is taken on board vessels to trim them particularly when they are sailing light or empty of cargo.

Beam. Referring to the width of a vessel.

Beaufort Scale. Scale depicting wind strength from zero to hurricane force.

Belay. To make fast a rope.

Berth. Safe place to moor or tie up a ship.

Bight. Loop in a coiled rope.

Bitts. Iron bollards usually in pairs on a ship, which are used to make fast, that is secure, the mooring ropes run to tie the ship alongside a berth or quay.

Boathand. The legal term for a Liverpool Pilot Apprentice.

Bollard. Squat iron post on the quayside used to moor a ship.

Bow. The front end of a ship.

Bring up. To stop a vessel dead in the water.

Buoy. A floating marker to indicate a safe channel or an obstruction. Literally: signposts of the sea.

By the head. A ship is said to be so when she is trimmed with a deeper draft forward than aft.

By the stern. As above, but trimmed with a deeper draft aft than forward.

C

Cable, 1. A very large diameter rope.

Cable, 2. A measurement of distance at sea. 100 fathoms, or 200 yards, or 183 metres.

Call sign. Every registered ship is allocated a group of letters, or letters and numbers to identify her.

Cant. The term given to a ship when turning to port or starboard, particularly when the engines are going astern or in reverse. Used by ship handlers to control a vessel.

Capsize. The term used for a vessel, which for whatever reason overturns.

Cargo ship. Vessel for carrying dry cargoes.

Cast off. The act of letting go mooring ropes holding a ship to the quay.

Chart. Map of an area of sea and the adjacent coastline.

Clear and away. The state when a vessel has cleared all hazards and is in the open sea.

Compass. The instrument used to ascertain true north on the Earth's surface from which a ship may then be steered on a course from one point to another.

Competent Harbour Authority. A port authority to which the government has given the powers to manage a port of the United Kingdom.

Course. The direction, in which a ship is to be steered.

Current. The directional flow of water.

D

Davit. The small crane, usually employed in pairs, used to both lower and lift small craft, particularly lifeboats, on board a larger, mother craft.

Deadline. Last possible moment possible for docking or sailing.

Derrick. Shipboard lifting device, now in the main replaced by cranes.

Deviation. An effect on the magnetic compass due to the magnetism of the individual ship, which alters with every new direction of the ship's head. Magnetic compasses are adjusted, and a table is made to allow for the necessary compensation to be made to the course or bearing.

Dock. Enclosed area in a port in which a ship berths. Liverpool, with the Georges Dock, was the first port to have an enclosed tidal dock where ships would float at low water of the tide.

Dog Watch. The half watch used to divide the working time fairly between the crew of a ship, usually during the hours of six to eight in the evening.

Dredger. A vessel used to deepen channels or enclosed docks with the use of grabs or suction pipes.

Drift. The distance and direction a ship moves as a result of the effect the wind has on the vessel.

Dry-dock. A dock, in which a ship may be dried out for repairs or maintenance.

E

Ebb. The outward going tide.

Echo Sounder. An instrument used to bounce sonar pulses off the seabed to determine the depth of water, in which a ship is floating.

Even Keel. This term describes a vessel, which has been loaded to an even trim.

F

Fairway. The navigable channel leading to or from a harbour.

Fathom. Unit of measurement, approximately six feet, used to mark depths of water. Now obsolete with the adaptation of metricification. A fathom is equal to 1.83 metres.

Fix. The process of obtaining a ship's position at sea by taking bearings of landmarks or by taking celestial sights.

Flood. The incoming tide.

Flow. Referring to the direction and strength of a tidal current.

Force. Referring to wind strength.

Freeboard. The distance measured between the main deck of a ship and her waterline.

G

Graving Dock. Similar to, and now better known as a dry dock.

H

Hand. Referring to a crewman or crew-woman.

Hatch. Opening in a ship's deck, into or from which cargo may be passed. A hatch cover is the wooden or metal cover, which closes the hatch opening in the ship's deck.

Hawse pipe. The pipe through which the anchor cable passes.

Head. The middle point of the bow, thus the ship's head indicates in which direction the ship is "heading".

Heave-to. To ease off speed and stem the seas in heavy weather in order to ride out a storm.

Heaving Line. A light line thrown by a member of the crew for it to be the means, or link, in the passing of a heavier line to a tug or to a boatman.

Helm. A ship's wheel or tiller. Hence helmsman: one who is steering the ship.

Hold. The compartment below decks for storing cargo.

I

Inward bounder. A vessel proceeding inwards, or towards the port.

J

Jack Staff. A short mast mounted at the forepart of a ship to carry a small flag, such as the company's house flag. In the merchant navy, flag etiquette insists that only when a ship is moored in harbour can this flag be flown, it being lowered upon departure from the quay.

Jacob's Ladder. A rope ladder usually with round steps, used to climb up or down the side of a ship. Not to be confused with a pilot ladder, which has flat rungs and international safety specifications.

K

Kedge. A method of manoeuvring a vessel by using an anchor, hence the term to "kedge anchor."

Keel. The strake running along the bottom of a ship. Also bilge keels may be fitted for stabilisation on the hull.

L

Lead. The 7lbs. weight on the end of a lead line, used to take soundings.

Leadsman. Term used for a trainee on a training trip, taken from the time when one hand would "swing the lead" to ascertain the depth of water under a ship.

Leeway. The speed and distance, which a ship experiences in being taken off her desired course as a result of the effect that the wind has on the vessel.

List. The amount a ship heels over due to an imbalance in cargo loading or discharging or indeed through a cargo, which has shifted.

Log. An old method of determining distance covered by streaming an impeller over the stern, the other end of the rope streamed being connected to a log clock, which the impeller then turns recording distance covered.

Log Book. Book, in which to record events, which have taken place in diary form.

Long shore. Term used for the period when pilots were working taking ships outward bound from the port.

Lynas Point. Point of land on the north coast of the island of Anglesey, off and in the shelter of which is the western station of the Liverpool Pilots.

M

Merchant Navy. Commercial vessels of a country carrying cargo.

Minesweeper. A naval vessel designed to sweep and explode mines out at sea.

Moor. To make a ship safe and fast, either with anchors in a seaway, or with ropes in a harbour.

Muster. To assemble the crew of a ship.

N

Navigation. The art of conducting a ship safely from one point on the Earth's surface to another.

Neaped. A vessel, which is unable to dock because of insufficient water for her to float in through the approach channels on a given tide, is described as being neaped.

Neap tide. A tide with a low range of tidal difference between low and high water, which in Liverpool Bay can be around seven metres.

O

Offing. The safe distance a ship may be from the dangers of the shore.

Outward bounder. A vessel proceeding outwards, or away from the port.

Overhaul. To overtake, pass or indeed even to start to catch up with a vessel ahead.

P

Pilot. One authorised to pilot ships.

Port 1. Harbour where ships load and discharge cargo. A safe haven.

Port. 2. Referring to the left hand side of a ship.

Poseidon. Greek God of the sea.

Punt. The name given to the pilot's boarding boats, slung from davits on the mother ship. In these craft the Liverpool pilot, as a boathand, first came to learn about ship handling.

Q

Quarterdeck. The deck at the after end on a ship. Hence: Starboard quarter or port quarter indicating the side of the after end of the ship being referred to. On warships, often the point where a pilot will board.

R

Radar. Electronic instrument used to detect targets around a vessel at sea. A "picture" composed of returned electronic waves, which have been sent out from a radar scanner, and have struck obstructions, such as another ship, or landmasses, is shown on a radar screen. This can be interpreted by the trained navigator and is particularly useful in conditions of reduced visibility, such as dense fog. Not so efficient, any more than the eyes are, in heavy snow.

Reefer ship. Refrigerated ship.

Ro-Ro. Roll on roll off.

Royal Navy. Vessels of Her Majesty used to defend the realm.

Rudder. The moving "flap" at the stern of a ship operated by means, which allow it to pivot from the centre point to the left or to the right, thus enabling the vessel to alter course.

Rules of the Road. The set of rules, which constitute the "International Highway Code of the Sea."

S

Salvage. The name given to a reward for a person or persons who save a ship and her cargo from loss.

Scuppers. Draining holes or ports cut into the sides of a ship on decks to allow seawater to flow safely away over the ship's side.

Sea turns. Term used when the pilot was bringing ships into the port. (Usually considered the more difficult of the two directions. Presumably because the ship was running ever nearer to the dangers not encountered in the "open" sea.)

Sextant. Instrument used in celestial navigation to take sights of heavenly bodies.

Shackle. A u-shaped iron closed with a screwed pin used to secure the looped ends of ropes, or the ends of a chain, to other fittings such as anchors.

Sheer. An unexpected alteration, usually a drastic one, which a ship takes away from her intended course.

Signal Letters. The four numbers or letters, or combination of the two, used to identify any particular ship.

Sill. The "step" at the ends of a lock on which the lock gates sit.

Slack water. The period, either at high or low tide, when little or no stream runs.

Slings. Equipment in the form of a net used for handling cargo.

Snotter. Equipment in the form of a rope loop used for handling cargo.

Soundings. The depth of water recorded from instruments recording depths.

Splice. Method of joining ropes or forming loops in the ends of them by using the ropes themselves.

Spring. A rope employed to assist in the manoeuvring of a ship in leaving a quay. Also the name of a rope leading from forward or aft, away from the extremity of a vessel, which help to hold her securely to the quayside when she is moored.

Spring tide. A tide with a high range of tidal difference between low and high water, which in Liverpool Bay can be in excess of ten metres.

Spurling Pipe. Pipe leading the anchor chain down to the anchor locker on the inboard side of the windlass.

Starboard. Referring to the right hand side of a ship.

Steer. To guide a ship in the required direction.

Steerage way. The lowest speed required for a vessel to answer her rudder.

Stem. The foremost part of a ship's bow.

Stern. The after, or back end of a ship.

T

Tank or tanker. Vessel for carrying liquids.

Tide. The ingress and egress of water into a port dependent on the attraction of the sun and the moon on the earth's surface. In Liverpool tides are semi-diurnal, that is; they occur twice in a twenty-four hour period.

Tide tables. The pilot's bible! Published lists of tides for each day of the year. With knowledge of the time of the tide, which the pilot is working on, I have always maintained that an experienced pilot could go out to sea stark naked, with no need for anything save his body, brain and his knowledge to be present on the bridge of a ship.

Tideway. Out in the tidal flow of the approaches to a port.

Tow. The operation of one vessel pulling another by means of a rope.

Trim. The way in which a ship floats in the water.

Tug. Small but powerful craft used in the towage of a vessel.

U

U boat. German submarine.

Underway. A vessel, which is moving through the water.

V

Variation. The angle contained between the true and magnetic meridians is the variation of any specific place on the Earth's surface. It is caused by the geographical and magnetic poles not coinciding. This varies over the years.

Veer. Word used in the expression, "to veer" relating to the direction of the wind altering in a clockwise fashion.

W

Warp. A rope used in moving, or "warping" a vessel along the quay.

Warship. A vessel used in warfare in the defence of a realm. In the United Kingdom one of the Royal Navy, belonging to her Majesty the Queen.

Watch. The twenty-four hour period at sea is divided between the crew into watches.

Well found. A vessel, which in a good seaworthy condition.

Windlass. Winch mechanism for heaving anchors.

X

X-Boat. Inflatable carried by the R.N.L.I's All Weather Lifeboat Fleet.

Y

Yardarm. The outer extremities of the spars or yards, from which sails were hung on board a square-rigged sailing ship.

Yokahama Fender. Large form of a floating fender intended to keep ships off the quay. Also to be placed between two ships moored alongside each other to reduce the risk of damage between them.

Z

Zenith. Important in celestial navigation when the heavenly body, the sun for example, is at its 'zenith', that is at its highest point, a sight may be taken with a sextant to help fix the ship's position on the Earth's surface.

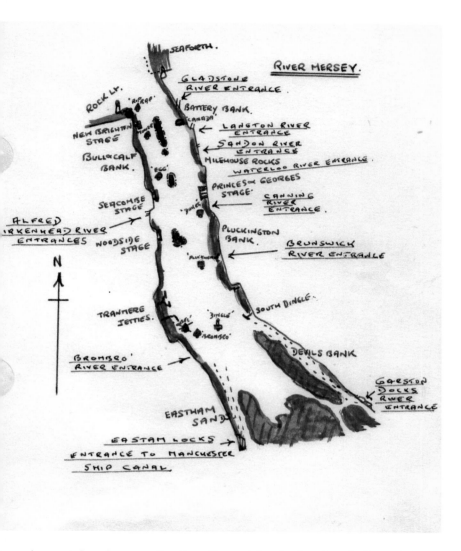

rough map taken from my Boathand's mark book, showing the River Mersey
ith some geographical features, and indicating the river entrance locks
ferred to in the text.

BIBLIOGRAPHY

Suggestions for further associated reading:

Beyond the Bar. A light History of the Liverpool Pilot Service. Youde. B. Laver. Liverpool. 1994.

Heart of Darkness. Conrad, J. Bantam. 1969.

History of the Liverpool Pilotage Service. Rees. J.S. Southport Guardian. 1949.

Life on the Mississippi. Mark Twain. Harper. 1896.

Marine Pilot. Foot, J. Henry. 2004.

The Ellan Vannin Story. Stafford, R. Mannin Media. 1999.

Unplanned Passage. Russell, J.D. Pen Press. 2011.